OUT OF THIS wORLD

The Alternative South African
Spiritual Experience

Alexandra Levin

PENGUIN

VIKING

PENGUIN BOOKS
Published by the Penguin Group
80 Strand, London WC2R 0RL, England
Penguin Putnam Inc, 375 Hudson Street, New York, New York 10014, USA
Penguin Books Australia Ltd, 250 Camberwell Road, Camberwell, Victoria 3124, Australia
Penguin Books Canada Ltd, 10 Alcorn Avenue, Toronto, Ontario, Canada M4V 3B2
Penguin Books (NZ) Ltd, Cnr Rosedale and Airborne Roads, Albany, Auckland, New Zealand.
Penguin Books India Pvt. Ltd, 11 Community Centre, Panchsheel Park, New Delhi – 110 017, India
Penguin Books (South Africa) (Pty) Ltd, 24 Sturdee Avenue, Rosebank, Johannesburg 2196, South Africa

Penguin Books (South Africa) (Pty) Ltd, Registered Offices:
Second Floor, 90 Rivonia Road, Sandton 2196, South Africa

First published by Penguin Books (South Africa) (Pty) Ltd 2003
Copyright © Text Alexandra Levin 2003
Copyright © Photographs: as per individual credits
The Acknowledgements on page iv constitute an extension of this copyright notice
All rights reserved
The moral right of the author has been asserted

ISBN: 0 670 04785 6

Book and Cover design by Mouse Design
Printed and bound by Formeset printers, Cape Town

This book is dedicated to the memory of John Kanter,
the kindest, gentlest and most compassionate soul to ever walk this earth.
Although he is now out of this world, his loving spirit will remain forever
within the hearts of those who loved him dearly.
RIP

Copyright Acknowledgements

Contents

Acknowledgements   **vi**

Preface   **vii**

T. Dr Shado Moses Dludlu – Mngoma   **1**

The Reverend Donna Darkwolf Vos, High Priestess of Kali – Witch   **9**

Lionel Berman – Psychic Counsellor   **17**

Jeanne Stock – Psychic, Channel, Clairvoyant   **23**

Evans V Brown – Grand Master Hypnotist   **29**

Hofit – Spiritual Healer & International Medium   **35**

Mouneen Forrester – Tarot Reader & Teacher & Channel   **39**

Colleen-Joy Page – Intuitive Spiritual Counsellor   **45**

Renée Fouché – Reiki Master & Mystic   **51**

Rozelle Mazetti – Dream Interpreter & Tera-mai Seichem Master   **57**

Shui Tseng – Medical Doctor & Feng-Shui Practitioner   **63**

Judy Le Cash – Crystal Healer, Abuse Counsellor & Channel   **69**

Michelle Serafino & Alison Effting – Aura-Soma Therapists & Teachers   **77**

Sandy Smith – International Numerologist   **83**

Mpumi Khumalo – Sangoma   **89**

Dr Mark Harman – Psychic, Parapsychologist & Strega Witch   **95**

Dr Melanie Polatinsky – Grief Counsellor, Spiritual Philosopher, Inner Child Therapist   **101**

Jayshree & Mellissa Mallaya – the Mystic Sisters – Intuitive Palmacologists   **109**

Chris Tokalon – Sound Healer   **115**

Nandiva (Wendy) Wood – Yoga Teacher & Natural Healer   **121**

Durgana/Magda Inglethorpe – Yoga Teacher, Kinesiologist, Reflexologist   **127**

Corina Loe – Natural Animal Healer   **135**

Bernie Rowen – Complementary Natural Healer   **141**

Irma Bellingan – Clairvoyant, Clairaudient, Astrologer   **147**

Rod Suskin – Astrologer and Sangoma   **153**

Mirabai Devi/Jane Blecher – Spiritual Teacher, Healer & Intuitive   **159**

Contact details   **167**

On the Path to Spirit, by Cara Faye   **168**

Acknowledgements

I would like to thank all the very special esoteric practitioners featured in this book who had sufficient faith in my abilities to come along for the journey when the whole concept of the book was little more than a dream and I had no guarantee of finding a publisher.

There were days when I doubted that *Out Of This World* would ever see the light of day, and then I would play the tape that I had recorded of my reading with Lionel Berman. 'I never get involved in projects that do not succeed,' he stated.

His words were echoed by the remarkable Jeanne Stock during a trance reading that she did for me. 'What you are doing with your book will be a success,' she said, 'for you will take something of the essence of what each one [of the practitioners] does and it will be in your heart, your mind, your being.'

I thank both Lionel and Jeanne for replacing my uncertainty with certainty.

Indeed, I have learned so much from each and every one of the practitioners I interviewed. All of you have offered me new insights and some of you have counselled me, and those close to me, unselfishly and with so much love that I do not know how I can ever repay my enormous debt of gratitude. I am only sorry that there was not sufficient space to accommodate various other people I met during the course of this spiritual journey who are undoubtedly worthy of inclusion in a book of this nature. God willing, I will yet get to write about more of you who are blessed with special powers.

I would like to thank the photographers who captured the hearts and souls of their subjects: the late John Kanter, Francki Burger and my daughter Oriana Levin in Johannesburg, Jaco Wolmarans in Cape Town, and Terence Hogben in Durban. My heartfelt gratitude to Alison Lowry of Penguin Books South Africa for so readily embracing the concept of *Out Of This World*; and to my editor Pam Thornley for her enthusiasm and for her understanding not only of the text but also of the emotions in my heart. I must also mention the rest of the Penguin publishing team – Claire Heckrath and Jane Ranger, Kerrin Wilkinson and Marlize Cary – who worked with such professionalism and dedication to produce the book. And if you find beauty in this production, it is thanks to the discerning eye of designer John Dangerfield.

During the course of writing this book I showed initial drafts of each chapter to my zealous team of proofreaders – my daughters Daniella and Oriana, and my friends Barbara Bird and Helen Ofsowitz. Thank you for giving so freely of your valuable time and for your worthwhile comments. I would like to thank Helen particularly for her strong belief and unquenchable faith in this project.

When the book was nearing completion, I asked Cara Faye, former website researcher for *Odyssey* magazine, if she would like to contribute a list of esoteric websites. She fulfilled this task with thoroughness, taking pleasure in being able to bring those who are searching into touch with the spirit realm. I do not have words to thank her.

I would also like to thank Chris Erasmus, editor of *Odyssey*, for permitting Cara Faye to open new worlds to readers. From the initial conception of this project, Hilda de la Rosa, editor of *Namasté* magazine, has given support and encouragement, as has Erica von Greunen, organiser of the highly successful Exploring Consciousness Film Festival. Thank you both for believing that people are eager to nourish their souls in alternative ways.

I thank Arlene Tannenbaum for the loan to my photographer of her treasured crystal and Warren Lieberman for the loan of his irreplaceable drum.

I thank my spirit guides, especially Tahika, who I believe helped guide me to the people that I should interview. It was always my intention to interview only the Living, for I wanted my readers to be able to consult these esoteric practitioners and be helped as I have been. Thus, hard as I tried, I was unable to secure an interview with the Rain Queen, Modjadji, who died unexpectedly in the winter of 2001. An unseasonable rainstorm, punctuated by brilliant lightning and violent thunder, accompanied her on her journey from this world to the next.

Finally, I thank God for a period of adversity in my life which led me to seek understanding of our brief sojourn in this world. If it had not been for the pain of the surrounding darkness, I would never have explored alternative ways to find the healing Light. May the flame never be extinguished from my heart!

Love and Light, *Alexandra*

Preface

I have fought against white domination, and I have fought against black domination. I have cherished the ideal of a democratic and free society in which all persons live together in harmony and with equal opportunities. It is an ideal which I hope to live for and to achieve. But if needs be, it is an ideal for which I am prepared to die.

Nelson Rolihlahla Mandela

On 10 May 1994 Nelson Mandela was inaugurated as the first democratically elected State President of South Africa and, as if by the magic of one man, the restraints and restrictions that had oppressed the nation for so long under the tyrannical apartheid regime seemed to vanish in a puff of smoke.

The Rainbow Nation was born and with it the freedom to believe in gods and goddesses and deities and spirits not laid down by orthodox religion and, particularly, by the rigid doctrine of the Dutch Reformed Church. Now at last the traditional healers, the *sangomas* and *mngomas* could once more hold their heads high.

With the advent of this New Age, there was place for the psychics and Tarot card readers and astrologers to make their predictions known without fear of persecution and ridicule. It was time for the alternative healers – those who offered cures from the bounty of Mother Nature rather than drugs fashioned in pharmaceutical laboratories – and those who practised Reiki and Reflexology and Acupuncture and Aromatherapy to soothe the heart of a nation ready at last to throw away the burdens of a dark past.

I believe that the twenty-six people interviewed in this book, with their varying views, opinions and beliefs, represent the free spirit of this new nation. Despite growing pains and problems, South Africa is an example to the world that people of different cultures and beliefs can coexist in relative harmony. We have an inspiring and courageous example to follow. After twenty-seven years of imprisonment Nelson Mandela rose above recrimination to show the world that tolerance and forgiveness are the most powerful weapons a true leader can possess. You will read of many extraordinary things in this book, but there is surely no greater miracle than this.

Alexandra

T. Dr. Shado Moses Dludlu – Mngoma

'Like my ancestors, I believe that there is a continued existence of the soul. It is this soul, together with the body, the environment and the life energy that constitutes a complete human being.'

Shado Moses Dludlu

Photographed by John Kanter

For a great master healer of the body, the spirit and the mind, a herbalist and a prophet like T. Dr Shado Moses Dludlu, a man chosen by his ancestors to receive a spiritual calling, there was a tremendous pull between the lure of the so-called civilised western world and the centuries-old traditional healing system of Africa.

During the authoritarian regime of apartheid South Africa, with its narrow-minded thinking, the country's white population regarded traditional black healers with deep suspicion.

It is only now, nine years into democracy in a country which is troubled by escalating crime on the one hand, but on the other is basking in the openness that has come from reconciliation, that black healers, the *sangomas* – or those elevated to an even higher calling, the *mngomas* like Shado Moses Dludlu – are receiving the recognition and respect they so richly deserve.

My first meeting with Shado took place in a nondescript, scantily furnished office in downtown Johannesburg. This was the headquarters of SAGDA, the South African Graduates Development Association, an organisation battling with the immense problem of placing the growing legions of black university graduates in viable employment.

With his combined BA Honours degree in social anthropology and film & drama from the University of the Witwatersrand, Shado is an invaluable asset, contributing his insight and authority to the SAGDA development team. When I first met Dr Dludlu I was also introduced to dreadlocked Vukile Nkabinde, a director of SAGDA. My later dealings with Shado were coordinated by Ronnie Midaka, another key member of SAGDA.

Like a king or president, Shado is constantly surrounded by

his entourage of loyal followers. Gaining an interview with so exalted a personage was no easy task, particularly as his ancestors, the deceased family members who are with him constantly in spirit acting as his guides and counsellors, must also sanction any meeting between us.

Curious to learn more about his miraculous powers, I ask Shado to 'throw the bones' for me. These are actual bones, often those of a goat, which are used in the healer's graduation or initiation ceremony. Other artefacts may include coins, a symbol of a foot or the actual foot of a rooster or a monkey, seashells, small smooth stones and any other object which the healer's ancestors may have told him to add.*

The bones are used to diagnose illness and to reveal the state of the heart – both healthwise and in matters of love and romance. Many other matters of concern, such as travel plans, financial status and employment opportunities, can be divined by these all-knowing tools.

For the throwing of the bones, Shado dons a leopard skin hat and a brightly patterned tribal apron or skirt. The others leave us and we sit on the office floor. An age-old practice in a modern office block is about to commence.

'Gllllllaaaaaaaah. Glaaaahhhhhh.' I am startled by the gasps coming from Shado's throat. They sound to my uninitiated ears at the very least like deep burping or, at worst, like signs of acute discomfort or physical distress. Shado closes his eyes. The noises are the spirits of his ancestors entering his body. Without the omnipresent ancestors the bones have no story to tell.

After my (accurate) reading, I am filled with curiosity. I ask Shado what sort of person would come to him for a reading.

He replies: 'Any human being who is concerned with life. Those who seek functional harmony within the vital organs of

*Reference: *Called To Heal* by Susan Schuster-Campbell.

the body or the balance of the vital human energy system. In essence, you don't really need to have a problem to consult a sangoma.'

My next concern is how divination using his bones would differ from a diagnosis by a medical doctor, a psychiatrist or a psychologist. Shado thinks deeply for a moment before relating the following story:

'An Indian woman came to consult me. Her business was not running smoothly – she attributed this to her dysfunctional relationships with men.'

'When you threw the bones, what did you see?'

'As a *mngoma* I view sickness as a moment of self-discovery and misfortune of the soul. When I saw that she had a pain around the groin and kidney area that was particularly severe before her periods I knew that I had to address this problem. I felt that this premenstrual syndrome was having a negative impact on her ability to function effectively as a businesswoman.'

'To what did you attribute this malady?'

Shado then tells me that he 'saw' that the Indian woman had had an abortion some years previously, an assumption strenuously denied by his patient. Shado, however, stood his ground. Finally, the woman burst into tears and confessed to having had her unborn foetus removed.

'Aha!' Shado exclaimed. 'Whoever performed this procedure might have removed the infant's body. However, what about the baby's spiritual side? Your baby's soul was not detached and reaffirmed. Therefore, the bodily pain that you are experiencing is at the point where the baby's soul was connected to your body. It is this soul that is causing you so much anguish today.'

'What were you able to do for her?'

'I advised her on the ritual that she needed to perform in

order to detach and reaffirm the baby's soul. I administered some herbs – by the way, herbs for me are like *muti* or medicine – to recondition and balance her body energy in order for this energy to flow smoothly through her body once more.'

'How did she respond to this process?'

'After the reconditioning process, her womb was warm and fertile once more. Men who had previously found her frigid were now attracted to this warmth. Her body was now ready to receive affectionate and loving vibrations. I had restored her sex appeal. Then I had to balance, ground and create a protective seal around her.'

'Have you seen your patient since this healing?'

'Yes, indeed. I am pleased to say that today she is happily married and running a successful business. She also has a wonderful child from this union.'

Shado looks at me and says with a small laugh, 'I have changed someone's life for the better. You know, I think I like myself.'

By general consensus, it was agreed that my next meeting with Shado should be in Barberton, site of his *ndumba*, his home and that of his ancestral spirits. Barberton is situated in the province of Mpumalanga, close to the Swaziland border and near the Kruger National Park.

Once famous for its rich gold deposits, present-day Barberton comprises little more than a few streets – unlike its near neighbour, the city of Nelspruit, which is enjoying unprecedented growth.

The residential area consists of rather unprepossessing houses, many of which have clearly seen better days. Here and there, however, one can observe the work of enthusiastic renovators, some of whom have a garish eye for colour.

Shado lives in the township, not more than five minutes away from the town's centre. His house is modest, not very different from the others in the dusty street – although it boasts the luxury of a western-style flushing toilet, a television set and a pretty impressive computer set-up.

The great *mngoma* might be most at home here, surrounded by majestic mountains of heart-stopping beauty, where the plants and herbs he needs to perform his healing grow in wild profusion, but this does not stop him from keeping in touch with the global pulse.

The other houses in the street seemed quiet on this sleepy Saturday afternoon, but Shado's place was a hive of activity. The group of men sitting outside in the sun – amongst them Ronnie Midaka, Vukile Nkabinde and fellow *sangoma* Joel 'Ndumezweni' Mkasi – were cooking meat over an open fire, drinking beer, chatting and smoking.

In addition, many of the young children of the neighbourhood had gathered around, obviously attracted to the *mngoma*'s magic. They were very small, ranging in age from two to five years. Their clothes were clean but ragged and they were playing together without the benefit of any toys – except those their imagination could manufacture – and seemingly without any adult supervision.

Yet these children, who might have had little in the way of material comforts, appeared extremely happy and uncomplicated. Vukile told me: 'This is how we all grew up in the townships. We learned to fend for ourselves from an early age. But these kids are lucky . . . they know exactly where their mothers are should they need them.'

In the outside yard chickens were running around freely and wooden drums were being beaten with ferocious intensity by Mgahbaza Manana, a drummer and fellow *sangoma*.

Despite his great knowledge and learning, Doctor Dludlu would not grant this interview alone. It was important that all the questions that were asked should be carefully considered and discussed before they were answered. This was true democracy at work, with everyone present mindful of the fact that the ancestors are powerful and not to be trifled with.

Shado came forward to greet me and photographer John Kanter. He led us into the *ndumba*, the rondavel-shaped hut that he had built to honour the spirits of his ancestors. We took off our shoes before entering this dwelling, for we were well aware that the ground we were about to walk on was holy.

The approval of the ancestors was needed to sanction the meeting of the white woman and the white man who wished to interview and to photograph the *mngoma*. If we had come to mock traditions and customs as old as the hills themselves, the meeting could not proceed.

Thus *phahla*, an introduction and greeting to the ancestors, had to be made. Money was offered. I had to state my intentions, so that the ancestors could decide whether my motives in writing this book were honourable.

After I had spoken, an audible silence filled the *ndumba*. Finally, I heard Shado's deep burping '*Gillllllllaaaaaah Glaaaahhhhhh.*' The ancestors had entered his body. They had accepted my request. Permission for the interview had been granted.

'Tell me about your childhood, Shado,' I say.

'I was born here in Barberton. Nature in all its power was my first teacher. As a very young boy, I stayed outside all day in the veld. I learned to look after the chickens and goats. Then I looked after the cattle. This job is more important than you might think. Here, a man's wealth is measured by the cattle he owns.'

After this idyllic period spent amidst the nature he reveres, Shado went to school in Komatipoort.

As was all too common with young black children, his mother, a domestic worker, was obliged to stay at her place of work which meant that the boy had to stay with a relative. Thus Shado moved in with his aunt, his mother's sister.

The young Shado soon dazzled with his brilliance at school, obtaining full marks in many of his examinations. Thus when it came to electing a headboy, he was the obvious choice. Shado smilingly maintains that this studiousness was not due to his diligence, but rather to the guidance of his omnipresent ancestors.

The boy Shado was already having many dreams in which he 'saw' his ancestors. 'First I saw an old man. Then I was visited by my great-grandmother of my mother's line. Then I saw her son. Plenty of ancestors or, as we say, *Amadlozi Ndawe*.'

Even when he attended church the young boy was 'different'. He didn't pray in the restrained manner of the other worshippers during services, but as soon as the spirits of the ancestors possessed him, Shado danced and clapped and sang with wild abandon.

The rest of the congregation attributed this unconventional behaviour to boyish enthusiasm, but Shado says: 'Because of the power that filled me, I was simply more charismatic.'

After completing his schooling, Shado wanted to attend a conventional university before becoming a traditional healer. But, as in everything he did, he had to seek out the ancestors and ask their permission. Negotiations with the spirit world took place and the ancestors agreed that they were happy to let him study for a Bachelor of Arts degree.

Three years passed. Then, when Shado was doing his Honours degree, the ancestors became impatient. They felt the pact that Shado had made with them was being broken. It was time, they felt, that he reconnect with the spirit world. He could no longer ignore his calling – he *must* become a *sangoma*.

'In what way did their displeasure manifest itself?' I ask.

'I became ill – emotionally, spiritually and physically. I felt estranged in every part of my being. My blood pressure was too high. I suffered from arthritis. Being a being became unbearable. It was like drowning in the ocean. I wanted to die.'

Shado's malaise was not imagined. Malidoma Patrice Somé in his book *The Healing Wisdom of Africa* writes:

> Methods of healing must take into account the energetic or spiritual condition that is in turmoil, thereby affecting the physical condition. If you address only the physical problem, then perhaps you end up with a cure, which fixes the physical condition, providing a momentary sense of victory over debilitation. But this act denies the need of the energy, the adjustment of Spirit needed to make the cure last.

'And when you appeased your ancestors and agreed to go to the University of Thwasa . . . ?'

'Then I felt good. Fine. Excellent. The ancestors were happy with me once more. I was fulfilling their prophecy. I was becoming a traditional healer.'

'Where is the University of Thwasa?'

Shado looked at Joel and Manana, fellow *sangomas* who were sitting on either side of him. They all laughed. 'The University of Thwasa is here.'

'Here?'

'Yes. Right here in this room.'

Finally, I understood. Wherever the ancestors lead you, wherever there is a traditional healer qualified and experienced enough to teach you, that is where your university is.

'What did you learn at this university and for how long were you there?'

'I was there for six months. During the first three months I learned to throw the bones but, more importantly, I learned that the bones are the ancestors. You and your ancestors are one and the same. As it is written in Genesis: *This is now bone of my bones and flesh of my flesh*. Also, I learned that your ancestors are the source of all your knowledge. You can only learn by knowing that which went before.'

'And in the following three months?'

'I learned about the herbs and plants and how they can heal you. You know, there are two types of illness. The physical and the non-physical. Hate, jealousy, happiness, grief, these are all diseases. I learned, through the power of nature and all its bounty, to cure both the physical and the emotional.'

'In the western world a doctor must study for at least six years before he is qualified, a psychiatrist for even longer. Yet you are saying that you knew everything in just six months?'

'You must understand that the ancestors gave me my knowledge, my wisdom and my insight. So I do not have the knowledge of six months, I have centuries of emotional, physical and spiritual knowledge within me. Thus I am able to practise *kufemba* – a tradition that is 30 000 years old. When a patient comes to me I am able to see their pain. In the west you would call this scanning.'

'Can you give me an example of this?'

'I recently had to work with a troubled soldier. Seemingly without reason, he would go on the rampage, shooting and killing. He appeared to be schizophrenic and insane. This troubled the army officials greatly, particularly as the boy came from a family that saw the army not as a profession, but as a calling. The male members of his family had served in the army for four generations.'

'How did you "see" the soldier's problem?'

'Through the power given to me by my ancestors, I saw that he had killed people whom he was not supposed to kill. People whose earth work had not been completed. He had to take responsibility for cutting short these people's earth mission while they still had work to do here. It was necessary for these people's souls to be released from him so that they could go back to their original life path.'

Shado looks at me carefully to see if I am able to grasp this concept, before continuing with the soldier's story.

'In addition to this heavy burden, there was also the problem of his calling. His great-grandfather had been a soldier and he had inherited the former soldier's psyche and memory. These inherited traits, together with the problem of the people he had killed, were overpowering his body and overwhelming his unconscious. Through rituals and cleansing, I had to ensure that the wildness of these traits be contained and controlled.'

'Were you successful in this?'

'Today, this man is back with the troops working in a commando as an army reservist. In fact, on the strength of this soldier's healing, I have been requested to give a lecture to a group of senior army psychologists in Pretoria.'

Shado hands me an invitation from the South African National Defence Force.

I think to myself that in the days of apartheid South Africa an invitation such as this would definitely not have been forthcoming. The divide between traditional and modern

medicine would have been allowed to remain as wide as the gulf between the different races.

South Africa is today a country healing itself from the sickness that was apartheid. A man like Shado Moses Dludlu – youthful, intelligent, articulate and well educated, is very much in the forefront of this process.

As part of an ongoing educational programme, SAGDA is using Shado's skill to bridge the enormous cultural divide that exists between black graduates who grew up with a strong belief in their tribal customs and those who grew up in the city or townships with no knowledge of spiritual matters.

With the great gift of prophecy and healing from his ancestors comes the heavy mantle of social responsibility to his people and his community – a nation able, on the one hand, to reap the fruits of equal education for the first time, and on the other hand, a nation suffering from a great plague – the scourge of Aids.

Working with the roots and plants and herbs with which he is so familiar at his Emagulubeni Healing Centre in Mpumalanga, Shado has formulated his own special herbal mixture, which has a concentration of leucocytes that help maintain and boost the body's white blood cells.

His recently formed non-profit organisation, *The Mngoma Walk*, is responsible not only for providing this medication to HIV-positive patients, but also for instigating income-generating projects and job opportunities.

With traditional healers like *mngoma* Shado Dludlu spearheading a nation recovering from the ills of apartheid, perhaps the cure for Aids will yet be found, rooted in traditions as old as the hills.

Bewitched but not bothered or bewildered

Darkwolf, pioneer of the public Pagan movement in South Africa and author of *Dancing Under An African Moon*, the first book on Paganism and Wicca in this country, sits on her ordinary suburban sofa, her bright kohl-ringed tiger's eyes gleaming as she recounts the story of her extraordinary straying from the path of conventional religion. Worshipping at her feet lies Borg, her pink-eyed white bull terrier.

Clad in a floor-length black robe trimmed with a leopard skin print, Donna's slender taloned fingers are adorned with two unusual rings – the first a present from a former boyfriend; the other, an even longer and more pointed one, doubles as both ornamentation and a wand.

Around her neck Darkwolf wears a large pendant in the shape of a pentacle – the ritual five-pointed star enclosed in a circle. The pentacle symbolises manifestation, realisation, proof, prosperity, the fruits of one's labour.

Today she displays this symbol with pride. In apartheid South Africa, before the rigid barriers of conventionalism crumbled, Donna would have faced condemnation and possibly persecution – the pentacle pointing out those heretics who were regarded as anti-Christ.

'We are all connected to cosmic energy. There are many different names for this energy. Some call it The Great Spirit; some call it God; others know it as 'Wakantanka'. Our purpose in life is to find the path that will best connect us to this energy and then to discover what we need to return to this earth with all its manifold bounty.'

Donna Darkwolf Vos

Photographed by John Kanter

Born Donna Deniel Vos, Darkwolf began her life in the small town of Worcester in the Western Cape. (Interestingly enough, Worcester, which was founded in 1820, was established because of the development of agriculture and the importance of communication to the eastern valley of the Brëe and the Hex* Rivers.)

Ignoring the companionship of her younger brother, Donna found much to occupy her days as a child. Behind the house lay the forest where she could commune with nature and frolic with the birds and rock rabbits.

Able to read from an early age, Donna immersed herself in the teachings of the Bible. Music filled her soul and she played the piano; but her temper rose to an angry crescendo when her teacher one day smacked her small hands for playing the wrong notes. Furious, Donna retaliated by slamming the lid of the piano down on her teacher's hands – an act for which the unrepentant child was expelled from music school.

High school saw Donna as a prefect at Fairmont School in Durbanville. She was a born leader, an active member of the choir, the drama team and the Student Christian Association. She was also heavily involved with the Docks Mission – a movement which enabled her to meet regularly with the sailors from the passing ships and, with unswayable conviction, she attempted to convert them to Christianity. Luckily, her Guardian Angel was at the helm, for her faith and her virginity remained intact.

School ended and Bible College in Kalk Bay began. And with it, more questions than answers. Why did the Bible denigrate the role of women? Why didn't the College members do more and pray less?

'We used to visit the mentally handicapped people at the New King's Residence in Camps Bay and the Elders would pray. But what good is prayer when one needs to get shopping done or a letter written?' Donna shrugs.

Sexual trouble was also brewing. Why did the Old Testament forbid sex outside marriage? What the hell was wrong with sex? And what was wrong with her? The first time she slept with her boyfriend at Bible College there was no pain, no fire, no brimstone, and no guilt. Yet once under the sheets, her partner wrapped himself in shame. 'I was only guilty because I wasn't guilty,' says Donna.

Instead of graduation, expulsion loomed. 'But why was I threatened with expulsion for having sex, while my boyfriend was free to continue with his studies? Don't they know it takes two to tango?' Donna demands.

Her father's intervention kept Donna at Bible College, but her disenchantment with conventional Christianity was growing. 'We had church service three times a day. The Eucharist. The consecration of the bread and the wine. Yet the Bible says you mustn't eat and drink while you have sin in your heart.'

Finally disillusioned with the Church, Donna went on to do a postgraduate diploma in librarianship and information science at the University of Cape Town. Yet she still hankered after the Good Book. So she followed the diploma with an Honours degree in theology by correspondence through the University of South Africa. But God wasn't enough for her. Where, Donna questioned, was the Goddess?

Still seeking Nirvana, Donna turned to the East, looking for answers in the Koan System – the instruction technique of the Rinsai School of Zen Buddhism. Her search took her north to Johannesburg where she fell head over heels in love with a Tantric Yoga Master and, for a while, she lived and breathed the wisdom of the East.

Then one day Donna found herself in a second-hand bookshop. Idly browsing amongst the dust and cobwebs, she picked up a book on witchcraft. She read of the things that witches did, like burning

*Pronounced in the same way as *heks* – Afrikaans for witch.

candles and creating small talismans. A shiver ran down her spine. Her moment of enlightenment had dawned. She knew instinctively that she was a witch.

Wicca is a contemporary religion. Its practitioners revere the God and Goddess as the creators of the universe, as tangible, conscious beings. Wiccans accept reincarnation and magic, and venerate the Earth as a manifestation of the Goddess and God. Their religious ceremonies are held in accordance with sacred cycles of the Sun and the Moon.*

Embracing this new religion, with its acceptance of the feminine aspect of the Divinity (the Goddess), Donna immediately felt at home within its magical circle.

'When I think back,' she says, 'I wasn't rejecting Jesus Christ, but I was rejecting the Patriarchy. Bible College was no more than a one-stop hypocritical shop.'

The Darkwolf rejoiced in the enlightenment that entered her life, but her wild spirit was still not completely satisfied. So in 1996, after working behind the scenes for some time, Donna Darkwolf Vos started the Pagan Federation of South Africa. She soon found herself persecuted by the more conservative elements of the community. Troubled by what they did not understand, there were those who harassed her and her fellow pagans, breaking into and searching their houses for signs of their collusion with Satan.

'They did not understand,' Donna says. 'Paganism is simply a nature-based religious-spiritual system of beliefs and practices which recognises and acknowledges nature as a manifestation of divinity. Paganism is for those for whom diversity is a cause for celebration and not division.'

Spreading the teachings of Paganism to her growing band of followers, now numbering in the hundreds, is a full-time occupation for Donna. In addition to convening Wicca/Pagan workshops, giving counselling and guidance to those who request it, reading the Tarot cards – an exercise greatly enhanced by her strong psychic powers – her duties include occupying herself with magic, rituals and spells.

Working either on her own or with a coven of witches, Donna creates certain of her spells using dolls known as poppets. These small talismans are carefully filled with herbs. Choosing the correct herbs is part of the witch's art and the poppets are used to cast different spells. The nature of the spell will decide the dolls' fate: for a love spell the poppets will be bound together; for the exorcising of evil spirits, the dolls might well be burnt to a cinder.

I ask Donna what type of person would visit her to receive her unique brand of therapy.

'All sorts of people,' she replies. 'Anyone from housewives, to scholars, to businessmen. The people I see range from teenagers to people in their seventies. I usually find that their problems are linked to a spiritual cause.'

'Can you give me some examples of people that you have helped?'

'A young girl who was deeply troubled came to see me. Her lack of self-esteem led to bulimia. After counselling her and performing a ritual she is almost fully healed and now has the courage to leave home.'

'What sort of ritual?'

'The nature of the ritual must remain private . . .'

'Do you do love spells?'

Donna tells me the story of a man who came to see her because he had been on his own for a number of years and was extremely lonely.

'I performed a ritual asking the universe to provide this lonely

*Reference: *The Truth About Witchcraft Today* by Scott Cunningham.

soul with someone he liked.'

'Did it work?'

'Within the allocated six-week period he found the woman he was looking for,' Donna says with a smile.

Like the leaders of more orthodox religious orders, Donna performs various rites of passage, such as ceremonies for births, deaths and marriages. More unusually, when I spoke to her, she had on her agenda the single-sex nuptials of two male witches.

This wedding was to be held at Waver's Roost, a retreat tucked away within a wand's throw of the majestic Magaliesberg Mountains. The ceremony formed part of the weekend celebrations of the Beltaine Pagan Fayre. This fair, which I attended, is an annual event that marks the ripening and new growth of the Earth with laughter, song and dance.

I noticed that there were many witches attending Beltaine, both male and female, some in traditional black and others in robes of purple or blue. The second day of the festival was a balmy Sunday and the May Queen, decked in flowing white with a garland of flowers in her hair, danced joyously around the maypole. Children dressed in similar attire danced with her. Her year-long reign had come to its end and she was required to hand over her crown to the incoming queen. The new May Queen and her partner, the May King, were then ordered by a laughing Donna to go off and procreate. For Beltaine is the festival that celebrates bountiful harvests and fertility.

As I watched the celebrations it occurred to me that Donna, as the founder of the Pagan Federation, must have been responsible for the induction and training of many of the witches present. I thought it would shed light on Donna's work if I could meet and interview a witch she personally had instructed in order to prepare her or him to follow the path of Paganism.

I was able to arrange an interview with Kerry Hill, otherwise known as Kerry 7th Hawk, who had learned her witchcraft from Donna Darkwolf Vos.

The woman who opened the door of the suburban cottage did not look anything like my preconceived idea of a witch. Casually dressed in jeans, tackies and a T-shirt, a beaded bracelet knotted at her wrist, her brown hair coiffed into fashionable curls, she looked surprisingly 'normal'. Even more surprising was the news that both she and her ex-husband Anton, now a reflexologist, Reiki Master and holistic masseur, had both defected from the high-tech computer industry.

As her first venture into the esoteric world, Kerry studied feng-shui. Disenchanted with what she perceived to be its crass commercialism, she thought that she would like to learn more about Wicca, her main motivation at that stage being to learn more about herbs and their manifold uses.

Who would be the best witchcraft teacher? Anton swung his pendulum and everything pointed to Donna. So Kerry enrolled for Wicca 101, a course that started with the screening of *Burning Times* – a video about the persecution of witches at the hands of Christians related by various well-known witches.

The course went on to deal with the detailed theory of witchcraft. Subjects Donna covered included the history of the deities; Wiccan traditions and Paganism; spells, magick and ritual; meditation and visualisation.

Happy in the realisation that she was utilising both her developing psychic and intuitive powers, Kerry was hooked. She went on to do Wicca 102, a more practical course that covered, amongst other subjects, divination; the Tarot; candle magic; herbs and their uses; talismans, amulets and poppets.

'What was Donna like as a teacher?' I ask.

'Truly amazing,' Kerry enthuses. 'Her knowledge is unsurpassed.'

Today, Kerry is a fully fledged witch and spiritual counsellor. Judging from the number of calls during our interview, I gather that, because of her genuine concern for her clients and her empathetic manner, she is extremely busy and successful in her new career.

Kerry

Inspired by her love and knowledge of herbs, Kerry has also opened *The Source – the Pagan's Haven Shop*. 'To the best of my knowledge,' she says, 'this is the only shop in the country that caters solely for Pagan requirements.'

Housed within her home, the shop is filled with an eclectic array of merchandise – jars of herbs, herbal creams and balms, essential oils, witches' robes, magic spells. Tucked away in one corner is a wide selection of coloured, handcrafted candles. Each colour has a special meaning: pink is for love, red is for strength, orange is for success, green is for money, white is for purification, and purple is for power.

I find the vast array of herbs particularly fascinating. Some are well-known herbs like basil and thyme; others, while unfamiliar to me, would be readily recognised by a trained witch as vital ingredients for various spells.

Slippery elm is meant to hold gossip; *imphepho* (Kerry has recently started developing her knowledge of herbs used by South African traditional healers) is used to cleanse negativity.

'You must understand,' says Kerry, 'that this shop is not only

for witches. I also sell quick "takeaway" spells, although I don't feel these are nearly as effective as a spell that I would make especially for someone.'

'Tell me about these special spells.'

'Ideally, before I make a spell, I prefer to do a counselling session with the person. That way I will know intuitively what they are *really* looking for – the cause of their problem, rather than the problem itself. After this consultation, I know exactly which herbs to use to make this personalised spell both powerful and effective.'

'Let's say, for argument's sake, that I came to see you about money problems. What spell would you make for me?' I ask.

'Hmm,' Kerry cogitates. 'Here's a quick money spell. Firstly, I would make a concoction of herbs. I would definitely use basil in the recipe. Every plant or herb has its own meaning and basil means money. I would put these herbs in a glass jar and instruct you to add copper and silver coins to the mixture. Starting on a Thursday evening . . .'

'Why Thursday?'

'Thursday is traditional for money purposes. I would tell you to light five green candles – remember green is for prosperity – while shaking the jar and saying "Herbs of money, copper and silver, bring my money to me." You would then blow out the candles and repeat this ritual for the next five days, preferably at the same time.'

I ask Kerry what inspired her to open her amazing shop.

'Some time ago, Donna had a stand at Bruma Lake where she did Tarot readings. At the time I was dabbling in herbal creams and Donna asked me to take a stand too. I soon saw that there was a demand for the creams and so my shop seemed a logical progression.'

As I take my leave of Kerry, I think of her teacher and mentor, Donna Darkwolf Vos, with increasing respect. From small beginnings, Donna has, despite hostile criticism and controversy, been dogged in her pursuit of bringing the philosophy of Wicca, and more particularly of Paganism, to her growing band of followers.

One of the reasons for the hostile response of others is the fact that Wicca is often linked to Satanism. The first paragraph of *Aradia*, or *Gospel of the Witches* by Charles G Leland, originally published in 1899 and one of Wicca's main sources of reference, reads: *Diana greatly loved her brother Lucifer, the god of the Sun and of the Moon, the god of Light, who was so proud of his beauty, and who for his pride was driven from Paradise.*

Wiccans steadfastly maintain that their horned god is not Lucifer, the Christian devil, but is just 'the god of the Sun and of the Moon'. When asked to comment, Donna reiterates: 'Our creed clearly states "And it harm none, do what thou wilt . . ." '

Although seemingly contradictory, Donna performs a daily consecration to the Hindu deity Kali, the 'dark mother', and her consort Shiva before the small shrine in her home. Kali is a fierce and terrifying aspect of Devi (the supreme goddess) who, in other forms, is represented as tranquil and pacific.

Which side of Kali does Donna represent? The chicken's foot hanging from the front mirror of her car, together with a medicine wheel and a small broom on the back ledge, convey a contrary message. 'Mess with this woman at your own peril' is what these symbols seem to say.

Lionel Berman – Psychic Counsellor

'The way that I see it is that there is much beyond us; that physical life is a courageous choice and that we need to find balance between the paradoxes that the physical life offers. We need to understand the greatness of the Creation and our place within it. For only with this knowledge can we gain a sense of purpose and meaning within our lives.'

Lionel Berman

Photographed by John Kanter

Lionel Berman is a small, compact man, yet when he enters a room his presence is immense. One notices his ready smile, his glistening dark hair framing his swarthy, handsome face, the silver earrings glistening in his lobes. But it is his eyes that mesmerise.

For these astonishing green orbs with their translucent intensity appear to have been fashioned not by the make-up artist, but by the Divine Creator himself. Through these instruments Lionel can look not only into your soul, but he can also see people who dwell in other realms and other worlds. Lionel communicates with spirit guides, and with those who have died and left this earth who appear to him as living and complete.

'Do you know the film *The Sixth Sense?*' Lionel asks, casually leaning back against the sofa, his arms folded. When I nod, he says, 'Well, I am like the little boy in the film, Cole Sear. But there is one vast difference. Cole could see the dead and it terrified him. I have always seen dead people, but I was never frightened. Not now or at any other stage. In fact, when I was a kid I couldn't even distinguish between the living and the dead.'

'Tell me about your childhood,' I say.

Lionel talks with fondness of his family. Of his Lithuanian Jewish father who worked in the rag trade; of his mother who, although Jewish by birth, was unconventional and unorthodox enough to be considered a 'shikse' by his father's very traditional family.

'When my parents married in Johannesburg in 1950, their immediate desire was to be fruitful and multiply. Yet the years went by and to their great disappointment there were no children. In desperation, they consulted doctor after doctor, even going to see a Harley Street specialist. Finally, after about five years, they came to accept the sad truth . . . their marriage would be barren.'

'Yet you are here . . .'

'One Sunday evening, so the story goes, my mother and father went to visit friends where they played the game "Glassy Glassy" with a Ouija board. This is a primitive way of contacting the spirits. Anyhow, the glass suddenly moved and spelled out a message from the spirit: YOU ARE PREGNANT. My mother shook her head. She had given up all hope of ever having children. But the spirit in the glass was adamant. YOU ARE DEFINITELY PREGNANT.'

Exactly nine months after this astonishing event, nine months during which his mother began exploring the immense possibilities of the spiritual world, sitting in circles and investigating the reality of guides, Lionel was born.

Because of the way in which his birth was announced, it was accepted that this baby would be deeply spiritual, a miracle soul, particularly as his birth took place on Rosh Hashanah, the Jewish New Year and holiest time in the Jewish calendar, a time of revelation and redemption.

Indeed, when he was only three or four the young boy began throwing his 'Linus' blanket on the ground and then telling his enthralled audience what he saw. And he saw many things. His drawing guide, Marguerite, soon appeared to him and, using the young Lionel as an instrument, gave him the ability to draw other people's guides.

These inspirational drawings are a source of comfort to the many people who flock to see Lionel, seeking his wisdom and guidance. Today Lionel is renowned as a shaman, psychic counsellor and teacher.

Today he regards his life as charmed, but as a young schoolboy he experienced confusion and loneliness. His school years were his personal hell, filled with his heartfelt cry: 'Let me be stupid. Don't let me see beyond what others see.'

His teachers and fellow pupils found it difficult to relate to the strange boy who insisted on having an empty seat at his desk for his guide, Kurt.

Kurt, a German soldier who died in the First World War, is a source of enlightenment not only to Lionel, but also to those who come to listen to Lionel channel Kurt's energy. At these well-attended lectures – which are held in Lionel's smallish house, with a sign in the window warning that the place is protected by snakes – those with open minds can listen spellbound to Kurt's messages of spiritual wisdom, delivered with intelligence, compassion and a fair measure of humour.

'Kurt,' Lionel says with a wry smile, 'always refers to me as Aaron, a reminder that while I am Lionel in this space-time dimension, like all other beings, I have a spirit that is more than Lionel. We have all lived past or parallel lives. We have all been mothers. We have all been fathers. Each life offers different experiences which add to the greater whole, thereby enabling one to understand oneself in deeper and more complex ways.'

'Can you give me an example of this?' I ask.

Lionel pauses for a moment. 'You must understand that I will not mention names. Just as a person's visits to medical specialists and doctors are confidential I, too, respect the privacy of my clients.'

'I understand.'

'Good. Then I will tell you the story of a young man of about twenty-six who came to see me. He had had a miserable childhood because seemingly everything he touched went wrong. When he became an adult his life circumstances did not improve – in terms of his work, his recent retrenchment, his relationships – his life was a mess.'

Lionel looked at this unfortunate person and immediately 'saw' him as a woman living in the sixteenth century.

'Do you believe in curses?' he asked.

The young man looked at him in astonishment. 'That is actually the reason that I came to you. I believe that I am cursed.'

'Yes, you are cursed,' Lionel corroborated. 'There is a whole scenario being played out. You are standing there in your long dress and bonnet while the crowd is hissing and spitting and throwing stones at you. They are actually cursing you. They are telling you "Whatever you touch will turn to lead".'

Lionel emphasises to me: 'For a woman of that time, this was an extremely serious curse. She would believe every word of it.'

'But that curse happened centuries ago. How can it continue to affect the young man's life today?' I ask.

'Your belief system from this and from other time spaces will determine your reality,' Lionel explains. 'Because he believed this age-old curse, it continued to affect his present life. What I needed to do with him was to identify this belief and replace it with a more positive affirmation of his role in life.'

'How long did it take you to re-establish his belief system?'

'I saw him for three sessions of one hour each.'

'And how is he today?'

'He's found a decent job. Also, he seems to be establishing a good relationship with a woman. Yes, a woman that he likes is coming into his life. I guess that you could say that he is feeling a helluva lot better.'

Back to his boyhood. The young Lionel, filled with insatiable curiosity, explored some of the world's major religions including Anglicanism, Judaism, Hinduism and Islam, looking for answers to some of the many questions that perplexed him.

'At the age of six I went to study in the Anglican Church and I continued with these studies until the age of twelve. This, coupled with subsequent studies, gave me a deep understanding of The New Testament. At the same time I went to Cheder classes to learn for my Barmitzvah* portion. This meant that on Tuesdays and Saturdays I went to Hebrew School and on Sundays I went

*When a Jewish boy reaches the age of thirteen, he is required to read his portion of the Torah – the Jewish law – in synagogue.

to Sunday School.'

'Did you have your Barmitzvah?'

'Yes. And I think the portion I was required to read was fairly significant. I read the first portion from Genesis: *In the beginning God created the heavens and the earth . . . And God said "Let there be light! And there was light . . ."* '

But the darkness did not lift until Lionel completed his schooling. His mediocre school reports gave way to brilliance and distinction in all his further studies.

'I have always had the ability to exclude that which I do not like from my reality,' he says.

Somewhat surprisingly for someone who loathed his school days, Lionel realised that his vocation lay in teaching. After attending the University of the Witwatersrand, not only did he teach primary school and later biology and mathematics at high school, but he was one of the very few men in South Africa who both studied nursery school teaching and taught it.

The latter may seem a strange choice to some. But perhaps this path is explained by Brian Weiss in his best-selling book *Messages from the Masters*. Dr Weiss writes:

If we allow them, children can show us the way out. There is a well-known story in which a mother enters her infant's room and finds her four-year-old child hovering over the baby's crib. 'You must tell me about heaven and about God,' the toddler implores his sibling. 'I am beginning to forget.'

Lionel's time as a school teacher was followed by three years as a senior lecturer under the University of the Witwatersrand at Giyani College of Education in Venda. Promoted to the position of acting head of department, he taught philosophy, psychology, sociology and history of education.

He then moved on to develop Learning For All, a non-governmental organisation which enabled the mothers of preschoolers, many of them illiterate, to learn to teach their toddlers. 'I think I learned more about the African sensibility from these tribal woman than they ever learned from me,' he remarks with a wry smile.

Living in villages like Patantswana in rural Sekukuneland, Lionel began to learn the ways of black traditional healers. Today he is permitted not only to call himself a *sangoma*, but is regarded by many as 'a black man in a white skin'.

In the fullness of time, Lionel had a traditional Jewish marriage in a synagogue and although the seven-year union did not last, his friendship with his ex-wife continues, as does his enduring love for the progeny of the relationship. For the past eighteen years, Lionel has lived in a committed and loving relationship with Tom Swart, an educational consultant.

Judaism. Anglicanism. Hinduism. Buddhism. Spiritualism. The belief systems of tribal Africans; the lore of Native Americans. A lifetime of study to get him to the point in his life where he is today.

Lionel is like a tree with many branches, offering spiritual guidance rooted in immense knowledge. During one-on-one readings, he not only draws one of your personal guides, he also helps you draw wisdom from his spiritual advice. Troubling questions are answered and confirmation is sought in the Tarot cards, which he uses to give clients a visual representation of spiritual messages.

His clients are often astounded when the message is given and then the specific card that exemplifies the message is turned up. When cynics accuse him of manipulating the deck, he reminds them that they shuffled the cards!

'Tell me about someone that you have helped through a reading,' I ask.

Lionel reflects for a moment before telling me the story of a woman who had been in an abusive relationship for many years.

Her husband was extremely violent and often beat her.

'One night, while she was preparing the evening meal,' says Lionel, 'the husband came into the kitchen, drunk and itching for a fight. The woman could stand it no more. Taking the kitchen knife, she plunged it into her husband's heart and killed him.'

'Did she go to jail?'

'Owing to the extenuating circumstances, she was found guilty of manslaughter, rather than murder. She was nevertheless given a five-year jail sentence. I didn't know this when she came to see me. All I knew was that my guide was saying to me that she had had to go to prison to get her freedom.

'She was a white woman and she was placed in a cell with black women. This situation forced her to confront her racial prejudices. To her surprise, she found that her fellow prisoners were just like her – they had the same hopes and fears; pains and problems. But they kept asking her to write letters for them. And when they received mail, they asked her to read the letters to them.

'Soon the woman started a literacy programme in the jail and she got so much joy, satisfaction and fulfilment from this that she actually found her life purpose . . . Now the question remains "Where was the prison?"'

He looks at me quizzically. 'I could explain to her that the prison was not the physical jail, but rather that she had been imprisoned within the confines of her relationship. She herself was able to identify that she got her real freedom in jail.'

'So how did you finally free her?'

'By explaining the role her dead husband played in the story. I told her that he was the one who actually gave her the gift. By pushing her over the edge and sacrificing his life, he got her to the place where she was supposed to be.'

'How did she react to this?'

'She was finally able to forgive him. Her anger and resentment dissipated. She was grateful to him for triggering the situation that allowed her to find her purpose, her power and her freedom. In short, her soul was healed.'

The hours I spent with Lionel passed all too quickly, for he is a fascinating man, a great raconteur, with an astonishing breadth of vision and insight into the purpose and reasons for our being here in this space and time frame.

I had one last question to ask him: his feelings concerning conventional religion.

'Too many religions are based on fear,' he replied. 'The shaman, the priest, the rabbi, the *sangoma*, all are revered, yet feared. My teachings, my lectures, my psychic readings – which I, incidentally, refer to as psychic healings – are designed to teach people and give them the necessary tools to communicate with their spirits or their God/Goddess themselves.'

His cigarette smoke and his voice rise, giving emphasis to his next statement. 'The new shamanism is about empowerment, not disempowerment. Once you are in control of your spiritual life, your need for high priests, gurus et cetera falls away.'

Lionel leans forward to bring his message closer. 'In the new millennium the role of the interceder between you and spirit becomes redundant. Marianne Williamson in *A Return to Love* says: "Our deepest fear is not that we are inadequate. Our deepest fear is that we are powerful beyond measure. It is our light, not our darkness that most frightens us." '

He is silent for a few moments before concluding: 'When you can understand your own life, your own growth process, I will be redundant. When I am no longer needed, I will know that I have succeeded.'

Jeanne Stock – Psychic, Channel, Clairvoyant

'Our bodies are our temples. By going within ourselves we find the truth and essence of self and when we identity with it, we become whole in the light and love of the universe. All truth is flexible and so are we.'

Jeanne Stock

Photographed by Francki Burger

It is a warm Monday night in January. The small lecture theatre of the Hypnosis and Psychic Centre in Bedfordview in Johannesburg is packed to capacity. More chairs are hastily being brought in.

Standing before the audience is a small woman with shortish blonde hair, penetrating hazel eyes and a ready smile. Psychic Jeanne Stock clasps her hands together, her long, carefully manicured nails varnished a shocking pink. This evening she will be assisted by her cousin, clairvoyant Peter Attwood.

'Let us meditate,' Jeanne says in a soft voice. Although she has lived in South Africa for many years, her accent pinpoints her British origins.

Strains of Eastern music fill the room. In order for the messages of the spirit guides to come through, Jeanne needs to create an abundance of energy. Thus the meditation focuses on the chakras – the centres of energy that lie along the axis of our spines, just outside our physical bodies, in what is called the etheric sheath.

'Close your eyes and let us begin with the crown chakra,' she intones. 'The centre of your eternal, spiritual self. We then move down the forehead into the Third Eye. Everything you see, you see through this eye. Now we move down into the throat area. The throat is an expression of all you say. Next we come to the heart chakra. This chakra expresses what you feel. Begin to like and accept yourself. Find your truth in your heart chakra.'

Jeanne traces a downward movement with her hand. 'Now we move into the region of the solar plexus. Feel the energy within and then release it. Next we come to the base chakra, which connects you to life energy, sexuality and creative power.'

There is a sound of softly tinkling bells. 'Let the music you're hearing herald peace and light. Bring the energy you're feeling down through your legs and the tips of your toes and fingers. Feel wonderful love. Be at one with the cosmic energy and the Father/Mother God. Be at peace.'

Slowly Jeanne and Peter open their eyes and Jeanne focuses on a grey-haired woman sitting in the middle of the third row.

'Have you recently lost your daughter?' she enquires gently.

The woman nods, bravely trying to control the trembling of her upper lip. 'Yes, she died last month.'

'And do you still go into her room each day?' asks Jeanne.

'Yes, I do.'

'Well,' Jeanne continues, 'your daughter wants you to know how much she appreciates the fresh flowers you put there. She says to tell you that they mean a lot to her.'

'Thank you,' says the woman as her neighbour takes her trembling hand and squeezes it.

Jeanne then focuses her attention on the woman sitting next to me. 'Eli,' she says, 'your mom's here with us. She's quite a chatty lady, isn't she?'

Eli nods in surprise. 'Well,' Jeanne says, 'your mom says you've got to stop worrying about your daughter, Alexandra. She is going to be fine. Oh . . . and you won't be alone when she leaves home. By the way, your mom says to wish you happy birthday. You are about to have a birthday, aren't you?'

'It's next week,' Eli smiles.

'Your mom wants you to enjoy your birthday. And she says that even if she's not here with you, she's with you in spirit.'

'Thank you, Jeanne,' Eli says softly. I notice that her eyes are filled with tears.

In this manner, Jeanne works the room, ably helped by Peter. She pauses to give special messages to her family – daughter Cheryl, granddaughter Tamarin, grandson Nicholas, who are all sitting in the back row. Nobody in the audience is left out, for even if her guides don't have a particular message, there is still time for individual questions.

'Jeanne, can you see my father?' a teenage boy demands.

'Was your father a very good-looking man?'

The boy nods.

'Are you thinking of moving from your home?'

'Yes.'

'Follow your heart. Your dad's behind you. "Talk to me, son. I'm still here," he says.'

The youth's slender shoulders began to heave with uncontrollable sobs.

Everyone is eager to tap into Jeanne's psychic powers and the questions continue. They range from the mundane – 'Jeanne, can you see where I left my watch?' 'Jeanne, do you know where I've mislaid my passport?' – to the more serious.

'Jeanne, my husband drowned in the Vaal River a couple of years ago. They've never found his body. Can you see it?'

Jeanne narrows her eyes. 'They're looking in the wrong place. They must move further down the river. To a clump of bulrushes. His body is there, entangled in the reeds.'

'Thank you,' replies the widow gracefully. 'I'll only be able to truly accept his death when his body is recovered.'

Born in the quiet village of Presbury in the English Cotswolds district some six decades ago, Jeanne seems much younger than her physical years. Not only does her diminutive stature enhance her youthful figure, but when she finds something amusing (her humour tends towards the slapstick) she collapses into giggles like a schoolgirl.

Her late father was a rider, trainer and racehorse owner. Her mother, who is still alive and a sprightly ninety-something, was a housewife. She has one older sister, Maureen.

'From whom did you get your psychic gifts?' I ask.

'Probably my grandmother on my father's side. My mother also "sees" things. She will say, so and so is about to happen. But then she'll quickly add the proviso, "Of course, you knew that that was going to happen. It's just a matter of common sense." '

'Was your childhood happy?'

Jeanne reflects for a moment. 'I was very lonely. Even though I had a lot of friends I was always "different". I saw things. I saw spirits. They looked light, transparent. Not solid. They always talked to me. They were my friends.'

'What did your family make of your behaviour?'

'When I was seven or eight I "saw" that one of my mother's friends was pregnant. I told her: "You're going to have a baby." There was a stunned silence because this was during the war years and her husband was away fighting. I was scolded and smacked and sent from the room.'

'How else did your psychic powers manifest themselves?'

'I always knew who would be present in class and who would be absent before I got to school.'

'Can you tell your own future?'

'Alas, no. I can't predict anything that's going to happen to me.'

After leaving school, Jeanne found employment in a small hosiery shop in the Cotswolds.

'I enjoyed the work. I enjoyed the customers. I liked visiting the mills and learning about the different yarns and spinning processes. It was during this period that I got engaged. All the preparations were under way for our wedding in March. But on Boxing Day I broke our engagement off. My fiancé was devastated.'

The young Jeanne was enjoying life, working and socialising and during this time her psychic ability seemed all but forgotten. Then when she was about twenty-two, she suddenly had a vision of a girlfriend who had died when they were both eighteen. 'My friend came in and said "Tell everybody I'm happy." My friend's mother had the same vision. At exactly the same time.'

News of Jeanne's psychic powers quickly spread around the

small village. 'I was invited to join a circle which was led by Caroline Carr. She was a well-known psychic.'

'What happens in a circle?'

'We usually sit with seven people, some mediums and some laymen. We put on meditation music and open up all our chakras. We bring in the colours and then, when we are all totally relaxed, our guides come in with messages.'

When Jeanne was twenty-two she married Graham John Stock and the young couple emigrated to South Africa. Her new husband busied himself with his work at the Atlas Aircraft Corporation just outside Kempton Park and with his sporting activities.

Jeanne continued sitting in circles. 'I remember a woman and her husband who used to sit in the circles. The husband was thoroughly disenchanted because he never "saw" anything. Then one night he announced in a shaking voice that he'd just seen his first spirit. A boy playing with a stick. I looked outside. It was my husband playing with our dog.' Jeanne wipes the tears of laughter from her eyes.

After a time Jeanne and her husband left South Africa and went back to the UK. Later they moved to the USA, to Newport Beach, California, where Jeanne worked in the glamorous Gloria Marshall's health spa in the mornings and did readings for people in the afternoons. Word of her remarkable clairvoyant ability soon spread and in no time she was reading for the rich and famous, becoming a guiding light to the stars.

Jeanne then went to work at the Temple of Healing and Light in Florida – seeing, reading, channelling, healing. It is a tribute to her remarkable ability that she continues to receive calls from people asking for spiritual guidance, not just from the USA, but from all over the world.

When she returned to South Africa Jeanne's psychic workload grew in leaps and bounds. In addition to her readings for private clients, she is a frequent guest on radio shows. Every time her name is mentioned, the station's switchboard is inundated with calls.

'Hi, Jeanne can you help me. My son was killed eighteen years ago. Does he have any messages for me?'

'Did your son have a small dog?'

'Yes.'

'He says he remembers this dog very well. And he says that he's very happy and very proud of you.'

I ask Jeanne if she is asked to communicate with the dead. 'Yes. When I do private readings' – (Jeanne is often booked up for weeks, sometimes months, in advance) – 'I go into a trance and my spirit guide enters my body. In this way I am able to channel the spirit's energy.'

'Do you have a particular guide?'

'Unlike some mediums or psychics, I never know which of my guides I will be channelling. But through my guides, I am able to communicate with the spirit world. I frequently communicate with the dead, especially with dead children – mostly matric students who've committed suicide. More boys than girls, somehow. I like to think that the messages I receive from them are of comfort to their grieving parents.'

Although most people are grateful for the messages Jeanne gives them, a few sceptics become angry, feeling that communication with the dead is both unChristian and unbiblical. Others think that Jeanne is nothing but a phoney, without any real psychic powers.

After one particular show on East Coast radio, an irate radio listener berated Jeanne for talking to the dead, maintaining that it was evil practice.

Quoting Ecclesiastes Chapter Nine, Verse Five – *'For the living know that they shall die: but the dead know not anything . . .'* the caller demanded to know what gave Jeanne the right to presume to talk with the dead.

Jeanne calmly replied: 'The spirit world communicates with me. I don't ask for it. It happens. I've helped hundreds of people who've lost loved ones, lovers or whatever. I've given them the confirmation that there is life after death. And I'd like to say to you, caller, that all roads lead to Rome. You walk your road and I'll walk mine.'

Late one Friday evening on Radio 702, another angry listener phoned in. 'I've been listening to your programme and I think Jeanne is nothing but a phoney. No one can sit on the other side of a phone and tell people the things that she told them. I think that it is plain rubbish. See if you can give *me* concrete proof.'

Headphones on her head, Jeanne leaned back, thought for a few moments, then said: 'Your mother has passed on. She is with you now and she is telling you that she gave you a painting when you were young and you've loved it and treasured it and it's hanging in your lounge.'

'Yes,' came the answer.

'Your mother is telling me that if you go to the lounge now, you will see that the picture she gave you is hanging crooked on the wall.'

An audible silence filled the studio. 'I will go and look and call you back.' Immediately, the talk show host, Aki Anastasiou, interrupted. 'Although we have a lot of calls waiting, I am going to keep this line open. I want you to go into your lounge and then come back and tell us what you found.'

Jeanne answered two more calls before the caller returned to the line.

'I don't believe it. The picture *is* crooked. How did you know?'

'I saw it quite clearly,' smiled Jeanne.

Extremely modest about her abilities, it is not Jeanne, but her associate hypnotist Evans Brown, who tells me that Jeanne is a fully qualified hypnotist. 'And,' says Evans, 'not only is she extremely competent in this field, but for a time she performed on stage. She is the *only* woman stage hypnotist in the world.'

'Do you still perform?' I ask Jeanne.

Jeanne shakes her head. 'It was a fun period of my life, but I won't do any more hypnosis on stage.'

Her working days at the Hypnosis and Psychic Centre are not without their fair share of high drama. On one of my visits to the Centre I witnessed Jeanne in what is perhaps her most challenging role – that of an exorcist of evil spirits.

A beautiful but troubled Indian woman of the Muslim faith had been brought to the Centre by her husband to consult Evans Brown. The worried husband hoped that hypnosis would cure his wife of her depression and fainting spells.

After observing the lady under hypnosis, Evans said that he believed her depression was caused by negative energy inhabiting her body. 'Do you mind if I bring in my colleague Jeanne Stock?' he asked.

The husband agreed. I, too, was allowed into the healing room as extra energy was needed to exorcise this powerful spirit.

The patient lay on the bed, seemingly in a deep trance. Her eyes rolled back in their sockets and she was moaning softly. She was clearly in a state of extreme agitation.

I watched as Jeanne laid her hands on the woman. Her body immediately became warmer for Jeanne's hands carry the heat of a healer. Suddenly, Jeanne's whole countenance changed. She seemed to grow taller, the shape of her eyes altered and she began talking in a strange dialect.

'What is happening?' I whispered to Evans.

Jeanne is channelling the energy of her main guide, White Eagle. He will help her exorcise this energy.'

I watched with a mixture of fear and fascination as Jeanne ran her hands soothingly up and down the woman's body, talking to her all the time in what sounded like a Native American dialect. At first nothing seemed to be happening. Then suddenly Jeanne staggered back, exhausted.

'Is Jeanne all right?' I asked Evans anxiously.

He nodded, whispering, 'Jeanne's taken on the entity. However, she has great control. She will be able to rid herself of this negative force later.'

After much coaxing, the Indian woman eventually awoke from her trance. She began coughing violently. 'That's right,' said Evans. 'Spit it out. Release it from your body.'

With trembling hands, the woman took a glass of water and began to sip. Slowly she turned to me and said sadly, 'This curse has been ruining my life.'

Her husband shook his head. 'People do not want to visit us. They cannot cope with my wife's depression. It is tearing our family apart.'

Trying hastily to tidy her luxuriant long black hair, the woman rose slowly from the bed.

'How do you feel?' Jeanne asked gently.

With unshed tears in her large brown eyes, she replied, 'I feel much better. Is the spirit really gone?'

Jeanne nodded.

'How can I ever thank you?'

'Be happy,' said Jeanne, clasping the weary woman's hands. 'Simply be at peace from now on.'

Evans V Brown – Grand Master Hypnotist

'For the man who has conquered his mind, it is his greatest friend. But, for the man who fails to do so, it will become his greatest enemy.'

Evans V Brown

Photographed by Francki Burger

Are you trying to quit smoking? Do you want to stop drinking? Are you wrestling with bulimia? Is asthma making it difficult for you to breathe? Do you suffer from low self-esteem? High blood pressure? Are you depressed? Are your school marks below average?

If you are battling with any of these problems, the person you should probably see is sitting before me – a large, softly spoken grey-haired man who appears totally relaxed in his oversized pastel armchair.

Evans Brown was born in 1936 in Jeppe in Johannesburg. Little in his early years prepared him for his present life of healing and helping others through hypnotherapy. Evans was a star sportsman at Malvern High School, excelling at cricket, boxing, soccer and shooting – the last skill standing him in good stead during his stint in the army when he served with the Witwatersrand Rifles Regiment in Potchefstroom.

When his army training ended, Evans began an apprenticeship in the printing industry and continued to make his mark in the sports world. He was a Springbok softballer who also boxed and played baseball and soccer for his province, the former Transvaal.

After working for various companies, Evans opened his own printing business, Tribune Press, and settled into domestic life with his family – wife Judy, son Mark and daughter Jacqui.

A chance visit to the late Max Collie's hypnotist stage show in Port Elizabeth changed his life.

'I watched in amazement as Max told the people on stage to do all manner of mindless but amusing things. I immediately thought that I would like to control people as I saw Max controlling them.'

With his interest in hypnosis aroused, Evans searched for a teacher and eventually found one close to home – Tom Phillips, who taught self-hypnosis.

Not yet aware of the true essence of hypnosis, Evans thought that Tom would soon have him under his control. 'I thought that if he wanted me to, he'd be able to persuade me to rob banks. I had no idea then of the tremendous healing power of hypnosis.'

'What can hypnosis actually do?' I ask.

'Well, last year I saw two patients who were HIV-positive. At the end of their sessions with me they were HIV-negative. The blood tests showed no trace of the Aids virus.'

'You must be very powerful.'

'No. I am not very powerful. The mind is very powerful. When somebody comes to me, they must want to do something, whether it's to stop biting their nails, to stop drinking, to stop stammering, or whatever. If they don't want to heal themselves and if their mind isn't made up, there's nothing I can do.'

'What happened at Tom Phillips' Monday night sessions that altered your mindset about hypnosis?'

'I went to Tom's classes with a friend of mine, Robin Evans. When I arrived at Robin's home on the night of the second session, I found that he had been playing soccer over the weekend and had injured his back. I had to help him out of bed. He was in such agony that he could hardly get in or out of my car.'

During the course of the evening lecture, Tom Phillips asked Robin to sit in an easy chair and put him under hypnosis. He told Robin that when he woke up he would be able to bend and stretch, touch his toes and reach for the ceiling. Tom added that Robin would feel no pain, but that he should not be silly and do anything rash. He should rather let nature take its course and heal his body.

'What happened?' I wanted to know.

'Robin stood up and touched his toes and stretched to the ceiling, after which he walked without assistance. I said to him, what about the pain?' Evans smiled. 'Robin said, what pain? That was the turning point for me. Robin's positive mental attitude, coupled with his remarkable physical recovery, changed my whole perspective. I realised then that hypnosis wasn't about controlling. Hypnosis was about healing through the mind.'

Inspired by the 'miracle' healing he had witnessed, Evans began to take a serious interest in hypnosis, reading every available book on the subject. He began hypnotising willing guests at parties and news of his prowess soon spread.

He was asked to do his own stage show and as a result of their enormous popularity, he began performing all over the country.

'What happened at these shows?' I asked.

'Oh, I would invite members of the audience to come up on stage and let them believe that they were famous performers. I would tell them that they were Elvis, Michael Jackson or Tina Turner. Sometimes I would send them fishing. The women would catch mermen, while the men were told to catch mermaids. The reactions to these suggestions were hilarious.'

He smiles at the recollection. 'We had a lot of fun. Especially when I told some of the participants that they were world-renowned artists. When they were under hypnosis, I told them to paint horses in a meadow. Then, as they ran their brushes over an imaginary canvas, I told them that their horses had galloped away. They ran frantically all over the stage, searching for these imaginary missing horses.' Evans chuckles.

Becoming serious once more, Evans tells me: 'A hypnotist has an enormous responsibility to see that nothing goes wrong. Particularly a stage hypnotist. You must know exactly what you're doing, or you could have your hypnotised subjects falling off the stage and injuring themselves. Hypnosis in the wrong hands can be extremely dangerous. I remember seeing a woman who had been led to believe, by an unethical so-called hypnotist, that her late father, whom she adored, had raped her.'

'How did she react to this?'

'She was so upset that she went home, got into a bath and slit her wrists. As fate would have it, a friend found her and took her to hospital. When she recovered, the friend brought her to me. Through regression, I was able to reassure her that her father had never touched her in a sexual way.'

As he became increasingly well known for his skills as a hypnotist, Evans was elected president of the South African Association of Hypnotists, a position he held for ten years, and he is now president of the South African Society of Hypnotists. A respected teacher of hypnosis, he started his own school about twenty-eight years ago.

'Who comes to your school?' I asked him.

'Professors, doctors, psychiatrists, housewives. A wide spectrum of different people – professional people as well as laymen who simply want to learn how to use the art of hypnosis to help themselves.'

'How long is the course?'

'One hundred and twenty hours of both theoretical and practical components. After you've attended the lectures, done your practical sessions, written examinations and satisfied the examiner of your abilities, you obtain a certificate. The Traditional Healers Association of South Africa recognises this course, thus enabling you to become a member as a traditional medical practitioner.'

An association Evans formed with English-born psychic Jeanne Stock approximately nine years ago led to the establishment of the Hypnosis and Psychic Centre in Bedfordview. From these homely headquarters, in addition to his routine hypnosis, Evans, assisted by Jeanne, began to work on more complex cases. These included helping the police with criminal investigations, as well as working with extraterrestrial beings and exorcising evil spirits.

'Are there beings from other planets on this earth?' I asked incredulously.

'You would be surprised how many aliens there are masquerading as "normal" people.'

'Can you give me an example?'

'Late one Tuesday afternoon an extremely tall woman, aged about twenty-six, came to my rooms. Her skin was very white, she had high cheekbones and she was so thin as to be almost anorexic. However, the most remarkable thing about her was that her arms, hands and wrists all seemed to run into one. She appeared to have no joints.'

'How did you know that she was an extraterrestrial being?'

'As I started my hypnosis instructions, she just sat there gazing at me with soulful brown eyes. It was then that I decided to ask Jeanne for help.'

Jeanne sensed a very unusual magnetic field surrounding the woman and began to speak to her. 'I am aware of a large flight deck with lots of lights flashing in different panels. There is no one at the controls. Strange as it may sound, I believe that you are from outer space.'

'Yes, I do have space ship connections,' said the woman. 'In fact, the ship was forced to make a crash landing. Only two of us survived. I now need to contact the other survivor urgently as we are due to leave earth.'

'How have you survived here on earth?'

'To be able to move around freely, I took control of a human body. I can go without food for days; I seldom eat cooked food and I can live off certain plants.'

'Where did your space ship crash?'

'The ship came down in the mountains,' the woman said. 'The urgency now is to find my partner and get back to these mountains so that we may return home.'

I stared at Evans in amazement. He looked so 'normal', like a favourite uncle. I could hardly believe what he was telling me.

'Evans,' I said, 'you're having me on.'

'Well,' replied Evans, 'a few days after this incident I got a call from Dave Larson, a man very much involved with space research. In answer to my questions, he confirmed that there have been many sightings and landings of spacecraft in the mountains.'

Of Evans' many successes in his decades of treating people through hypnosis, there were two stories that particularly captured my imagination.

The first concerned a woman who came to the Centre suffering from chronic asthma.

'When I could find no apparent reason for her asthma,' said

Evans, 'I decided to regress her to a past life. You know, sometimes the problem lies with a difficulty that the person experienced during a previous lifetime.'

'Please explain this.'

'Through regression, I found that in a previous life she had been an Indian squaw. As a teenager, she was crossing a river with a group of her peers when she slipped, hit her head on a rock, passed out and drowned. This is what caused her asthma.'

'Were you able to cure her?'

'After her regression, I told her to throw away her asthma pump. She didn't believe me. However, once we had established the cause of her asthma, she never had another attack.'

'She must have been delighted with the treatment.'

'Yes. So much so, that she decided to train under me and has become a leading hypnotherapist.'

But perhaps the greatest testimony to the power of the human mind is the story that Evans told about his father, eighty-seven-year-old William Brown.

When the elderly man fell and broke his arm in August 2000, he could not undergo surgery because his heart and lungs were too weak to withstand the trauma of an operation. The attending surgeon put the fractured arm in a cast, hoping that the bones would knit, but after six weeks his arm showed no improvement.

Then and there, Evans decided that hypnosis was the only option left to give his father relief from the excruciating pain he was experiencing. Every day for one week Evans worked with his father, directing him through various stages of hypnosis, preparing him for the operation. 'We needed to clean his lungs and strengthen his heart.'

'On the day of the actual operation,' said William, 'Evans started the hypnosis by putting his hand on my forehead. He told me to concentrate on him and to relax. I guess that I must have floated off into some kind of trance for I felt no pain while the surgeons were working on my arm.'

As the operation was about to begin, a muscle in his arm began to twitch and the surgeon suggested that a local anaesthetic be administered. Evans agreed.

'The surgeons then pushed a steel rod through my dad's shoulder to just above his elbow,' explained Evans. 'They also pushed two steel pins through the top part of the arm just above the elbow.'

After the operation, William was wheeled into the recovery room where the nurse rather anxiously reported to Evans that they were unable to wake him up.

'Wake up, Dad,' ordered Evans.

Oh hearing his son's voice, William half opened his eyes and mumbled: 'Evans, tell these guys that you are the only one who is allowed to wake me up.'

About seven months after the surgery I met William Brown senior.

'How does your arm feel now?' I asked him.

He held it up for my inspection. 'Well, as you can see, it's a bit crooked. But I've got no pain and at least I'm able to use the arm.' He demonstrated the flexibility of his limb by raising it and opening and closing his fingers.

'Are you proud of your son's achievements?'

'Hypnosis saved my life,' declared William Brown. 'No doubt about it. I wouldn't be here today if it weren't for Evans.'

Clearing the sickness of the mind

Photographed by Oriana Levin

Hofit, intuitive spiritual healer and gifted international medium, greets me at the door of her apartment. Born in Israel in 1973, she looks younger than her years, her long red hair hanging schoolgirl-style down her back. Behind her glasses her brown eyes twinkle.

In her arms she is holding a pretty, curly-haired child. This is her three-year-old daughter Adi. Her son Itschak is five years old. I think that Hofit must literally have her hands full, trying to settle in a foreign country with her husband Israel and two small children.

When I ask her if emigration to a new land was difficult for her, she replies: 'In Israel, I had everything. A nice place to stay, a car. I was a nurse at the Sheba hospital. I worked with old people. I love old people. Here, I must start over. But I realised that if I must come here, there must be a reason.'

Hofit believes that she receives her inspiration from her two guides – her beloved maternal grandmother Sophia, who has now passed on into the spirit world, and Yoshafat, the distinguished judge from the Torah.

When she was thirty years old, Sophia lost one of her legs in an accident. With the rest of the family occupied with the task of putting food on the table, it was left to the four-year-old Hofit to keep the crippled woman company.

'I believe in the Jewish God. I believe that I was sent to this earth to help enlighten people with the knowledge given to me by the guides that God has sent me. I believe that the more enlightened people are, the more peaceful this earth will be.'

Hofit

'Didn't you mind this?' I ask. 'After all, you were very young. Surely you wanted to join your friends playing outside?'

Hofit shakes her head emphatically. 'No, I loved being with my grandmother. She was a very spiritual woman. She could read your fortune from coffee cups and she taught me all about life's lessons; about things from the spirit world; about codes of behaviour; about angels.'

'You must have been much grieved by her death.'

'Yes. My grandmother died when she was seventy-three years old and I felt as though I had lost my best friend. In my grief, I started to meditate and I was able to connect with Sophia's soul. During her funeral I saw a white bird and I heard my grandmother saying that only her physical body was gone and that, from then on, she would be my guide. So now, in her death as in her life, we are always together.'

Initially, when Hofit started on her spiritual path, her guides were content to let her make prognostications and do Tarot readings for her clients. However, as her spirituality developed, Sophia and Yoshafat demanded more of her. Recognising her dedication and love of humanity, her guides gave Hofit the power to unblock and heal people's emotional problems – the root cause, so Hofit believes, of most of humanity's physical ills.

'How are you able to do this?' I ask.

'I get to the bottom of the blockage by speaking directly to the soul of the person involved. This is something that is not done in psychology. I believe that within three sessions, I can help a person suffering from a deep depression, even if they have been undergoing years of therapy.'

'Does this mean that you do not advocate people going to conventional doctors and mental health practitioners?'

'Not at all. I believe that the spiritual healing that I do – the purpose of which is to enable people to lead a healthy, clean, confident and productive life – can often be complementary to more orthodox medical practices. It is well known that cancer patients who combine their treatments with spiritual practices recover better and are often cured.'

'What exactly do you do in one of your healing sessions?'

'Firstly, I will ensure that the room in which I work is cleansed of all negative energies which might have been accumulated from previous patients. I have powerful incense, which I import from Israel, especially for this purpose.

'Then I will say prayers to ensure that God and my guides are with me throughout the treatment. After praying, I will let the patient lie down. It is so important that they feel comfortable and relaxed. I help them achieve this with special breathing techniques.

'Once they feel completely at ease, I do a spiritual analysis, followed by the actual healing session where I use various techniques, including Reiki. If I think it is necessary, I am even able to perform psychic surgery, removing physical blockages without using an operating theatre, anaesthesia or surgical instruments.'

'How successful are your methods?'

'I think you should put that question to some of the people I have treated,' replies Hofit, with an air of quiet confidence.

It is my great honour to have this opportunity to tell you about a very special and amazing woman who has impacted on my life so greatly.

I was referred to Hofit by a friend who had been deeply touched by Hofit's amazing connection to G-d and her incredible healing abilities.

Hofit came into my life when conventional medical practitioners had failed me. For months I had been suffering from terrible digestive complaints, ranging from persistent constipation to bloatedness and an inability to lose weight, despite following a strict eating and exercise regime.

At first I attributed my health difficulties to a mild bug and thought that they would soon pass. However, the problem grew progressively worse and I began responding less and less to medication. (Even my doctor, a homeopath, was unable to prescribe a successful remedy.)

Meanwhile, I was suffering a great deal, not only physically, but emotionally as well. I became severely depressed, seldom leaving the house. I was moody and irritable, even towards those I loved.

I truly felt that I was fighting a losing battle. I knew inside that something was wrong with me. There was something inside my stomach over which I had no control and which was slowly ruining my life.

My eating was in a state of confusion from the various diets that I had tried to eliminate the supposed problem. I had tried everything from anti-candida, to lactose-free to wheat and gluten-free diets. It had got to the point where everything I ate, even in insubstantial amounts, would result in cramps.

This is how I came to Hofit.

At first I was amazed at how young she was – and how pretty! She has a wonderful, warm energy, which I found to be very soothing. The healing began the minute I walked through her door.

After chatting over a cup of herbal tea, Hofit did an initial treatment in which she performed Reiki on the affected areas. Whilst unblocking my crown, heart and solar plexus chakras, she would pray for me, using special, potent Hebrew prayers. Throughout the treatment, Hofit was in constant communication with her spirit guides to assess the situation.

At the end of the first treatment, Hofit told me that I was in need of a spiritual operation that she decided to perform the next day. That night, after many troubled evenings, sleep came to me in welcome peace.

The next morning I woke up feeling refreshed and with a renewed sense of hope. I looked forward to the evening's operation with a sense of nervous anticipation.

Hofit's healing room was beautifully adorned with candles and filled with the aroma of exotic incense. In the middle of the room was positioned a mattress on which I was to lie.

At the start of the procedure, Hofit laid her hands on my stomach. I could feel the heat exuding from her hands before her actual touch. She then began making what I can only describe as an incision into my stomach with cutting-like movements of her bare hands.

To assist her Hotfit used healing crystals and special oils and blessed water.

The 'operation' lasted approximately forty minutes, during which time (to my great relief) Hofit announced that she had found the problem.

She described it as a 'little devil', a spiritual animal or beast, living inside me for quite some time now, which had been 'placed' there to teach me some much needed spiritual lessons. A kind of test from the Universe.

Hofit told me that in order to fully expel it, I would have to start transforming certain fixed thought patterns and beliefs as well as going on a 'diet', channelled to her by her guide, which she noted down on paper after the operation. I say 'diet', although it seemed to me more like a feast, including many foods which I had restricted myself from for a long time, years even. She also gave me a special ointment that she concocted under guidance for me to dress the 'wounds'.

Hofit's treatment was so effective that the change could be noted almost immediately. My bowel movements began normalising for the first time in months and the cramping subsided.

Despite the fact that I was feeling much better, Hofit recommended that I have a follow-up 'operation' during which she received what she later described as the equivalent of a sharp puppy bite across the centre of her right palm. Indeed, when she showed me her hand after the operation, there was a definite reddish line across her palm, which disappeared an hour or so later.

Following these treatments, Hofit instructed me to phone her every day with any dietary questions and also to let her know how I was feeling. Depending on my responses, she would then pray and do healing for me on her own, until our next session. She showed genuine concern for my well-being and peace of mind.

I continue to see Hofit on a regular basis as she helps me in many other areas of my life. I still have many lessons to learn and fears to conquer. I find that Hofit has been instrumental in my spiritual development as she is not only a healer, she is a teacher as well. She has taught me the gifts of prayer and meditation, enabling me to draw upon the strength and the G-d within myself. To be touched by Hofit is to be touched by an angel!

Name withheld by request

It is a Thursday night. Meditation evening at Hofit's apartment. In her kitchen refreshments that include Middle Eastern delicacies are being served to the dozen or so people attending the meeting. Each meditation session has its own theme and is always designed to work on The Inner Self.

'Alexandra,' Hofit welcomes me, 'have you had anything to eat? Anything to drink?'

When I shake my head she says, 'Come, you must eat, you must drink.'

Hofit is filled with an enormous generosity of spirit, which is reflected in the fact that she and Israel have already established a wide circle of friends – her phone never stops ringing.

A fellow Israeli, Lea, comes up to me. 'I believe that you are writing an article about Hofit. When I nod, Lea says: 'Well, let me tell you about Hofit. I came to Hofit for a card reading and a channelling session.'

'Yes,' interjects Hofit. 'The cards I saw were bad. Lea had cancer.'

'Sure enough,' continues Lea, 'the doctors confirmed that I had breast cancer and it was decided that I was to undergo a lumpectomy. I was devastated. I am still a young woman and I have small children. But I had not reckoned with Hofit.'

'What did Hofit do?' I ask.

'She gave me a specialised Reiki healing coupled with meditation. After the Reiki, she told me that the doctors would not operate on me.'

'Was she correct?'

'Yes. However, the doctors decided that to be on the safe side I must undergo a course of chemotherapy.'

'How did you react to the chemo?'

'It made me very ill. I was grumpy and moody. My family couldn't cope with me. But Hofit never gave up on me. She came with me to all the chemotherapy sessions and afterwards she did Reiki. Today I am cured. I thank Hofit from the bottom of my heart. She is an angel. My guardian angel.'

'What do you say to this, Hofit?'

'Everyone has a purpose,' she states. 'I believe I was put on this earth to help people. Yes, helping and healing is the reason that I am here. You know, G-d sends little people into this big world with torches to light the way. Hopefully, I am one of those torches.'

Mouneen Forrester – Tarot Reader & Teacher & Channel

'I believe in reincarnation and karma. Whatever you put into this life, whether good or bad, that is what you will get out. I try never to be judgemental and to love unconditionally. For, sinner or saint, we are all fashioned by the one Divine Creator.'

Mouneen Forrester

Photographed by Francki Burger

Do you want to know what the future holds? Do you want to know about a problematic love affair? Does he really love you? Is your wife being unfaithful? Should you stay in South Africa or should you pack for Perth? Should you change your job or is a major promotion looming in the organisation where you are currently working?

If you are looking for the answer to these and other similar questions, a visit to a Tarot reader could well be on the cards for you.

There are different theories about the origin of the Tarot cards. One theory, explored by Court de Gébelin, a French intellectual of the eighteenth century, linked the Tarot to Egyptian hieroglyphics, seeing a link between the Tarot and the Book of Thoth, the Egyptian god of science.

In the mid-nineteenth century the work of de Gébelin was developed by Alphonse Louis Constant, another Frenchman with an interest in the occult. Constant developed a system for interpreting Tarot cards that inspired the printing of many Tarot decks, including the most popular one in use today – The Rider-Waite deck.*

I am sitting with Mouneen Forrester in the small back room of her suburban Johannesburg home which she uses for her readings and she is explaining her understanding of the Tarot to me – an understanding which developed from her early interest in the spiritual world. By way of illustration, she is using her favourite pack – seventy-eight small Rider-Waite cards.

'Where did you learn about the Tarot?' I ask her.

'It was after my divorce – I was married for sixteen years and I have one son, Michael – I've always had an interest in spiritual things. But the first time I became really aware of the spiritual world was when I went to pay the rent for the house my mother, stepfather, two sisters and five brothers lived in in Roodepoort.'

'What happened on that day?'

'I recall that the rent collector was a Mr van der Merwe. After I had paid him the money, and as he was handing me a receipt, he suddenly said to me: "You know, Mouneen, your father is standing behind you." My father had died when I was four and my mother had remarried when I was six, so this was pretty disturbing news. I turned around in the small office, but I saw nothing.'

'What happened next?'

'With an odd smile on his face, Mr van der Merwe continued conveying my father's message to me: "Your father wants you to know that he is always with you, that he is looking after you and that he loves you very much."

'Terrified, I ran home as if six devils were chasing me. When she saw my anxious face, my mother explained to me that Mr van der Merwe was a spiritualist. This was my first knowledge of such things.'

Mouneen left home at seventeen and after a spell of working for the City Council in Johannesburg, she moved to Pietermaritzburg in KwaZulu-Natal, a beautiful city of historical buildings, green parks and bright flowers. It was here that she began in earnest to search for the ways of the universe.

'I broke away from the Afrikaans Gereformeerde Church in which I had been brought up and confirmed. I started making new and interesting friends. I went to the Hindu ashrams with my Indian friends. I went to talks with swamis. I even did a ritual fire walk.'

'Tell me about that.'

'For several weeks before the walk, I followed a special diet and cleansing ritual. I started meditating. On the day of the walk, we were told to be silent for an hour before our actual walk.

'When the time came, I was so psyched up, I managed the short journey across the burning coals with ease. It was an unforgettable experience.'

*Reference: Geddes & Grosset, *Guide to the Occult and Mysticism*.

It was at this impressionable stage in her life that Mouneen became deeply involved with a man who was a spiritualist. He took her to hear medium Nina Merrington talk. Jasper Swain, a well-known lawyer in the town, had lost his son Mike in a car accident. A transfiguration medium, Nina was able to assume Mike's personality and talk as the dead boy. Tapes were made and Jasper Swain wrote a book entitled *Mike*, which was later reprinted as *On the Death of my Son*.

Mouneen, fascinated by this, bought her first pack of Marseilles Tarot cards and began sitting in psychic circles. However, her subsequent marriage to Philip Forrester put an end to her quest for esoteric knowledge and it was only after her divorce (she divorced her husband on their sixteenth wedding anniversary) that she was able once again to turn her mind to spiritual matters.

Mouneen moved back to Johannesburg and began attending meetings at the Spiritualist Church. Here her interest in the spiritual way of life was truly awakened. She bought herself a Rider-Waite deck and began trying to teach herself to read the cards. This was successful only up to a point, so she enlisted for a course with the respected psychic counsellor and teacher, Kate Rheeders.

Kate's divination course touched on Tarot, Numerology, Palmistry and African Divination, the latter including throwing the bones and prognostication through the Yoriba Shells.

I ask her to explain about the Yoriba Shells.

'The Yoriba tribe lives on the west coast of Africa. They are a very old tribe and their folklore consists of a host of different deities and is in many ways similar to Greek mythology. In order to read the future, the Yoriba diviner uses sixteen cowrie shells.'

'How do you use the shells?'

'The smooth serrated opening on one side is regarded as the "mouth" of the shell. The rounded side of the shell is broken open. A sharp pointed object is poked through the fragile surface and the shell is broken away to leave a rounded opening. This is the "eye" of the cowrie. The prepared shells are shaken in the hands and cast into a circle drawn on the ground or on a piece of cloth or paper. Questions are answered according to how the shells fall.'

'Are the Yoriba Shells an accurate means of divination?'

'Yes, if you understand it fully. But of all the lectures Kate gave, the Tarot most appealed to me. I went on to do both an intermediate and an advanced course in Tarot reading with her.'

By 1995, the year South Africa hosted the Rugby World Cup, Kate felt that her protégée was ready to go public with her Tarot prowess.

Kate was manning a table at Bruma Lake and she asked Mouneen to read the cards at a similar stand at the Johannesburg College of Education.

Somewhat apprehensively, Mouneeen agreed and was delighted to find that her readings (which included three readings for Radio Five disc jockeys) were an unqualified success.

She began reading Tarot for her friends and, as her confidence increased, for clients.

'Can a card reading really help solve a person's problems?' I ask.

'Most definitely. A client – let's call her Linda – came to see me. She had recently come out of a messy divorce from an abusive husband. Following her divorce, Linda had met up with her childhood sweetheart, who was married, but not very happily. She had feelings for this man, but she did not want to have an affair with him if there was no hope of them being together.'

'What did the cards show?'

'I immediately saw that Linda was still recovering from her divorce. She was carrying a lot of emotional baggage. Her self-confidence and self-esteem were at a very low level and this made her extremely vulnerable. The cards gave her a distinct warning that she should be very careful about starting an affair with her old flame as it could cause great upheaval in her life.'

'What did you advise?'

'Linda needed to work on her self-image and on building up her self-confidence. Only when healing had taken place would she be ready for another relationship. I suggested that she should start meditation and also do some affirmations. The affirmation I gave her was as follows: "I am worthy of and ready to receive the abundance of the universe. I am a unique person and I love myself the way I am." '

'Did you get any feedback from her?'

'I saw Linda six months later. She was a changed person. She had joined a meditation group and in this group she had met a very nice man and the relationship was progressing smoothly. The positive vibrations that she was sending out had spread to other aspects of her life as well. She was succeeding in her job and she had recently had a salary increase.'

As we progress through life, we are all bound to face certain unpleasant realities such as illness and the death of loved ones. Thus I asked Mouneen how she conducted a reading when the querent drew 'bad' or negative cards.

'I have never seen death in a reading. I will never say to a person that you or somebody close to you is about to die. When I asked my guides about this they explained that only the Father God knows the exact time and manner of somebody's death.'

In recent years, as her ability to read and interpret the Tarot increased, Mouneen found that she was able to channel the energies of her four spirit guides, thereby giving greater depth and meaning to her readings. Sketches of these guides hang on the walls of her reading room and she speaks of each one of them with great affection.

'One of my guides is Li. He is a Tibetan monk and he often channels through me. My main guide, however, is Hazar, a very highly evolved spiritual being. I also have two lady guides. Lucia, who is a Sister of Mercy, and a Native American guide called Lady Blue Feather.'

'How do you know which guide you're channelling?'

'Li always refers to me as "My beloved friend". When Hazar appears I get a lovely warm feeling as if I'm being hugged. He calls me "My beloved". Lucia always greets me with the words "I'm the bearer of light". Lady Blue Feather says, "I'm the practical one." '

'You've already explained that you will never foretell a death,' I say. 'What if you see other negative things, such as financial ruin, for a particular person?'

'Some people come to me and say they want to know everything. Others say they want to hear only the good things. But if I feel great negativity in a reading, I will always try and give that person a healing affirmation.'

'Such as?'

'Well, if I see great financial difficulties, the affirmation I give them might be, "I am worthy and ready to receive the abundance of the Universe." '

Mouneen then goes on to tell me the story of Amy, a widow in her forties, who was experiencing financial difficulties.

'Amy,' Mouneen explained, 'had had a high-powered position in a financial institution, but she left this job to start her own business. This business had been going for six months, but not very successfully. The question Amy asked me was whether she should cut her losses or whether she should carry on working on her own.'

'What did the cards say?'

'I told Amy that if she stayed in the business a few months more, big contracts would be coming her way. It would cost her money, but the rewards would be great. I felt that if she closed the business at that point, she would just about break even. She would get another job, but she would always feel that she had failed.'

'Did she follow your advice?'

Mouneen smiled as she replied: 'With reluctance. Amy simply could not see her business improving. However, she said that she would continue working for herself for another three months and then she would reassess the situation.'

'What was the final outcome?'

'She phoned me a month later and told me that she'd recently been awarded two big contracts from a bank and that things were looking better. Three months later she phoned me once more to say that the business was doing very well – there were more big contracts in the pipeline.'

If I needed further proof of the accuracy of Mouneen's predictions, I got verification from a most unexpected source – my older daughter Daniella.

Daniella was going overseas to work as a camp counsellor in America. She would be teaching tennis to a group of young girls at a summer camp in Vermont. Now, although she had been overseas before, she had always been accompanied by her parents or by her friends. This was her first solo excursion and Daniella was understandably feeling somewhat apprehensive.

I suggested that she consult with Mouneen, hoping that a reading would allay her fears. When Daniella saw Mouneen, who reassured her that a whole bunch of new friends would be waiting to welcome her in the States, my daughter had a further question for the Tarot reader.

'Do you know where my watch is?' she asked.

Mouneen narrowed her eyes. 'Is it a watch with silver links? Does it look like a bracelet?'

Daniella nodded. 'Last night, I was going to a party at a club.

I was in a hurry, so I didn't fasten it properly. It was late when I left and I was tired – I didn't notice that it wasn't on my wrist.'

'Well,' said Mouneen, 'it's not lost or stolen. It fell off your wrist and it's lying in a dark place. Probably in soil. It will be returned to you.'

A search for the missing watch was instigated. It was not found in soil – although it was found in a dark place. The watch had slipped behind one of the sofa cushions in the restaurant.

A relieved Daniella put her recovered watch on her wrist. This time she made quite sure that it was securely fastened.

I had spent many pleasant hours with Mouneen. It was now getting late and the afternoon shadows were lengthening across the carpet. Mouneen picked up the Tarot pack and carefully placed the deck in a plain wooden box. This is a gift she cherishes almost as much as the cards themselves.

Within this box she has also placed a quartz crystal for energy; a turquoise to provide her with the ability to speak the truth; a rose quartz for healing and an amethyst for clarity of mind and psychic power.

For Mouneen does not see the Tarot as a mere pack of cards. Rather, she regards each card as a familiar friend who is to be cherished and treated with great respect for its amazing power to divine hidden secrets.

'For me they are alive,' she concludes with a gentle smile.

'I believe that the greatest act of love
you can bring to the world is to be
visible. Show others what a person
looks like without a mask. Remind
others of their wholeness by being
whole.

Colleen-Joy Page

Photographed by Francki Burger

Have you ever had the feeling that you need to phone a friend because they're in trouble and they need you at that moment? Dr Colleen-Joy Page believes in these empathetic moments – only she likes to take them into another realm.

She likes to look beyond the obvious; further than what the lips are saying; she likes to journey into the depths of the soul. She listens to what the soul is saying and she is able to convey its message. She even teaches those who are open to it to tune in to the music of their own soul.

From the Academy of Metaphysics near Fourways in Gauteng, which she founded in 1998, Colleen-Joy offers students of the esoteric a variety of spiritual growth development options. In addition to one-on-one intuitive counselling, step-by-step home study courses are available.

Subjects covered in these powerfully transformative audio cassette tape courses include: Developing Your Intuition; Past Lives and Destiny; Emotional Healing. Colleen-Joy also gives workshops and lectures on a wide variety of metaphysical topics, covering everything from practical facilitation for spirituality and soul integration, to fear management and transformation, to an exemplary understanding of astrology.

With her strong academic bent, the path of learning has been one of straightforward achievement for Colleen-Joy, culminating in a PhD in Metaphysics from the University of Metaphysics in the USA. Her road through life thus far has, however, been a mixture of pleasure and pain.

Born into an ordinary middle-class home in Alberton and the oldest of three children, Colleen-Joy Brandon, with her big blue eyes and ready smile, was a very appealing toddler. Indeed, she was most aptly named – Colleen is an Irish name which means 'pretty little girl'.

However, tragedy struck when Colleen-Joy was four. She developed a fibrous dysplasia tumour behind her right eye. Although the tumour proved to be benign, it grew rapidly until it was about the size of a large egg. Owing to her extreme youth, doctors were hesitant to operate. Ashamed of her unusual appearance, Colleen-Joy changed from a happy and carefree little girl into a shy and withdrawn child.

Within a year a CT scan – technology that had only just become available in South Africa – revealed than the inner tumour was larger than the outer one and perilously close to the optic nerve. Unless an operation was performed, Colleen-Joy would be blind. Today, as I interview her in her sunny sitting room, Colleen-Joy makes the telling comment: 'It was near blindness that taught me to see.'

When she was just five years old and not yet ready for school, Colleen-Joy underwent a dangerous and complicated operation that took more than ten hours. A team of surgeons, that included a neurosurgeon, a plastic surgeon and an orthopaedic surgeon, was in attendance.

After some hours had elapsed, her anxious mother went in search of someone who could give her information about the progress of the operation.

'How is the Brandon child doing?' she enquired of a passing nurse who had just emerged from the operating theatre.

Not realising that she was speaking to Colleen-Joy's mother, the nurse replied, 'Oh, it's such a fascinating operation. Do you know, we nearly lost her?'

It transpired that for a period on the operating table, Colleen-Joy was technically dead and had to be resuscitated by means of hot paddles that shocked her back to life. The burn marks on her back, still visible after all these years, bear testimony to the depth of her distress.

Resurfacing from her harrowing ordeal during the recovery

period, Colleen-Joy began to draw tunnels of coloured light. Today, she believes that these were the classic tunnels people see during near-death experiences.

This was her first indication that there was a non-physical spiritual world beyond this one. Even at that tender age, she began to ponder on the bigger questions, asking herself 'What exactly is life?' A precocious maturity had been forced on her by her unfortunate experience.

Starting school was a difficult time for Colleen-Joy. Her hair had been shaved off for the operation and was still painfully short when she started school. She felt extremely self-conscious and became even more shy and withdrawn. Turning inwards, she found that more and more she was developing an inner life.

A 'friend' – a small ball of pink light – appeared to comfort her and was always there for her in times of dark despair. Only later would Colleen-Joy realise that this was an early manifestation of becoming acquainted with her spirit guides.

At the age of seven or eight, Colleen-Joy shared a psychic experience with a close friend. The two girls had the same dream. Her friend dreamt that she was in a kitchen playing with paper boats in a basin. When she related this dream the next day at school, Colleen-Joy realised that her dream of the previous night had been identical. 'How is this possible?' she wondered. Once again, she instinctively felt the presence of the spirit world.

Before the advent of television in South Africa, Colleen-Joy 'saw' space travel, people conquering space, astral travel. Her dreams at this stage were as vivid as her inner life. She began to play telepathic games with her friends. She would write down five numbers and tell her companions at the other end of the playground to write down their five numbers. More often than could be put down to coincidence, the numbers were identical.

Friendship. Laughter. Happiness. By the time Colleen-Joy was nine years old, it seemed that she could at last enjoy a 'normal' childhood.

Then tragedy struck once more. The tumour grew back.

There would have to be more surgery. Colleen-Joy panicked, not so much about the implications of the operation, but about whether the doctors would shave her hair off again so that she would once more be different from her friends.

The surgeons did not shave her head this time, but the operation required the reconstruction of a portion of her nose. Colleen-Joy was only finally given a clean bill of health when she was sixteen.

Today, Colleen-Joy is a good-looking and self-assured young woman. Unless you look very closely, no scars are visible. But what grew from this childhood trauma was empathy for those who needed help; for those experiencing difficulty; for those in pain. People from all walks of life come to consult Colleen-Joy – people ranging from CEOs to radio personalities, to parents, to fellow members of the esoteric and healing professions.

Not that Colleen-Joy, with her amazing psychic powers – she

began reading the Tarot for clients when she was only sixteen – will give a conventional fortune-telling reading. She prefers to reach deeper.

Why have you really come to see me? What pathway are you choosing to follow? What is the state of your energy systems? What is your soul purpose?

If this concept is difficult to grasp, perhaps the following story will better illustrate Colleen-Joy's intuitive understanding of the soul's journey through this time space.

Bronwen, a counselling psychologist who was feeling unfulfilled in her career, began consulting Colleen-Joy. Two months later, her twenty-one-year-old sister Bianca was involved in a serious car accident. There was doubt as to whether or not she would survive.

Coincidentally, Bianca was a friend of Colleen-Joy's brother Richard, who phoned in a distressed state and asked his sister if she could help.

'Is it a head injury?' Colleen-Joy asked her brother.

'Yes,' he said.

Colleen-Joy sat quietly by herself for an hour to gather her intuitive energies. She saw that Bianca's eyes had been pushed in and damaged; her right arm was smashed; she had a fracture in the lower part of her skull at the back of her head; her bones were injured; her ribs were bruised.

Realising that her energy alone would not be enough, Colleen-Joy asked her mother and brother to support her – to send an energy line to Bianca throughout the day. Intuitively, Colleen-Joy knew that as Bianca hovered between life and death, her soul was making a decision whether to stay on this earth or to return 'home'.

It was not an easy choice. In this world, Bianca had to face the unpleasant reality that she had suffered extensive physical damage that might not be fully overcome. The rehabilitation process would be arduous and might not be altogether successful.

As Bianca's soul wrestled with these problems, Colleen-Joy continued to send out healing energy. 'But,' she told me, 'I did not interfere with the soul's choice. I let it be known that I would support this choice, whatever it might be.'

By four o'clock that day, Colleen-Joy realised that Bianca's soul had elected to stay on this earth in order for Bianca to meet the many tests of life as a physically challenged person.

The next day Colleen-Joy went to visit Bianca in hospital. Taking her hand she told the unconscious, paralysed girl that she saluted her courage and respected the choice her soul had made.

For months Bianca lay in a coma. She was paralysed and could not speak or communicate in any meaningful way. Various forms of therapy – occupational therapy, physiotherapy and speech therapy – were introduced to facilitate healing.

Brownen says of this time: 'Every small movement Bianca made was a celebration. We watched as she managed a slight twitch of her little finger to manoeuvre herself into a sitting position. We watched her being weaned off a ventilator, tracheotomy, gastrostomy and catheter. We watched her utter her first words. We laughed, we cried, we celebrated.'

However, in the midst of their joy, there was one great sadness – Bianca was blind. Bronwen brought the wheelchair-bound Bianca to see Colleen-Joy. The sightless girl told Colleen-Joy that while she was lying in hospital her guides had appeared to her and had offered to show her the world as it truly is.

Bianca then explained to Colleen-Joy how she had been exposed to a world of great beauty and light and that this had calmed her and made her feel at peace.

'At first,' Bianca said, 'I felt pretty vulnerable being seen by others because of the limitations of my broken body. But then I realised something . . .'

'And what was that?' Colleen-Joy asked.

'People may judge me,' replied Bianca, 'yet I know that their souls do not.'

Colleen-Joy has been married to Chris Page for the past eight years. 'Our marriage, I believe, is a contract of our two souls. We complement each other. I believe that I am truly blessed.'

Chris, who is both a student of the spiritual and an artist, is able to relieve Colleen-Joy of some of the pressures of her enormous workload.

For in addition to her readings – and before each one she will consult with her guides so that she gets a more complete picture of the person's soul purpose – her teaching, her workshops and her public speaking, Colleen-Joy is a regular contributor to the blossoming esoteric publication *Namasté*.

To add to her other impressive qualifications, she was ordained as a minister in 1996 by the International Metaphysical Ministry of the USA. Somehow she also manages to find time within her busy schedule to conduct christenings, weddings and funerals for people who want a deeply spiritual, personal, yet alternative ritual.

Chris and Colleen-Joy have two small daughters – Eryn who is seven and Megan who is five. It says much for Colleen-Joy's strength of character that she is able to say to me with complete conviction and sincerity that there is a beautiful story attached to young Megan's life.

Megan was born with her bladder outside her body. Many reconstructive procedures were required to correct this problem and to re-establish the functioning of this delicate organ. Megan's operations began when she was just fourteen hours old.

Colleen-Joy's ability to take her mind to the quiet place inside her of peace, love and knowing, gave her the fortitude to cope throughout two years of surgical procedures which almost resulted in the financial collapse their business and also caused painful memories of her own childhood to resurface.

One particularly traumatic day, following a small dilation procedure to correct a bladder blockage, Megan lay sleepless and inert on the hospital cot. Her pain had gone beyond mere crying.

Colleen-Joy realised that the bladder procedure had not worked because it was not the problem. She instinctively knew that her daughter's discomfort was not being caused by the bladder blockage, but rather by a blockage of the bowel. This diagnosis was confirmed by the X-rays that Colleen-Joy requested.

The attending doctors immediately wanted Megan to have major bowel surgery to remove the life-threatening blockage.

With remarkable courage, Colleen-Joy was able to put aside her fear. Instead, focusing her energies and going deep within, she went past the small body of her daughter in order to get a soul perspective, rather than a purely physical, five-sensory perspective of the problem.

She then 'intuitively' realised that Megan's soul did not request the surgery, unlike the other operations to which her soul agreed. During those long and anxious hours Colleen-Joy worked with Megan, supporting her soul choice in her body.

Family and friends were called upon to pray and send healing thoughts to the sick child. Five minutes before the scheduled surgery, the blockage shifted and Megan passed a stool. For the first time in twenty-four hours, the child stood up and said, 'Mommy, hungry.' Checking her diaper, Colleen-Joy saw that the child's bowel had indeed worked.

With this tangible proof that her daughter was recovering, Colleen-Joy asked that the surgery be called off. Although the surgeon did not concur with the suggestion, he reluctantly agreed to wait until the following day.

As a result of new X-rays, the planned operation was cancelled. When the surgeon returned from his ward rounds the next day and saw that Megan was once again well with colour in her cheeks, he smiled a warm, rare smile. It was his tribute to Colleen-Joy's intuitive power.

There is no better story than Megan's to illustrate Colleen-Joy's core philosophy that is central to all her teachings: spirituality must be incorporated into daily living as a valuable and practical life skill.

The Pages believe that this experience was a life-changing one. Without words, small Megan showed those who love and prayed for her the awesome power of the soul. If it is true, as some say, that we choose our parents, then Megan could not have chosen more loving, intuitive and insightful parents than Chris and his remarkable wife, Colleen-Joy.

Renée Fouché – Reiki Master & Mystic

Photographed by Jaco Wolmarans

'I believe that the stories in the Bible are symbolic of what is happening in our lives right now. Just as the people in the Bible had to face their challenges and their temptations, so we, too, have to deal with our difficulties. It is how well we cope with these challenges that ascertains our level of spiritual growth.'

Renée Fouché

Reiki is a healing method that is both magnetic and radiatory. It operates on all levels of our being – physical, emotional, mental and spiritual. The energy that is channelled through the hands of the practitioner is drawn from a blending of REI (cosmic energy) and KI (the energy within).

A Reiki treatment might begin with the Reiki practitioner centring him or herself by taking a couple of deep breaths. Some people like to say a small prayer and ask for guidance in the healing that they are about to perform. They may even call upon their guides or angelic beings or the Reiki Masters to help them.

The person administering the Reiki will then run his or her hands over the patient's aura a few times in order to get the feel of the patient and so that the patient can get a feel of the practitioner's energy. This energy does not have to be directed into specific areas of the body as it will flow to wherever it is needed – just as the sea smoothes the sand on a beach, filling holes and levelling sand castles.

The origins of Reiki can be traced back to ancient Tibet, thousands of years ago. The technique was rediscovered in the mid 1800s by Dr Mikao Usui of Japan. Dr Usui's quest to uncover the source of this ancient healing technique led him to the University of Chicago. Here he gained a doctorate in Theology, but he did not find the answers he sought, for he wished to uncover the secret of how Jesus and his disciples healed the sick and performed miracles.

When he returned to Japan, Dr Usui realised that Buddha had performed the same type of miracles as Jesus. He began asking the various Buddhist sects if they knew how to heal both the mind and the body simultaneously. To his disappointment, he found that the Buddhists concentrated on the spirit and not on the body.

Finally Dr Usui sought admission to a Zen monastery so that he could study the Buddhist scriptures, the sutras, in his search for the key to healing. After mastering Sanskrit, Dr Usui began reading the teachings of the Tibetan Buddhist sect. From these writings he found the symbols, formulas and descriptions of how the Buddha healed.

But Dr Usui was still not satisfied. For although he had acquired the *knowledge* of how to heal, he still did not have the power to heal. He sought the assistance of a monk within the monastery and it was revealed to him that he should go to a designated place upon the holy Mount Kuri Yama. There he was to fast for twenty-one days and to meditate.

On the twenty-first day, Dr Usui saw a light approaching him from far off in the East. It became brighter as it came closer to him. At first he was frightened, but then he said, 'If that light is for me, I accept enlightenment.'

The light became very bright and streamed across the heavens and hit him in the third eye. Dr Usui saw many, many bubbles in all the colours of the rainbow. Then came the powerful, bright white light, followed by golden Sanskrit letters, the secret formula of the Universal Life Force and how to contact it. They came to him one by one, commanding him to memorise and preserve them.

On his way down the mountain, Dr Usui met a young Japanese girl. She had a bandage wrapped around her jaw in an attempt to quell the pain of an aching tooth. He asked her if he could give her a healing and she gladly accepted his offer.

Dr Usui gently put his hands around her jaw and within a short period of time both the pain and the swelling began to subside. To his great joy, he had uncovered the secret of how Reiki flowed through him to the healee and how the body became well.

For many years, Dr Usui used his power to heal the sick. In 1893, he decided to pass on the knowledge he had gained to Dr Chujiro Hayashi. Following in the footsteps of Dr Usui, Dr Hayashi began travelling, teaching and dedicating his life to Reiki.

In the fullness of time, Dr Hayashi trained two Japanese women, one of whom stayed in Japan. The other, Mrs Hawayo Takata was instrumental in spreading the teachings of Reiki to the United States and Canada. Today, as Reiki continues to gain new adherents, there are many Reiki Masters throughout the world. One of them, Renée Fouché, operates from her heavenly holistic retreat Avanti, in Upper Orange Street in Cape Town.

Renée comes forward to greet me, her long reddish-brown hair hanging down her shoulders, her hazel eyes sparkling, her lithe figure held erect with the grace and posture of a ballet dancer. She appears to me to be the epitome of composure. It is hard to believe that until she emerged from a deep depression, caused by the death of her fiancé, her life was disordered and undisciplined.

I ask Renée about her life and the path that ultimately led her to Reiki healing, which she believes to be the fulfilment of her life's purpose on this earth.

She was born in the East Rand town of Springs, the middle child of three. Her father worked in the mining industry and the family moved around a great deal. Thus, when it was time for her to go to high school, her parents decided to put her into boarding school.

'Did you like boarding school?' I ask her.

'I loved it! I was full of mischief and I had a little gang of friends and we got up to all sorts of pranks,' declared Renée animatedly. 'Unfortunately, however, in Standard 8 I developed a learning problem and my concerned parents took me out of the school. I then went to school in Barberton, where I matriculated.'

At this juncture, Renée decided that she would like to become either a nurse or a teacher. In the end she went to Teachers' Training College in Pretoria, where she took a course that would qualify her to teach all subjects to senior primary learners.

Renée taught for ten years, moving around the country. It was a career that she thoroughly enjoyed. But she began to feel restricted by what she perceived to be the narrowness of thinking in government schools and moved on to teaching Afrikaans in private schools, which she found to be much freer and more liberated.

'What happened to your love life?' I ask. 'After all, you were now in your twenties and obviously very attractive.'

'Yes, I had boyfriends. Then I developed a serious relationship with a medical student who was about twenty-five. He was manic depressive and he ultimately committed suicide.'

His death plunged Renée into a deep depression that lasted many months. One day a friend put his hand on her knee. 'What's wrong with you?' he asked. 'You are like one of the living dead.'

Renée suddenly started screaming and it was as if, at that moment, the scales fell from her eyes. She saw, as if a blindfold had been removed, the astonishing beauty of the world. She felt filled with tremendous energy.

For the first time, she found her time cycle was synchronised. She instinctively knew that she would no longer be late for work; late for her bus. She, the teacher, realised that she had learned her lesson. Despite her great sorrow, she knew that she had somehow found the inner strength not merely to survive, but to thrive.

It was time to travel. Renée visited Amsterdam, revelling in the freedom she found there as well as the cultural experience. It was the hippy era; flower power was in full bloom. Throwing her inhibitions to the wind, Renée blossomed.

She returned to South Africa three months later. She knew that her life's path was to be a teacher and a healer. Marriage was not part of her plans for she knew that, fertile as her mind was, her womb was barren.

She began nursing at the J G Strijdom Hospital (now the Helen Joseph Hospital) in Johannesburg, but soon became disillusioned with what she perceived to be over-zealous attention to discipline and order. Sheets had to be pulled straight in case the matron did an inspection. One day a sick baby was turned away from the hospital because her family was deemed to be too poor to pay the bills. 'Where,' Renée asked herself, 'was the love? The compassion, the heartfelt caring for the sick?'

Leaving the hospital world behind her, Renée returned to teaching. She started to do yoga and transcendental meditation. She also realised that she no longer wished to live alone. 'People need the nourishment of other people,' she decided.

She began to live in communes; in communities of people with whom she thought she would find much in common. Initially, she found some of the commune dwellers strange: 'They walked around saying things like "Praise the Lord",' says Renée with a wry laugh, 'although I learned to adapt. Community living was new to me . . . for years I had been a loner.'

Renée lived first with a community called the Emissaries of Divine Light in Illovo in Johannesburg and taught at King David School in Victory Park. After living with this community for a few months, she again decided to quit the teaching profession and joined a community on a farm in Paarl in the Western Cape. She decided that rural life was for her. On the farm she could be at one with nature, milking cows, ploughing the land, picking grapes and guavas.

Life on the farm turned out to be extremely hard work and the ten people living there decided that the premises were too small for the group to live in comfort and to host their in-house classes.

Deciding to move on, the group bought the Hohenhort Hotel in Constantia. They also bought the land adjoining it, intending to establish a community settlement. The first months were extremely difficult for none of the group had had any hotel training.

But Renée had made up her mind to succeed and did so by dint of hard work and sheer determination. During this time she also travelled extensively, visiting Canada, France and England.

Then, once again, Renée felt the need for change. Asked to run a chiropractic practice in Johannesburg, she returned to that city, settling with the Emissaries at a commune near Fourways.

At this centre, the Emissaries performed healing sessions known as Attunements. Plagued by bouts of ill health that included typhoid, septicaemia and other conditions that required fairly major surgery, Renée took a keen interest in these sessions.

'I believe all physical illness has an emotional root. Illness is a catalyst for change. Sickness may be given to us as one of life's challenges for each one of us gets one or two major challenges in life to test one's faith in oneself and in life.'

'What if we fail the test?' I ask her.

'Then we will have to repeat it. If not in this life, then in another. We all have lessons that must be learned.'

'Were you happy with the community?'

'Suddenly, I saw the pitfalls of living in a group. It was as if my shoes didn't fit any more. I knew that it was time for change. I believe that it was Reiki that eventually helped me leave the community and stand on my own two feet.'

'How did you come to Reiki?'

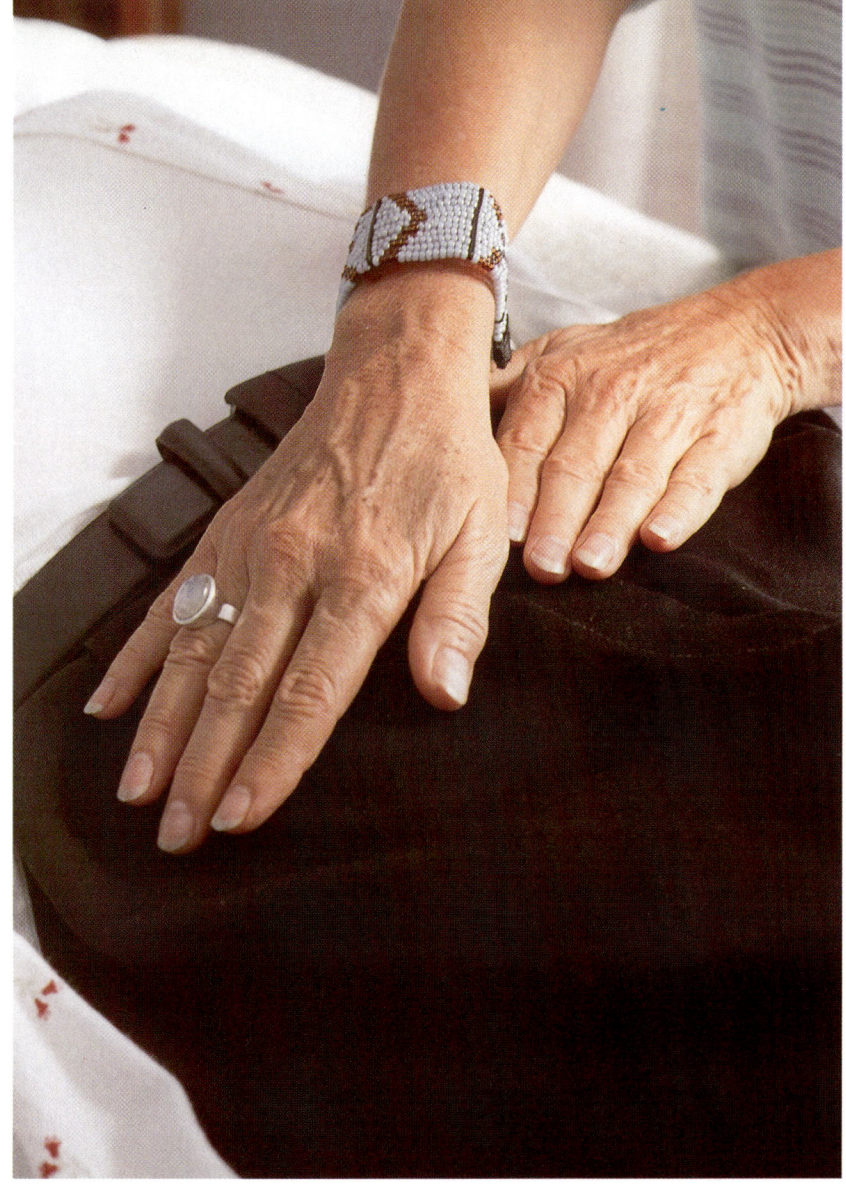

being was stripped away and my inner being was vibrating with the whole Cosmos.

'At the second ceremony it was as though black water was running down my body. Everything opened up. I had unbelievable energy – I felt as if I had been on a cleansing fast.

'After the third initiation, I could literally feel the warm sea water lapping at my feet as I stood in the ocean in Hawaii.'

'Hawaii?' I am puzzled.

'Yes. At first I thought it was a connection to one of the Reiki Masters who comes from Hawaii. However, when I went to see Horace Bree here in Cape Town who does Past Life Astrology, he told me that I had been a Kahuna Healer in Hawaii in a previous life. This made incredible sense to me. I love tropical weather, tropical fruit. I identify with these healers. Like them, I need a lot of time and space for myself.'

I look at Renée as she stands before me, serene and confident in one of the healing rooms of Avanti, the haven that she herself has created. Today she is a Reiki Master. She is what she always wanted to be. A teacher and a healer. Her path to her true destination was not always plain sailing. Finally, however, through trial and error, she has found her true spiritual home.

For the past ten years, since Renée has been practising Reiki, she has treated a multitude of people for a wide variety of ailments ranging from physical problems, such as whiplash, to emotional problems like depression.

I ask her to tell me about some of the people she has helped.

'A woman who had been involved in a bad car accident came to see me. She had chronic pain in her neck. She had seen chiropractors and physiotherapists, but to no avail. I am pleased to say that through Reiki she was completely cured. She was so impressed with Reiki's amazing healing power that she started studying Reiki

'There was a woman named Annie Issacs who used to come from Paris to the commune and she taught Reiki. At first I thought I wouldn't like it because I don't particularly enjoy workshops and also I found it too simplistic. It was only after I had the Reiki initiations that my whole life changed.'

'How was that?'

'For me, these initiations were the most powerful part of the Reiki experience. At the first initiation it was almost as if my outer and is today a Reiki Master herself.'

'How can Reiki help in the case of depression?'

'Well, with Reiki nothing is impossible – the only limit is our mind. Some time ago, a woman suffering from severe depression came to see me. The Reiki I did went hand in hand with counselling. Reiki itself stimulates the endorphins, one of a group of chemical compounds that occur naturally in the brain and have pain-relieving properties similar to those of opiates. I was able to help her reconnect with the Creator, with herself and with others.'

'How powerful is Reiki? What if someone suffering from a terminal illness comes to see you?'

'Firstly, you must understand that Reiki can be given in conjunction with other treatments – chemotherapy, for example. But in the beginning I felt terrible when one of my patients died. I felt as if I had failed.

'Later, though, I came to understand that we will all die. Death is a transition. We are like leaves on a tree . . . we will simply fall off when it is our time to leave this planet. I realised that what I had to do was help those patients accept their death; I had to comfort and counsel them and give them unconditional love.'

'If Reiki is the universal life force energy, can it also be of benefit to other living things?' I ask. 'Plants and animals, for example?'

'Most definitely,' Renée replied. 'Take my cat Shanti, for example. She had a bad accident and was paralysed for two weeks. The vet doubted that she would ever walk again. I started giving her Reiki treatments and today, although she is not one hundred per cent, she is able to walk and play. She is a happy cat. Why, she even assists me in some of my Reiki treatments.'

'Have you helped any other animals?'

'A friend of mine had a fish tank. One of the fish was lying at the bottom of the tank, listless and close to death. My friend asked me to apply Reiki. By using the Reiki symbols on my own hands, I was able to transmit energy through the glass. The next day, the fish was swimming around as if nothing had happened.'

I asked Renée if it was necessary to see a Reiki practitioner for a healing or whether one could apply Reiki on oneself.

'Anyone can heal themselves by simply putting their hands on themselves,' she answered thoughtfully. 'However, the Reiki initiation is a sort of energetic technology that amplifies the current of energy flowing from the hands. Therefore, in order to derive real benefit, it is important to have undergone the proper training.'

Renée firmly believes that merely applying the following five Reiki guidelines to one's life can truly make a real and positive difference to one's life and belief system:

Just for Today –

- Do not Worry
- Do not Anger
- Honour your Parents, Teachers and Elders
- Earn your living Honestly
- Show Gratitude to every living thing

'We are all like a walking hologram,' concludes Renée, 'so we totally create our own lives. Like intentions, thoughts and feelings shape light and energy. Practising Reiki really does assist in all these universal principles.'

As I took my leave of the healing centre and walked down the steps of Avanti towards my car, I could not help but notice that somehow the sky seemed bluer; the leaves on the trees seemed greener; the sunshine seemed more brilliant. My heart felt so much lighter.

'I hope that I am here to learn, to teach others the value of themselves, and, in some way, contribute to the magic of living. However, I suspect that I am just a tiny, drunk insect tickling the night. And I am fine with that.'

Rozelle Mazetti

Photographed by Jaco Wolmarans

Rozelle Mazetti, a pretty woman with black curls and laughing brown eyes, is a person of many talents. A teacher, a Seichem* healer, an artist and an author, Rozelle has over twenty years' experience as a dream therapist and interpreter.

We sat chatting in one of the healing rooms in Avanti, the holistic centre in Gardens in Cape Town where Rozelle, in addition to her private consultations, used to work on a part-time basis. In spite of her mystical ability, which manifested itself at an early age, Rozelle appears completely down-to-earth and approachable. She laughs frequently and her manner is warm and friendly.

I asked Rozelle why people should find it necessary to have their dreams explained to them. She replied: 'Understanding our dreams allows us to penetrate the mystery of life and the mystery of who we truly are. As we progress in understanding and cooperating with our dreams, so our true self unfolds layer by layer, thus enabling us to reach our full potential.'

The practice of dreaming as a means of gaining wisdom and insight is as old as the planet. The significance of dreaming is recorded in the Old Testament and in the history of various civilisations – the Egyptians, the Romans, the Syrians, the Chinese and the Japanese, to name but a few.

In Genesis Chapter 41 we read: 'And Pharaoh said unto Joseph, I have dreamed a dream and *there* is none that can interpret it: and I have heard say of thee, *that* thou canst understand a dream and interpret it. And Joseph answered Pharaoh, saying: *It is* not in me: God shall give Pharaoh an answer.'

In ancient Egypt the practice of dream incubation was widely carried out, as it was believed that dreams were the voices of the gods giving guidance, healing and visions.

Dream interpretation and incubation was very popular amongst the ancient Greeks. Sleep itself was revered as a mystery that led to communion with the gods. In the Greek dream world, Hypnos, the God of Sleep, was an important figure.

Dream incubation was also practised in Japan in both Shinto and Buddhist temples, several of which became famous as dream oracles. In order to receive a dream vision, the devout believed that it was necessary to practise abstinence and make pilgrimages to a sacred site where an offering would be made. The dreamer would remain at the site for a specified time, sleeping in a room adjacent to the inner sanctum.

The practice of sleeping in holy places to bring particular dreams was also common throughout Pagan Europe and early Christians followed the same procedure, sleeping in the shrines of saints who could send dreams of healing, transformation or enlightenment.

In many cultures, particularly indigenous cultures, children are taught from an early age to honour and remember their dreams. There is a thin line between the sacred and the secular and the conscious and unconscious aspects of the self are woven together in a natural way.

For Rozelle this culture of honouring one's dreams came naturally. 'I have always dreamed – even as a child my dreams were wonderful epics, colourful nightly pageants. Later, I realised that I could somehow travel in the Dreamtime, unintentionally entering into the thoughts and feelings of other people or discovering the whereabouts of lost objects.'

This clairvoyant ability seems to run in Rozelle's family. Her father's father came from Venice. Her mother came from a hardy, pioneering family who were founders of the little town of Postmasburg in the Northern Cape. Staunch defenders of their Afrikaans heritage during the Anglo-Boer War, the family were descendants of Paul Kruger.

'Perhaps that is where we inherited our clairvoyance. *Oom* Paul was known to have had visions and he had an uncanny ability of leading hunting parties towards unseen game. Both my mother

*Seichem is a supportive method of healing which utilises Universal Life Force to balance and re-energise the body's energy field.

and her brother had a gift of clairvoyance which manifested itself through dreams and an extraordinary connection with animals.'

This inherited gift has been passed on to Rozelle's two daughters in different ways. Her older daughter Annwen has had, from a very young age, a natural ability to interpret dreams. Her younger daughter Cara, aged nine at the time of writing, is able to see people's auras and has the ability, even at her tender years, to detect disease and stress in the body.

Dreams have always had a profound significance for Rozelle. 'I believe that our dreams are a window to the unconscious part of ourselves. They are an inner conversation between the different aspects or levels of the unconscious mind, sorting out information, making relevant connections and creating an inner map that helps us navigate our way through life.'

Rozelle believes that our dreams offer us a bridge to other dimensions, to divinity, to the future and to the past. She feels that through the dream realm, not only are we able to benefit from information and knowledge from the physical realm, we are also able to access wisdom from the spiritual world.

When she was in her thirties, Rozelle suffered a profound personal crisis which led her to seek counselling from a Jungian therapist who was particularly interested in dreams. Through this therapy, Rozelle realised the benefits of using dreams as a means of resolving personal conflict.

'Up until that time, my clairvoyant dream experiences had been random. Now, with my therapist's help, I was able to hone my skills and use my dreams as a guide to my inner and outer world. As I progressed in understanding and cooperating with my dreams, so I was able to unfold my true self, layer by layer. I believe that it is only by uncovering our real core that we are able to reach our full potential.'

Convinced of the benefits of dream therapy, Rozelle began to consult on a one-to-one basis. I asked her how she felt she could help people who were convinced that they did not dream.

'In order to access the dream world, we need to ensure that we get enough sleep. I recommend to people who wish to engage with their dreams that they have a bath or shower before retiring to a clean, uncluttered bedroom. It is a good practice to meditate or to pray before going to sleep.

'Most of all, one should clear one's mind of the anxieties of the day, particularly of feelings of anger and resentment. Drugs or an excessive amount of alcohol are to be avoided as they repress the REM* state of sleep which is when dreams usually occur.'

'What if you cannot remember your dreams?' I asked.

'A Dream Journal is an essential tool in assisting with dream recall. Apart from the exercise of recording the dreams, it also provides a record of the symbols, images and feelings that make up each person's unique Dream Language.'

Rozelle's personal journey into the exploration of the dream world has taken her to many mystical and spiritual sites. She has visited North and South America and the British Isles and Egypt. She was particularly fascinated by the time she spent in Peru.

'Peru is unique in that the line between sacred and secular is so thinly drawn that one is able to step easily into the realm of mysticism and dreams. The Andean and jungle healers of Peru, the *curandos*, use information received in dreams for healing and they are also able to enter the dream state of their patients to integrate deeper levels of healing or bring healing to completion.'

At a women's workshop in Mauritius it was suggested to Rozelle that she should run workshops to teach other people how to work with, understand and benefit from their dreams. Thus, at the start of the new millennium, Rozelle launched her ambitious new project – Dreamquest Workshops.

*REM sleep: A stage of sleep named for the rapid eye movements which are among its most salient characteristics.

'What type of person would come to see you, Rozelle?' I asked. 'Either privately or at one of your workshops?'

'I would have thought that only "alternative" people would be interested in the art of dreaming,' replied Rozelle, with a small laugh. 'However, this has not been my experience. I have had business people, professionals in all fields, as well as teachers and practitioners of complementary and alternative healing therapies. The common denominator amongst all my clients is that they are seekers – people who have the courage and drive to explore their inner world.'

'How have you helped them?'

'Dreams show us where we are in our journey through life – what is holding us back, what is tripping us up, and also how to reach our potential. Through dreams I will help clients discover their inner truth. Then I will journey with them through healing and transformation. I will help them take their rightful place in the world so that they may reach their highest potential.'

'What happens at your Dreamquest Workshops?'

Rozelle produces the programme from one of her two-day workshops which was held at Kagga Karma Private Game Reserve.

In addition to dream work, which included the writing of one's personal Dream Journal and the making of a Dream Shield – a shield regarded by Native Americans as a symbol of honour and protection – the programme included learning about the constellations of stars in the sky, access to sacred Bushmen sites and an explanation of the meaning and significance of their paintings, some of which date back over six thousand years.

Whilst I could see that this workshop had plenty to offer in the way of interest, I could not help but wonder whether or not it had fulfilled its prime purpose of bringing enlightenment and personal growth to the participants.

When I put my reservations to Rozelle, she brought forth a pile

of feedback correspondence from some of the participants, which commended her work in glowing terms.

This dream workshop was an unexpected treat. Rozelle is a skilled facilitator and drew our group together and then allowed an amazing amount of insightful nurturing to happen. The workshop was structured, but the flow of ideas from participants was encouraged. I was particularly impressed with how she drew in the archetypal energies, and their relevance to our dreams and to our hidden aspects.

The harmonious nature of the workshop encouraged even the most reserved people to open up and share, and thus allowed us to grow. The dream analysis that Rozelle shared with us has been very helpful to me. This was one of those amazing personal growth workshops that gave me a new way of thinking about things. Thank you for this gift.

Shirley Sudwarts, Reiki Master

Thanks for making a difference! Your workshop helped me to get to know the R I A in my life – that's Rest, Introspection and Action.

Bill Skinner, clinical psychologist

The more I think about the Dream Worskshop, the more I am able to process the happenings of that amazing weekend. Deep things within me were uncovered, parts of me that I really wished to hide, parts that I did not wish to acknowledge were all ignored and pushed down trying to be forgotten.

My dear, this weekend of dreaming has been a revelation to me. It is a precious gift that you presented to me. The gift to myself is one of release.

Shanti

Do I think that Rozelle's dream work has any real relevance in our frenetic, technology-based, modern lives? Yes, I do. Particularly if one takes into account the beliefs of the Native Americans and our own indigenous people in South Africa who believe that dreams are a form of guidance from our ancestral spirits, guides and teachers.

'Today,' says Rozelle, 'I work with abused children from squatter camps and townships on a voluntary basis. I do art therapy with them, as well as Reiki and dream interpretation. In this way I am able to use my esoteric skills in a totally practical way.'

One of our most talented musicians has written: 'I had a dream. I heard these beautiful sounds of people singing. The dream persisted for six months and I listened until I could imitate the voices. Then I could compose.' These are the words of Joseph Shabalala of Ladysmith Black Mambazo.

Shui Tseng – Medical Doctor & Feng-Shui Practitioner

Connecting your health, home and happiness

'I believe that your health is connected to the flow of energy through your home. For example, the front door of your house is like the mouth of your house. It must be easy to enter and it must catch only good energy. Otherwise you will suffer from poor health and bad luck.'

Dr S Tseng

Photographed by Francki Burger

Feng-shui (pronounced fung-shway) comes from the Chinese words FENG (wind) and SHUI (water). It is said that energy is carried by wind and retained when it hits water. This Chinese art of harnessing the heavens and the earth is believed to bring health, wealth and good fortune.

The practice of feng-shui dates back thousands of years and was originally limited in its use to the Emperor of China, his family and his functionaries. Other people practised it on pain of death. However, today its popularity has become widespread and it is used not only by the rich and famous, but also by ordinary people throughout the world.

The best-known writer and practitioner on the subject of feng-shui is Lillian Too. A lady with no mean credentials, she is the ex-managing director of the Grindlays Dao Heng bank in Hong Kong and the former deputy chairman of the billion-dollar company that owns the Knightsbridge store Harvey Nichols.

Throughout the East feng-shui is taken very seriously, particularly by businessmen, and it is interesting to note that many buildings in Hong Kong and Taiwan – states that have one of the highest per capita incomes in the world – have feng-shui inspired features.

Amongst the South African business community, too, feng-shui is gaining many adherents, although the captains of industry are reluctant to admit that they are calling in feng-shui experts to change their luck and bring in new business deals.

One successful businessman, whose name I am not at liberty to mention, called in Chinese feng-shui practitioner Dr Tseng when his business was experiencing a downturn. Dr Tseng's solution was simple. He told the businessman that he must move his office desk and that he must change the position of his desk chair. The businessman complied with these requests.

'Did it make any difference to his cash flow?' I asked the businessman's wife.

'Do you know, that very evening he received a fax from London containing a very large order that he had been struggling to obtain and had almost given up on?' she replied with a smile.

I made a few more enquiries about feng-shui practitioners working locally and once again Dr Tseng's name cropped up. A well-known restaurateur operating in Johannesburg's plush Hyde Park shopping centre was dismayed when she noticed a sudden decline in her business. Dr Tseng was called in. He told the owner that she must remove all the pictures on the walls (which were on loan from a local art gallery) and replace them with pictures of flowers.

'Why flowers?' she asked in surprise.

'Flowers will make your business grow,' explained Dr Tseng.

'Is there anything else I must do?' asked the restaurant owner.

Dr Tseng walked slowly through her premises, carefully studying his *lo p'an* or compass. Finally, he stopped in front of a ceramic lion near the entrance.

'This lion's belly is too fat,' he told the proprietor. 'It looks to me as if he has been eating up all your money. If you want to keep this lion, get two more little lions. The big lion needs to keep awake or your business will stay sleepy.'

Apparently, since following this advice, the restaurant's business has picked up very nicely, thank you.

I was intrigued and thought that I would like to meet the ubiquitous Dr Tseng. Consequently, I was delighted when a Reiki Master of my acquaintance gave me one of his business cards. The small white card with his name in black bore the inscription A.A. *Clinic and Chiness Medication Shop*.

Flipping the card over I read under the heading Physical Treatment:

*Oestopathy Nervous-pain Endocrire Digestive Urinary Reproductive Circulatory Headaches Insomnid (**Fun-sui**) Dislocation Paralysis Theumatism Articulation-pain Heemorrhoids Goiter & Edema Part-Atrophy Tendon-pain Other-pain Herbs etc.*

I immediately called the number on the card. Dr Tseng, whose grasp of the English language is somewhat tenuous, had difficulty understanding what I wanted of him. An interview is not, after all, a consultation. For a consultation one receives money.

Feng-shui, I was to learn, is very much about an exchange of energies – i.e. money. After some misunderstanding, and only once it was clearly understood that I was to recompense him for his valuable time, did he agree to see me.

I rang the bell at his modest house in Kensington, which was immediately answered by Dr Tseng himself. The good doctor turned out to be a small and charming elderly gentleman with a shock of grey hair. He was shoeless and as I entered what seemed to my uninformed western eyes to be a somewhat strangely positioned front door, I realised from the neat row of footwear lined up near the entrance that I, too, must take off my shoes.

After I had removed my sandals, Dr Tseng broke into a wide smile and bowed low. He led me down a long and almost bare corridor to the north-facing sitting room where his wife – all smiles and no English – greeted me. I was immediately offered tea. I accepted gladly but was disappointed to find that it was Five Roses. I always thought that nobody made better tea than the Chinese.

Born in Taiwan, Dr Shui Tseng studied Chinese medicine in Hong Kong. Feng-shui, which he learned from a Buddhist monk at the Sao-Lin Temple in Fugen, was part of his medical studies. When I expressed my surprise at this, Dr Tseng explained that medicine and feng-shui in China are intertwined. 'Like a river with two streams,' he explained poetically.

Thus a medical consultation with Dr Tseng could well consist not only of a visit to his A.A. Clinic – the rooms of his practice are situated in his garden – but could also include a visit to the patient's house in order to correct, via feng-shui, any negative energy that could be causing physical problems.

'Can you explain the connection between your medical studies and feng-shui?' I asked.

'Aha. Then you must also know about *ch'i*.'

'What is that?'

'It is the life force that flows through your body and departs only on death. Sometimes in China we call it 'dragon's breath'. Acupuncturists must study the flow of *ch'i*. When your *ch'i* is flowing smoothly, you will experience much good health, wealth, luck and happiness.'

This, then, is the basis of all feng-shui. The Chinese believe that straight lines or fast-flowing streams or roads deplete the *ch'i* which leads to the evaporation of health, wealth and luck. The ideal conditions for accumulating *ch'i* are slow, coiling, sinuous flows of water or wind that gather a good flow of life force in a suitably protected haven – be this shelter the body, the workplace, or the home.

After practising as a doctor in Taiwan for many years, Dr Tseng and his wife decided to come to South Africa about ten years ago. Of their four children, the two daughters stayed behind in Taiwan, but the sons accompanied their parents. Both sons are studying computer technology.

Also learning to speak good English,' Dr Tseng added, beaming at me.

When Dr Tseng is asked to do a feng-shui consultation for a house, he will come with only his *lo p'an* or compass and, some say, a good dose of psychic ability.

Amongst the things that he will check is the path to your front door. If it is curving, so much the better. A straight path, he believes, can cut your luck.

The front door is all important. It should be solid and protective and not made of glass. It should not open on to a narrow or dark corridor and the entrance hall should not have any wooden beams as these can be detrimental to the flow of *ch'i*.

A mirror in the entrance hall, Dr Tseng believes, sends good luck out. However, flower pots not only bring in money and good luck, they hold it and make it grow.

'Also important,' said Dr Tseng firmly, 'you must see that the front door is in the right position. A man phoned me and he was very sad because his luck had run out. He had no money. I went to his house. I changed the door to the money side.'

'Which is the money side?' I wanted to know.

'I need to see the house before I can say for sure. But you must know that once I change where the door is, I change the luck also. This man was very happy about his new good fortune.'

Another thing that Dr Tseng does not favour is a house on too many levels. 'For then, like the hills, your luck will be up and down.'

Nor does he like water features, particularly waterfalls, in the middle of a house. 'It takes out the heart of the home. It drains the energy. People with a house like this are always sick.'

Since water is an integral part of feng-shui, the position of the swimming pool is important. A housewife from Johannesburg's northern suburbs who believes implicitly in the power of feng-shui called in Dr Tseng when her husband's business was going through a difficult time.

'Dr Tseng immediately told me that the position of the pool was part of the difficulty. He said that it was easy for money to evaporate. I was so desperate that I was even prepared to close in the pool.

'However, Dr Tseng said that all I would have to do was place seven plants here in the corner like this' – she produced one of Dr Tseng's many rough sketches that he had made to correct perceived faults in her house – 'and the money, in his words, would no longer be able to run out.'

'What else did he suggest?'

'He has a profound knowledge not only of feng-shui but of other things like numerology and yin and yang, the negative and positive. When he came into our house, he asked the birth dates of my entire family. From these he worked out who was compatible and who was not. When he entered our bedroom the first thing he did was to remove the mirror that stood in front of the bed. He maintained that a mirror in front of the bed creates a double image and promotes discord.'

'What else did he say?'

'He changed the positions in which we slept. I used to sleep on the left side of the bed and my husband slept on the right. He said that this was the incorrect balance of yin and yang energy.'

'Did he change anything else in the house?'

'He asked how we sat around the dining room table. I showed him where I sat and where my husband sat. He asked us whether there was discord in the house. When I replied "Yes", he swapped our positions at the table. Dinner times are certainly a lot more peaceful now,' she laughed.

'You've had Dr Tseng go through your house from top to bottom. But feng-shui originated in the East. Do you really believe that it works in the West?'

'It was my son's birthday recently,' she replied, 'and we had a luncheon party at the house. One of the guests brought her four-month-old baby. She said that she hadn't had a moment's peace since the child was born because he was restless and always crying. The minute the baby entered the house, he seemed to sense a new energy. He became calm and was as good as gold. His mother said she couldn't believe the miraculous change in him. Does that answer your question?'

For Dr Tseng the birth dates of the occupants of a house are important. Everyone has one of the five elements – Fire, Water, Wood, Metal and Earth, the principal energies manifest in the universe – associated with the time, day, month and year of their birth.

From a feng-shui point of view, the year of birth and the animal represented in the Chinese horoscope according to this year will help to ascertain the compatibility (or otherwise) of the occupants in the house. For example, if you are a Fire person, then a water-orientated dwelling or workplace might not be advisable as Water destroys Fire.

According to Dr Tseng, the importance of numbers extends even to the number of fish swimming in your pond or in your fish tank. 'Two fish swimming together means money, but three fish is no good. For if the one fish swims away from the other two, your money also swims away. Do you understand?'

'I think so.'

'Another thing. In a house you must have the following number of animals or birds. Two, four, six, eight. Do you know why? Two dogs keep the peace. Three dogs cry. Four dogs make you lucky.'

I am well aware of the growing number of western feng-shui practitioners, some of whom have been privileged to study with Lillian Too. However, as I talk with Dr Tseng I realise how deeply rooted in Eastern philosophy and beliefs feng-shui is.

Consequently, despite the fact that I was not always able to understand the precise meaning of what Dr Tseng wished to communicate, I was pleased that I had interviewed him.

As I was taking my leave of him and his wife, he suddenly broke into a wicked grin. 'Tell me, do you always keep the lid of your toilet down?'

I shook my head.

'You must. Otherwise you will flush away your wealth. Your money will fly out. Fly, fly, fly.' With these parting words, Dr Tseng broke into a gale of laughter.

Judy Le Cash – Crystal Healer, Abuse Counsellor & Channel

Leading others towards the light

'I believe that for many incarnations I have been responsible for transforming negative energies into positive energies – darkness into light. This process has been carried out through incarnations as far back as Atlantis. In this current incarnation, I work with the Archangels Gabriel and Michael and also The Master Sananda who help me to assist people to transform and heal.'

Judy Le Cash

Photographed by Jaco Wolmarans

Like an angel of mercy, Judy Le Cash is on call twenty-four hours a day for clients who need counselling on a spiritual level for depression, anxiety, addiction, abuse and low self-esteem.

Judy also believes that through her three tools of psycho-spiritual counselling, healing and channelling, she is able to clear negative energies, restoring balance to the body and mind via the chakras and her omnipresent crystals, and thereby resurrecting the bright glow of a diminished aura.

In addition, her ability to act as a channel for the Archangels Gabriel and Michael and Master Sananda means that each person who comes to a private session with Judy will receive their own personal message of light and love from these Higher Beings. Soul enlightenment, she firmly believes, brings in its wake healing and transformation and a closer connection to God.

That Judy should find herself blessed with the ability to converse with such exalted beings would be extraordinary in any circumstances but is even more astonishing when one learns of her background.

For, light years away from the spiritual path on which she now finds herself, Judy's tumultuous early life was filled with all the sordid ingredients of the most depraved soap opera.

Brought up as a Jewess in England, pretty, blue-eyed Judy was abused by both her father and her grandfather. Her mother, seemingly powerless to act, simply stood by and watched the abuse that began almost as soon as the baby girl was born.

The adult Judy was in denial until her early forties, blocking out all memories of the abuse, and had been in psychotherapy for seven years. Today, Judy believes that her mother sacrificed her to lechery and debauchery because she felt that if her husband loved her daughter, he would not stray outside the family circle to satisfy his lust.

'I was a "soft" option,' she wryly maintains.

Inevitably, the horrors of her childhood resulted in behavioural problems. A high achiever in her early youth, by the time she was seventeen, Judy was, although she refused to admit it then, an alcoholic – a condition no doubt triggered by her unnatural relationship with her father.

While her father continued to abuse Judy throughout her formative years, one incident in particular wounded her greatly.

'I was about sixteen. My father came home and found me with a boyfriend. We were kissing and cuddling. Nothing more than that. My father was so angry that he sent the boy home and sent me off to bed. Then came into my bedroom and raped me, taking my virginity.'

Judy is talking to me in her turquoise, lilac and silver healing rooms in Observatory, in the shadow of Table Mountain and close to Cape Town's suburban railway line. With her tousled white, grey and brown hair, her loose, flowing purple outfit and shining crystals hanging from her neck, Judy is unlikely to go unnoticed in a crowd.

However, despite her somewhat flamboyant appearance, there is a calmness and gentleness about her that I find difficult to reconcile with her former wildness and promiscuity.

Following her father's death, while her career in the fashion industry was successful, Judy's personal life was a shambles. She entered into a series of abusive relationships. The first was with a man who, like her, had a drinking problem and consequently went along with her alcoholic tendencies.

Her subsequent marriage to her first husband, brought her into contact with an alcoholic man who was not only unfaithful, but used to beat her as well.

'He hit me on the night that he proposed to me. Until then, he had been my knight in shining armour. He was everything I could have wished for and more,' she recalls.

Seeing herself as a defenceless victim, Judy surrendered her body to the endless abuse. Frightened and alone, like so many battered wives, she lacked the courage to complain to anyone in authority about her husband's ill treatment of her.

After seven traumatic years, Judy obtained a divorce and started attending meetings of Alcoholics Anonymous. 'It was these meetings that pointed me in the direction of God,' she says now. 'They inspired me to search again for my Orthodox Jewish roots. I returned to the synagogue. I wanted to hear the cantor sing the songs that had inspired me as a child.'

But, still battling with the demons that haunted her, Judy entered into a period of unbridled promiscuity. Looking back on this time, she remarks that it was fortunate that Aids had not yet surfaced, as she believes that she would have undoubtedly contracted the disease.

It was at this stage, while searching for some meaning in life, that Judy began studying to be a Lifeline counsellor. 'It was here that I rediscovered my soul. A lot of like-minded people were doing the course at the time and I met people who are still my close friends today.'

Her second husband, whom Judy married when she was thirty-three, seemed to be a much more spiritual soul. He was a member of the Sufi Temple and Judy hoped that she had at last found some sort of peace. However, disillusionment soon set in: 'Not only was he a compulsive liar, he also had numerous affairs.'

Another divorce followed. And more affairs and, with them, more despair.

Judy's therapy helped her escape from the seemingly endless cycle of drugs, drink, sex, violence and abuse in which she found herself.

Her therapist decided to send her to a medium for a reading. Shortly after this Judy had her first spiritual experience.

'I was lying in bed. My late father came to visit me. I saw him clearly in the wall behind my left shoulder. He was very real to me. In therapy the issue arose that my father might have molested me. So, taking my courage in both hands, I asked my father why he had abused me. I remember him saying that he couldn't cope with his life – he hated it. He gave me and my mother such a hard time that he decided to leave.'

'What did he mean by that?' I ask.

'He had a heart condition which he decided to leave untreated. He died when he was fifty-seven.'

Judy's memory began to unlock. It would take seven years of therapy before all the buried memories of abuse were able to surface. A past life within a present life had been recalled.

With this recollection, came the opportunity for Judy to heal not only herself, but also the countless others who had suffered silently, as she had.

It is this first-hand and intimate knowledge of the darker side of life that has ultimately transformed Judy into the compassionate and understanding healer that she is today.

With her strong belief that regression helped heal and transform her previously chaotic life, Judy offers regression therapy to those whom she feels are ready to receive information that they may find disquieting or disturbing.

Those clients who are familiar with meditation Judy puts into a state of deep relaxation, allowing them to receive the information themselves. Since this type of regression will involve passing through death in the past life to which Judy regresses you into the life between lives' she always tells her clients: 'The question is not whether I do regression therapy, but whether you are ready to undertake regression therapy.'

For people who do not meditate regularly, Judy is able to offer the option of simply channelling past lives for clients who request this type of healing.

A most remarkable programme in February 2000 gave listeners of Cape Talk radio the unique opportunity of listening while Judy regressed a young woman named Jill live on air.

'Jill, why would you want to go through this?' demanded the show's anchor Shado Twala who despite her very public persona – or perhaps because of it – had declined to be regressed herself.

'It is something that has interested me for a very long time,' explained Jill in a clear and confident voice. 'I've done quite a lot of reading on it. It's just something that I think I've always been open to.'

'How long will the session take?' asked Shado, aware of the time constraints of radio programming.

'I don't know,' replied Judy. 'It depends how long it will take for me to connect with Jill's energy field. I'm not sure if I will be able to do it here, but I did ask my guides, the archangels, before I came into the studio if it was going to be possible. They agreed to let me try and, certainly, this crystal is really vibrating in my hands.'

'Jill, what is going on in your mind?' questioned Shado, while Judy asked God's permission to do this very public regression.

'My dad, who was dying of cancer, had a spirit guide called Sonny,' explained Jill. 'The doctors and specialists knew that nothing could be done to save him. However, Sonny helped him a great deal at this difficult time. Just after my dad died, before anyone else knew that he was dead, Sonny phoned my mom to say that he felt my dad's soul passing into heaven and how sorry he was that my dad had passed away.* Ever since then I've had a very relaxed, contented feeling about spirit guides and things in the other realm.'

'OK, Jill,' said Judy softly. 'Well, I can tell you that you have a very pure energy field. You are one of life's golden spirits and that

makes you very easy for me to work with.'

At this stage, Judy's voice broke as her feelings began to overwhelm her. 'I sometimes get a bit emotional when something like this happens because it's so wonderful to connect with someone at your level,' she apologised.

Controlling herself with difficulty, Judy continued: 'You have come here to do something very specific. You need to be out there working with children. I see you with black children. Helping them in some way. They look like they're eating. Maybe you're going to feed children. That's basically from this life . . .'

After a short pause, Judy went on to say: 'I see the angel who walks with you. She is actually part of your spirit. She is enormous. Of the greatest goodwill, the greatest intent, the greatest integrity – the most wonderful, wonderful being. She walks with you, right

*According to international medium James van Praagh, it is possible for those on the other side to communicate via the electronic media such as telephones and computers.

next to you, to assist you.'

Shado remained silent as Judy went on talking to Jill. 'Do you have any problems in your life right now?'

'Well, I'm still carrying mixed emotions about my dad's death. It's always something that's difficult to deal with.'

'Do you feel positive towards him? Or are you angry with him?'

'A little bit angry,' admitted Jill.

'Yes,' said Judy, 'I'm picking up your anger. I see you in a past life with him. You are on a battlefield. You are both in armour – as knights. It is a time we associate with King Arthur. It may have been exactly then. Somehow or other he is on a horse and you are trying to pull him off. There is a battle and he is fighting for his life. You are trying to kill him. The moment comes when he is at your mercy. You have a knife, a dagger, in your hand. He opens his eyes and looks at you.'

The silence in the studio is almost palpable.

'There is such a transformation in your spirit at this time. You drop the dagger and run. You don't know what's happened to you, but you have achieved enormous transformation. You run and run. You are, of course, now in danger of being killed yourself, although you do have a sword.

'Somehow the battle and the killing have lost their glamour and you just run. You run into a wood. You hide until the battle is over. Then you change your life completely. I could go on. . . but I think this is enough. God bless you!'

'Jill, how do you feel after this experience?' asked Shado.

'Strange. Actually, I felt very shaky throughout the whole thing. It's amazing. The legends of King Arthur and that period of time have always been of great interest to me. I've done a lot of reading about it and I felt a sense of knowing more about it than I found in books. Which is pretty freaky, really.'

'Jill, I just want you to know,' said Judy gently, 'that your father asked you to be here today.'

Any article on Judy would be incomplete without mentioning the crystals with which she works. Judy believes that she has been healing with crystals for centuries.

'During one of my past life regressions, I discovered that I'd been a healing master in Atlantis. I was a male and I worked in a pyramid-shaped crystal building. I had apprentices working under me and I helped many people.'

'How does crystal healing work?'

'Each mineral vibrates to an energy frequency that works to balance and harmonise the energy in the human energy field, or aura, that surrounds the human body. This energy, I believe, extends way beyond the human body, it embraces the earth and the planet as a whole.'

'I believe that you "stabilised" the energy of Table Mountain with your crystals. Could you tell me about this?'

'I was approached by the Save Table Mountain group who were very upset by that dreadful hotel that was planned and that has now been put up at Oudekraal. A group of us climbed the mountain and buried a giant amethyst on either side of the mountain. On the twelfth day of the twelfth month in 1998 we buried the first amethyst at sunrise on the eastern side of the mountain. Then exactly a year later we buried the second amethyst at sunset on the western side. Each "planting" was accompanied by a meditation and my sacred cry.'

'Why amethysts?'

'An amethyst contains within its violet or purple colour the ability to bring peace and serenity and to calm anger or rage. The buried amethysts are designed to hold the positive energies of the mountain and to bring healing and stop any further building developments.'

Judy Le Cash, quietly spoken but with firm conviction abouteverything she says and does, is a remarkable woman. She talks easily of lives past and present, some of which she clarifies in details that are disturbing, to say the least.

I was interested in speaking to people who have consulted her in order to find out whether or not they had benefited from her unique brand of therapy.

I obtained the following insights into Judy's work from Gita Mamba and Bianca Smith.

Gita's story is as follows: 'I began seeing Judy just over two years ago. The reason for my consultation with her was that I had recently discovered that I had cysts growing on my ovaries. Instead of going on the pill or submitting to the surgeon's knife, I took this medical problem to mean that my body was telling me that it was time for me to open my eyes and look at the harm I was doing to myself.'

'How were you harming yourself?' I asked.

'At the time I was in a destructive relationship with a drug addict and I was using loads of drugs myself. I believed that my relationship was fine and my drug habit healthy. In therapy, Judy opened my eyes to many aspects of me that I was ignoring, hiding, or denying. Learning about myself has been one of the most difficult things I have ever done.

'I know that Judy has made all the difference. From the beginning, she has given me room to be myself. Even when I refused to budge and carried on my self-sabotage, she respected and supported me and loved me unconditionally.'

'How do you feel about yourself now?'

'It has been one of the most confusing times of my life. I struggled to understand my feelings and the complex way in which I perceive the world. Judy helped me to simplify and understand. She has cleared away the cobwebs that were clouding my vision.'

From INTEC Student Adviser Bianca Smith I received the following e-mail communication:

I have been seeing Judy for counselling and healing for over a year. The changes that have occurred in this time have been remarkable. My whole mindset and being has been through a spiritual laundry spin. I have come out a different person in every respect. I am the very person I have always wanted to be. I have connected with my true self and I am living a life beyond my earlier dreams of freedom and security.

I have gained valuable insight into both myself and my relationships. All that I am, I owe to Judy's unconditional love for life which she has passed on to me. I cannot thank her enough and no money in the world would be sufficient payment to show my absolute appreciation.

Judy's lives within lives have been eventful in the extreme. I think back to the abuse, drugs, drinks and sexual promiscuity that clouded the first four decades of her present life.

Bearing this in mind, I am interested to find out at the conclusion of the interview how she feels about her life today.

'It's just been such a wonderful life,' she says. 'I'm so happy to be here. People say "But you had such a terrible childhood". I know that I had this childhood for a reason. The Course in Miracles that I studied as part of my therapy training taught me to become more positive. Everything that happens to us at any given point in our lives is part of our journey. We are all here to learn lessons. Life is completely perfect!'

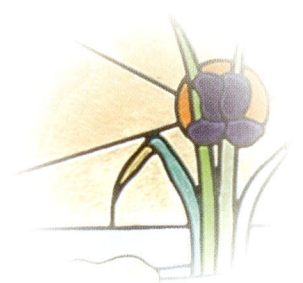

'I believe that All is One and that as each individual learns to shine their light a little more brightly by transforming their fears and becoming more peaceful within themselves, whatever their path may be, they are doing spiritual service for the planet.'

Alison Effting

'I believe we live in two worlds . . . one in which logical thought and the intellect reign supreme . . . the world of knowledge where things have to be scientifically proven and we have to "match up" and the other, the world of awareness where emotion, intuition and imagination are more important. We need to connect these worlds in order to live day to day in balance and harmony. COLOUR IS THE CONNECTION – the RAINBOW BRIDGE between the world of thought and the world of feeling.'

Michelle Serafino

Photographed by Jaco Wolmarans

The word *aura* is derived from the Latin word meaning *akin to air, a slight breath, light, vapour or shimmer*. Soma is the ancient Greek word for body. Aura-Soma therefore refers to the body of light or light body around the physical body.

Today Aura-Soma speaks a universal language through beautiful bottles of rainbow coloured oils called Equilibrium, and special essences called Pomanders and Quintessences.

Aura-Soma is a non-intrusive, self-selective, Soul therapy. Through Aura-Soma, one can discover for oneself what is at the root of any physical, emotional, mental or spiritual imbalance.

What causes this imbalance? If we accept that we are more than just our physical bodies, that we are, in fact, Light Beings made up of energy vibrating at different levels, each level resonating to a different colour, the theory behind Aura-Soma becomes clear.

Scientists have discovered that there is a Life Force flowing through us that keeps us vital and alive. This Life Force is managed by a series of spinning energy vortices called chakras, each of which resonates to a certain wavelength of colour and relates to a specific area of the body. When the chakras are functioning properly, one can enjoy good health and mental equilibrium. However, when the chakras are out of balance, one feels 'off colour'.

Aura-Soma provides a key to identify and correct these imbalances, empowering one to take charge of one's own healing process. The vibrational healing power of colour, herbal extracts, essential oils, gems and crystals contained within the Aura-Soma Equilibrium bottles enables one to grow in consciousness and self-awareness; to realise one's full potential and to become all that one can be.

As I sit in the bright, sun-filled room of Michelle Serafino's Aura-Soma consulting room in Cape Town chatting to her and Alison Effting, the distributor of Aura-Soma products throughout Southern Africa, my eye is constantly drawn to the shimmering brightness of the myriad of Equilibrium bottles on display. There are currently 103 bottles in this range which, as consciousness evolves, is continually being expanded.

It is a well-documented fact that healing with colour, or colour therapy, has been practised from the time of the ancients. From Heliopolis in Egypt, to Iran, to India and China, people recognised the healing properties of colour and used it in various ways.

In the temple of Heliopolis, for example, rooms were specially designed so that the sun's rays were broken up into the seven colours of the spectrum in order to be used for healing. In Iran, glazed ceramic tiles of different colours and geometric shapes were used architecturally in mosques for the upliftment and cleansing of the spirit and the teaching of natural law and consciousness.

'I know that colour as a healing tool has been used almost from the beginning of time,' I say. 'But how did modern Aura-Soma originate?'

'Aura-Soma as we know it today was founded by Vicky Wall in England around 1983,' replies Michelle. 'Vicky came from an extremely religious Jewish background and at birth she was given the name Devorah, although she later became known as Vicky. Vicky was the seventh child of a seventh child. Her father was a Chassidic rabbi. Her mother died of Spanish flu shortly after her birth. Her father, realising that he could not raise his large family on his own, remarried.'

'At first her stepmother loved Vicky and treated her as her own child,' continues Alison. 'However, one day one of her older sisters told Vicky that her stepmother was not her real mother. This revelation proved very upsetting to Vicky and resulted in her stepmother abusing her.'

'Did her father, the rabbi, do anything to help improve the situation?'

'He was unaware of the abuse. There was a deep bond between

the rabbi and his youngest child. He, too, could see the colours in people's auras.

'One day when Vicky was about eight, she went to her father, tearful and upset. She'd been talking to her fellow pupils at school about the beautiful colours she saw and the children started mocking her. Her father comforted her and told her not to worry about it, but to keep it a secret between them. "Some day," he promised her, "people will understand what you are saying."'

'Did the abuse at the hands of her stepmother continue?' I ask.

'I'm afraid so. When she was sixteen, Vicky could stand it no more. She ran away from home. Her father "sat shivah". This means that from that day forth he disowned her and would have nothing more to do with her. In his eyes, his beloved Vicky was dead.'

'Where did she go, without money or career prospects?'

'As luck would have it, Vicky found work in an apothecary. The chemist, Edward Smallbrook Horsley, was a very wise old man and taught her how to blend various lotions and potions – her father had already taught her a great deal about flowers and herbs – and Vicky became well known for her creams. She later trained as a surgical chiropodist and set up a practice with Margaret Cockbain, a cranio-sacral practitioner, who became her companion. She continued making foot and body creams.'

'Were these available to the general public?'

'Some of Vicky's original creams and lotions are now part of the Aura-Soma range. However, in the beginning she and Margaret used to sell the creams at fairs. Around this time, a friend approached them to invest their savings and they lost everything they owned.'

'I've read that Vicky became blind,' I say.

'Yes. One sunny day when she was walking along the coastline while on holiday she lost her sight. Her sight continued to deteriorate until she had no more than five per cent of her vision. She also had a heart ailment. She says in her book, *The Miracle of Colour Healing*, that she had about forty per cent of her heart function. Being physically blind may have reawakened her gift of auric sight.

'Vicky's father, whom she had not seen since she left home, died in the early 1980s and she felt that he then began communicating his spiritual knowledge to her from the "other side". As a girl she had not shared in the spiritual knowledge that was imparted to her brothers. And now she felt that he was sharing this with her.

'Vicky led a spiritual life and meditated regularly. One night during her meditation she heard a voice saying to her, "You must divide the waters, my child." This was accompanied by a vision of waves of colour approaching her and receding, like waves in the ocean.'

'What did this mean?' I ask.

'Vicky was perplexed and ended her meditation for that evening. The next night the voice called to her a second time. She questioned the voice. However, after the third night when once again she heard the voice with the same message, she got up and went into her laboratory and began to "work", making bottles of colour. She describes the process as if unseen hands were guiding her own hands.'

'What did she do in her laboratory?'

'Vicky found herself formulating a mixture comprising different layers and colours of natural ingredients. The next morning she could feel the resonant power emanating from the mixture she had created. Even more surprising was the fact that the morning sunlight revealed two distinctly separate and different layers. Vicky Wall, although blind, had created the miracle of Aura-Soma. The first Equilibrium bottles had been born.'

For Michelle, as for Vicky Wall, it was a health crisis that brought Aura-Soma into her life. A partial thyroidectomy in 1984, which became suspect again in 1997, coupled with the realisation that she didn't want further intrusive surgical intervention, led her to seek alternative avenues of healing.

An introduction to Aura-Soma so intrigued Michelle that she decided to do the Aura-Soma course – a decision that was to transform her life during the next few years into a full-time Aura-Soma practitioner and teacher.

Through Aura-Soma, Michelle found that she was able to gain a sense of mental and physical well-being. So much so, that when she was diagnosed with breast cancer, she found the therapy of great benefit in helping not only to cure the cancer, but also in helping her regain her spiritual, mental and emotional equilibrium. It has to be said that Aura-Soma does not claim to diagnose or cure. Michelle used Aura-Soma in addition to other complementary therapies to deal with cancer.

For Alison, too, it was a search beyond what conventional medicine could offer that led to Aura-Soma. 'As a radiographer, I came from a scientific background. But when science could not provide the answers to my health problems, I began to look into more natural healing methods. I believe that it was Divine Intervention that led me to Aura-Soma.'

'What were your health problems?'

'I was suffering from an iron deficiency which led to chronic fatigue. Eventually, I contracted hepatitis. A year after the hepatitis, my energy levels were still incredibly low. The doctors were considering all kinds of major surgery, including a hysterectomy.

I was only thirty-two. I thought there has to be some other way…'

Michelle provides a word of caution here: 'Aura-Soma does not claim to offer a physical cure. Rather, it provides insight into the underlying emotional, mental and spiritual stress patterns contributing to the physical imbalances and it helps to undo these stress patterns. Having said that, the use of the oils often contributes to an improvement because of the changes it helps to bring about in one's way of life.'

An Aura-Soma consultation with a qualified practitioner works in the following way: You will be invited to select the four Equilibrium bottles that attract you the most from the dazzling array of dual-coloured bottles on display.

Firmly believing that *you are the colour you choose*, the Aura-Soma practitioner will simply help you to explore what has been revealed through the colour selection you have made.

In an Aura-Soma consultation the focus is on awareness – there is no diagnosis or treatment of any medical condition or physical or psychological problem. The practitioner remains non-judgemental throughout, merely providing you with the tools you need to assume responsibility for your own well-being.

Of the four bottles, you will be given the one that the practitioner believes best reflects your present requirements. When you work personally with this Equilibrium Oil, shaking the bottle and rubbing its contents into your body, an energetic link is formed between you and your therapeutic bottle. Thus you should now be the only person to handle or shake your chosen bottle.

When applied to the skin, the selected Equilibrium Oil will be absorbed into the lymphatic system. It will then pass into the circulatory system to wherever it is needed in the body, and there help to re-establish the natural resonance of the cells, tissues, organs and systems.

Ideally, the Equilibrium Oil should be used in conjunction with other products from the Aura-Soma range — the Pomander and the Quintessence. The Pomander protects the energy field by imparting the positive energies of the colour in question. The Quintessence is an energy that invokes a particular spiritual quality, such as compassion or non-judgementalism.

'Almost,' smiles Michelle, 'as if you are enfolding yourself in the wings of an angel.'

Perhaps the following story that Michelle related will illustrate the unseen yet all-embracing power of this remarkable colour therapy:

'One of my clients who used the Equilibrium oils and then went on to do Aura-Soma Level 1 course, was surprised late one evening by an intruder standing in her lounge.

'Only a few hours before returning home she had used Quintessence of the Lady Nada. This pink substance protects the aura while acting as a very effective antidote to aggression and fear. So it was that when she found this man in her home, she remained calm and was able to prevent him from hurting her in any way.

'The Quintessence had filled her energy field with unconditional love so that the intruder simply could not succeed in his attempts at aggression. This story serves to illustrate that when we are at peace with ourselves, others will find it difficult to penetrate that peace with aggression or fear.'

'Still, if he wanted to harm her, he could have used brute force,' I say.

'Well, his next step was to look for a knife in the kitchen drawer, but he couldn't find one. She sensed his growing bewilderment as, one by one, each step he took to overcome her, failed. He did, however, manage to get a small amount of money from her.'

'Aha! So Aura-Soma could not prevent a robbery.'

Michelle gently shakes her head. 'When the police arrived, they found the money on the mat outside the door . . . However, I must stress that it is important to see Aura-Soma as a key to consciousness and not as a kind of magic.'

As I take my leave of Michelle and Alison, I look at the brilliant display of Aura-Soma bottles with new respect. Through the inner magic of these glistening dual-coloured jewels, these two women have both been able to overcome physical adversity and to reconnect with their souls and their spirits. If life's a journey, Aura-Soma has clearly shown them how to travel transformed!

Sandy Smith – International Numerologist

Photographed by Francki Burger

'As we progress along life's journey, I believe that people cross our paths to show us parts of ourselves – good, bad and indifferent. If one is prepared to listen, see and hear, we can become all that we want to be. As human beings, our potential is almost limitless.'

Sandy Smith

Numerology, the study of numbers and their supposed influence on human lives, is an ancient science dating back thousands of years. The most popular form of numerology in use today is based on the work of Pythagoras, the famous Greek mathematician and philosopher who lived during the sixth century BC.

Many great minds have been fascinated by the link between numbers and the events that shape our lives. Isaac Newton, for example, spent more of his time studying the numbers mentioned in the Old Testament Book of Daniel than he did developing his theory of gravity. The reason for this was that he was trying to discover the exact date that the world would come to an end.

One of the best known numerologists in South Africa today is Sandy Smith. She has appeared on many television and radio shows and has, since February 2001, been writing numerology and horoscopes for People Magazine. But she showed little sign in her earlier life that she would one day become a counsellor and spiritual adviser of note.

Amongst her many clients are heads of state and their families; captains of industry; celebrities and sports stars. Yet Sandy is equally at home reading for 'ordinary' people who need answers to life's manifold problems.

Her client base consists of both males and females of all ages – her youngest client is nine years old – and, assisted by the universality of the Internet, she is able to do readings for people all over the world.

Over the years, in addition to her skill with numerology, Sandy has studied the Tarot in depth, and has completed a course in astrology through the Airs Institute of South Africa.

The Tarot cards proved to be too vague for her. 'It's no good being able to tell a client that they are going to buy a new car. I want to be able to tell them exactly when they will buy the car and what colour it will be.'

Likewise, she believes that astrology is really only accurate if one knows the exact date and time of one's birth. So, searching for a way to pinpoint dates and time frames within a reading, Sandy perfected her own brand of numerology through endless study.

Unlike other numerologists, she doesn't need you to supply your name and date of birth days before your appointment in order to work out your blueprint. At your appointment, she'll simply ask you for your date of birth and the spontaneous reading will begin.

The more adept Sandy has become at numerology, the more her psychic skills have become honed, so that even the most sceptical and cynical of people are astounded by the accuracy of her predictions.

Tuesday, 11 September 2001. The truth of what happened on that fateful day may never be known, but the official story goes as follows:

Four Boeing passenger jets were hijacked within an hour of each other by nineteen Arab terrorists armed with boxcutters. Pilots among the terrorists then took control of the aeroplanes and changed course towards targets in New York City and Washington DC. Two of the Boeings were deliberately flown into the Twin Towers of the World Trade Center resulting in raging fires which melted the steel support structures and caused the complete collapse of the buildings. A third Boeing was deliberately crashed into the Pentagon. Passengers on the fourth plane overpowered the hijackers and caused the plane to crash in Pennsylvania.

This attack on America was planned and directed by Osama bin Laden, leader of al-Qa'eda, a previously obscure anti-US international terrorist organisation.

Writing for the media in June/July 2001, and basing her predictions on the name and birth date – 4 July 1776 (4/7/1776) – of the USA, Sandy's calculations produced the following:

The USA is going into a difficult year as it hits its life path number. Americans must change their attitude, expand their thinking. The country needs to turn to a more universal and spiritual way of thinking as their leaders have the power to heal on a massive scale. But their lower aspects are to threaten, push and shove. They need to start seeing the bigger picture. In order to avoid antagonising their enemies, the men in power have to stop thinking that they are the law, but rather work together to find balance and to deal fairly and justly.

In 1929 Black Monday occurred with the collapse of the American stock market. This is a similar year and October and November could be that time all over again as tumultuous events within the country lead to a major downswing in the economy.

Turning her attention to President George Walker Bush, born on 6/7/1946, Sandy wrote:

There could be a huge car, plane or boat accident around him. Something tells me that he is going to be very stubborn about many rules that he has and wants to set and he might just turn everything around for the USA. There is much anger and regret in his life. He has failed before and this time around, now that he is in high office, he might misuse his power . . .

Let us hope that, just this once, Sandy's predictions are incorrect!

Sandra-Jean Mary Smith, the middle child of electrical engineer Alexander Smith and his wife Margaret, did not give any indication during her childhood and early adulthood that she would develop into a deeply spiritual person, a counsellor and adviser, with strong psychic abilities.

As a child at school, at Parkview and later Blairgowrie Primary, she was downright naughty – the kind of kid who was always playing pranks.

When she arrived at Greenside High, Sandy was still having too much fun to get down to any serious work. 'I always studied for exams the night before and did a little extra work in the morning on the way to school. I passed exams by the seat of my pants . . . until I got to matric, when I failed the examination.'

'Didn't you display any mathematical ability?' I asked in astonishment. For, today, Sandy's mental agility with numbers is remarkable. A client simply has to mention their birth date and within seconds Sandy will have calculated their age and be able to fill them in on details of their life with astounding accuracy.

Sandy laughs. 'No. I was terrible at arithmetic. But you know what they say: "Your greatest weakness becomes your greatest strength".'

After rewriting the subjects she failed, and armed with a matriculation certificate, Sandy had no desire to go to university. Not that anyone could call her uneducated. A confirmed 'bookoholic' she will read anything she can lay her hands on, particularly subjects pertaining to biographical or esoteric matters.

Although her numerology is sufficiently advanced for her to have registered her company, Numerology by Sandy cc, she still reads every book she can find on the subject. 'Just in case somebody knows something that I don't,' she laughs.

Tall and statuesque with flowing red hair and long, manicured red fingernails, it was no surprise to learn that Sandy began her working career as a cosmetic consultant for Mary Quant. She subsequently worked for Estée Lauder and when the glamour of the beauty industry began to pall, her next career move was into the music industry.

Here Sandy encountered almost as many stars on this firmament as the stars in heaven that she had become acquainted with through her astrological studies. She casually mentions names like James Brown, Eric Clapton, Eddie Murphy, Ramsey Lewis, Michael Jackson, B.B. King, Gladys Knight and Randy Crawford, amongst others.

South African-born stars she worked with included Caiphus and Letta Mbulu, David Kramer, Jonathan Butler, Ray Phiri, Abigail Khubeka, Mara Louw, The Soul Brothers, Hugh Masekela and Miriam Makeba. It was a heady cocktail of glamour, fun, parties and people, mixed with strong doses of really hard work.

All in all, it was a life light years away from the spiritual path that she was subsequently to follow.

As is often the case with spiritual awakening, it was a crisis in her life that brought Sandy to the realisation that while her physical body was enjoying life to the full, her inner soul was hungering after something much deeper and more meaningful.

One Saturday morning in 1990 Sandy went to pick up some liquor at a warehouse on the West Rand for a promotional event that she was organising. It was early in the morning, a little after eight o'clock.

Eight men wearing long coats and jackets to camouflage their array of AK 47s, pistols and revolvers entered the store.

It was obviously an inside job for the men were well aware that there was over 300 000 rand in the safe. The robbers locked the people in the warehouse in a small office. Terrified, Sandy was forced to lie under a desk as a robber held a revolver to her head. The telephone lines had been cut, but fortunately a hunting line was still intact.

Someone phoned the police and they arrived at the warehouse in record time. 'There were two policemen,' Sandy recalled. 'A small white cop, almost a midget, and a large black cop. They arrived in the nick of time, for luckily none of us were harmed.'

'Nevertheless, you must have been pretty shaken.'

'Yes, I was. But at the same time, I was to learn a valuable lesson in forgiveness. It was a period in our history when a lot of black policemen were being killed in Soweto. Yet this African policeman told me that I must not fight violence with violence. He told me not to buy a gun or to seek revenge. He gave me his phone number and told me that if I needed trauma counselling, I should contact him.'

'Did this unnerving incident change your life?' I asked.

'Not immediately. About a year after the incident I went to a psychic fair in Sandton. I felt I needed some kind of support. There was an astrologer at the fair and I asked her to do my chart. I gave her the date and time of the armed robbery. She looked at me intently and said: "Do you know what the robbery meant?" I shook my head. She told me it was the Universe saying to me "Where are you going? What divine gift are you robbing yourself of?" '

Shaken to the core, Sandy Smith knew that her spiritual journey had begun in earnest.

Sandy's first attempts at numerology began with family and friends. She was Miriam Makeba's international manager at the time and as she became more deeply involved with the Tarot and numerology, she began to read for the musicians and technicians accompanying the star on tour.

'Miriam used to call me her "white *sangoma*",' Sandy informed me with a chuckle.

After about three years of this jet-setting lifestyle, Sandy literally 'burned out' and decided to come back to South Africa. From this time onwards, she decided to leave the music industry behind her and concentrate full-time on her readings.

With her warm and bubbly personality, Sandy made many friends in the entertainment and media industry over the years. As these people got word of Sandy's new profession, she was invited to appear on television and radio shows.

'Many of the media people were cynical. They didn't think there was anything in numerology. Initially, they used me as a sort of entertainer, a fill-in, if you like. However, the accuracy of my predictions, especially with South Africa's sporting performance in the world arena, astounded them. Even I was amazed.'

I asked her to tell me about some of these shows.

'Well, when I appeared on an SABC 2 Top Sport programme with Kobus Wiese in 1999 they asked me how South Africa, who was playing England at the time, would fare in their upcoming cricket match.'

'What was the date of this match?'

'Saturday, 22 May 1999.'

'What were you able to tell the viewers?'

'I was able to predict accurately who would be in the team. I said that Lance Klusener would be the Man of the Match. I predicted that the South Africans who would be bowled out were Hansie Cronjé, Jonty Rhodes, Gary Kirsten, Herschelle Gibbs and Shaun Pollack. I told the viewers that we would win the match and what the final score was likely to be.'

'How on earth were you able to do this?'

'Well, I've still got my notes. I wrote down the following: *South Africa as a country is in a 9/10-1 and going into a 10-1/11-2 year very soon on 31/5/1999. Due to SA's birthday being imminent, we have the flavours of the numbers 9,10 and 11, not excluding the 3,4, and an 8. The date says that there is an opportunity of gaining something great. Therefore, I feel very strongly about a win for South Africa. It is a win day that will highlight individual players' abilities. Steve Elworthy and Herschelle Gibbs are born on a 10/1 (good consequences) and Bob Woolmer (the team coach) is in a 10/1 year. PS Happy birthday to Graeme Hick for the 23rd.'*

'Whew! You must know a lot about cricket.'

'I know nothing about cricket,' admitted Sandy, 'but I do know something about numbers.'

Today, such is the demand for Sandy's services that she has begun teaching numerology to others from her home. This is not to say that Sandy Smith's work is not without its critics. There are those who say that to predict the future in this way is against the teachings of the Bible.

'What do you say to these people, Sandy?' I asked her.

'Like life itself, the Bible is full of numbers. On the first day of The Creation, God divided the light from the darkness. On the second day, he made heaven and earth. Also, why is one of the Books of the Bible called Numbers? Everything begins and ends with numbers – from the day we are born until the day we die.'

Mpumi Khumalo – Sangoma

From suicide to spiritual saviour

Photographed by Francki Burger

'For me, there is no heaven or hell. I believe that all creatures, visible or invisible, come from one central point. The energy that is amassed at this point experiments with creativity, fashioning all creatures, seen and unseen. This is why some people can see only human beings, while others have the ability to see spirits or ghosts or fairies or angels.'

Nompumelelo 'Mpumi' Khumalo

A man and his wife consulted a *sangoma* about their matrimonial problems. The wife, a career-orientated and ambitious woman, was earning more than her husband. For the man, a black African, this was a particularly bitter pill to swallow. His wife's success, he felt, threatened the very core of his being, his power as a male. Troubled and seemingly emasculated, he became impotent.

As a consequence, his wife grew increasingly frustrated. While she desperately desired sexual fulfilment, she was also wrestling with the dilemma confronting many modern-day career women – she was unsure whether or not she wanted to have a family. Children, she felt, would interfere with her career and hinder her climb up the corporate ladder.

On the other hand, for her husband, children were vital to the marriage, as not only did they ensure the continuation of his family bloodline, they were also living proof of his virility.

The *sangoma* listened sympathetically to these problems, much as a psychologist or psychiatrist would. She then began treating the couple with a special concoction of herbs that she had learned about at her Thwasa (the school where she had learned her craft) and with counselling.

With the *sangoma*'s wisdom to lead them, the couple's marital problems were resolved. After the birth of their first child, the husband, in a most extraordinary role reversal, particularly for a proud Zulu man, stayed home and cared for the infant, while his wife continued to be the breadwinner.

Helped and guided by the *sangoma* once more, the couple later had a second child. The husband carried on in his role as care-giver and child minder, while the wife continued to further her career.

The story of this modern-day marriage, which still relied on the centuries-old practices of the traditional *sangoma*, was made more unusual by the fact that the *sangoma* they chose to consult was Nompumelelo 'Mpumi' Khumalo – a young girl barely out of her teens.

Mpumi was born in Soweto in January 1978 to musician Stella Khumalo and a father whom Mpumi declines to name. Her father deserted her mother and Stella, faced with the problems of a small child to care for, an unstable career and no permanent home, was forced to take the toddler to live with her mother in Durban.

This was a difficult time for the young Mpumi. She felt abandoned by her mother and was unable to bond with her grandmother, a born-again Christian, who handled the young girl in a manner that Mpumi describes as unnecessarily harsh.

As a lonely child growing up in the township of KwaMashu, Mpumi sought solace in the company of imaginary friends. Her playmates were a drag queen, a young blind white boy named Billy, a Spanish man named Santos, and an old man who turned out to be her great-grandfather.

Reflecting on this somewhat eclectic choice of company, Mpumi says: 'What could I, a child of the townships, know of drag queens or of Spain? This small group were obviously more than just figments of my imagination. Looking back, I see that they were spirit guides, sent to help me in my pain and isolation.'

Her unhappiness meant that she was not the brilliant 'A' student her grandmother, a teacher, had hoped her to be. Her 'C' average angered her grandparent who angrily told the young girl that these marks were simply 'not good enough'.

These words were ringing in her ears when Mpumi's mother was able to fetch her and take her home and, rather than a joyous mother and child reunion, it was a time of conflict and rebellion. Even the family structure had changed – Mpumi's mother had given birth to Bafana, Mpumi's stepbrother.

There was animosity between mother and daughter. Although

Stella did her best to show her love for Mpumi, the young girl felt betrayed by what she perceived as her mother's abandonment of her.

Then there were problems at school. It was a time when black children were just starting to be integrated into the former apartheid educational system. Consequently, as a child of colour, Mpumi felt isolated in a predominantly white school. 'Although,' she concedes, 'I did make good friends there. People who are still my pals today.'

With all these changes in Mpumi's life, there was yet another major change. Her slender childish body was becoming more womanly – she was growing breasts and pubic hair. Instead of embracing her new-found womanhood, the thirteen-year-old Mpumi developed low self-esteem and a major eating disorder. 'Thirteen to sixteen were definitely the horror years,' she sighs.

Her imaginary friends, who had faded from her reality, now began to reappear. However, it seemed that nothing could give her comfort. Mpumi was diagnosed with clinical depression and bulimia. Desperately wanting to block out the pain, to be 'normal', she followed her psychologist's advice and began taking Prozac.

But not even this so-called miracle drug was strong enough to rid her of the omnipresent voices in her head that kept telling her she was psychic. Nor could she clear her head of the visions of lit candles in every room of the house – although she knew that there were none. In her despair, Mpumi attempted suicide.

'Were things really that bad?' I ask her.

'Yes. I took an overdose of sleeping pills and I slept for a very long time.'

'Did you feel completely alone at this time?'

'No. One day these spirits appeared. The familiar figure of my great-grandfather and with him, for the first time, two females. One female was as tall as my room. I remember she had an Egyptian headdress and she was suffused with a bluish green light. I never could see the other figure clearly. It was like watching a movie when they put Vaseline on the lens of the camera so that things appear ghostlike.'

It was during this dark period when Mpumi was at her lowest and most depressed that she saw what she believed to be God – a shaft of almost blinding silver light. The universal energy. The source from which, she believes, all creation sprang.

In time, Mpumi recovered and went on to complete her schooling successfully. She began a computer programming course and her family breathed a sigh of relief. Their problems with this strange girl seemed to be over.

They had however reckoned without the powerful presence of the ancestors. While Mpumi sailed through the major portion of the computer course, there was one section, Multiple Choice, reputedly the easiest module in the training programme, that she failed repeatedly.

'This can't be right,' thought Mpumi. 'Computers are obviously not where my destiny lies.'

While she wondered about her future, her mother had a dream. 'She saw a house – even the name of the street that the house was in and the number of the house – and she knew that she must take me there. When she awoke and took me to this place, she found it to be the residence of a fellow musician, Angie, who also happened to be a *sangoma*.'

'How did you feel when you got there?'

'Ecstatic. I heard drums. But not church drums, you understand. The drums of the *sangomas*.'

'How did Angie receive you?'

'She looked at me and said: "My child, at eighteen you are too young for this calling." She was about to turn me away when she heard the voices of my ancestors saying "Take up the bag of *isikhwana*, of medicine, girl. It is your gift from your great-grandfather,

91

the herbalist." '

'How did you feel when Angie decided to train you as a *sangoma*?'

'I was delighted. Nothing had ever sounded so good, so true. Suddenly it seemed as if everything had clicked into place. I said "Wow!" '

The stumbling student began to fly high. Mpumi's marks might have been average at school, but under Angie's tuition, and with the help of her ancestors, she soon realised her full potential.

Within the first month of *sangoma* tuition, the young apprentice was already 'throwing the bones' for people. Nor did she have any trouble learning about *mndawo* — the herbs traditionally used by the *sangoma*. After all, her great-grandfather, the alchemist, was there in spirit to show her how to heal people.

As for her psychic ability, it took little to bring that to the fore. 'I remember,' she says with a laugh, 'a friend of mine saying that she thought she would enter a local beauty contest. I told her that this would not be wise. She was angry with me. "Why do you say that?" she demanded. Because you're pregnant,' I told her. 'And I was right.'

Within three months Angie told Mpumi that she was ready to be a *sangoma*, concluding that there was nothing more she could teach her, for Mpumi knew it all.

'You must have been very proud of your achievements.'

'As part of the course, we had to learn to be humble, to learn self-control, not to display our emotions. The only time that you are allowed to express your emotions, is when you are in a trance and the ancestors are working through you.

'To be a healer does not make one special. It does not make you the king of kings. If you are prepared to open yourself to it, I believe that most people have this gift.'

The first day of Mpumi's two-day initiation as a *sangoma* in Bloemfontein dawned bright and clear and cold. In fact, the outside temperature was minus two degrees Celsius. 'It was freezing. We . . . myself and the one other woman who was being inducted that day . . . were not allowed to wear shoes. Also, for the ceremony, we were nearly naked..

'Our boobs (Mpumi's vocabulary is laced with contemporary slang) were exposed and we were only allowed to wear loincloths and beads. I was too busy to feel the cold, however. I was occupied in preparing everything I would need for the initiation, in seeing that it was all there in the correct order. In Western terms, one could say that I was getting ready for my final examination.

'That night there was a great celebration. Everyone came. There was dancing and drumming. We had to dance non-stop through the night until four o'clock in the morning. At one point I thought I was going to collapse with exhaustion. Somehow, though, I managed to get a second wind and I danced and danced.'

Mpumi continued the story of the induction by telling me that she had to go down to the river to bathe. Her naked body was coated with thick white mud and red clay was put in her plaited hair. (As we talk, she shakes her braided ponytail to show me that even after an interval of a couple of years, some of the red clay still remains.)

The initiation ceremony has many fascinating rituals, including the drinking of the contents of a twenty-five litre bucket of water. The initiates are expected to drink, then vomit, drink, then vomit. A goat is slaughtered and its blood is also supposed to be drunk and then vomited up.

Perhaps the most nerve-racking part of the ceremony for Mpumi came when she was introduced to her biggest test. She was required to drink the contents of a bowl that contained, within its specially prepared liquid, a rolled-up piece of *muti*.*

'I didn't know until I had to do this test that if the *muti* is vomited up whole, then this is positive proof that one has not cheated by coming into contact with, or having sex with a man, during one's period of learning. However, if the *muti* comes out in pieces or does not come out at all, it shows that one has not respected the whole process.

'I was terrified. My whole family – except, of course for my grandmother, who made a point of boycotting the ceremony – were there. What if I failed? What if I was disgraced before them? Yet I knew that I had honoured all the procedures . . .'

'What happened?'

'The roll of *muti* came out whole. My heart lifted. I had not let myself, my family or my ancestors down. I had passed one of the most difficult parts of the ceremony. I felt an overwhelming sense of relief.'

The interview moved on to the subject of exorcism. I asked Mpumi whether she had ever been requested to exorcise an evil spirit from either a person or a dwelling and how she tackled such an assignment.

Mpumi then told me the story of the *tokoloshe*† that she had expelled from the house of one of her mother's friends.

'There was a serious problem in that house. Certain things were being moved around without anybody touching them. Also, the place was full of unpleasant odours and smells. Unless one was very strong emotionally, it was extremely difficult to live there.'

'What did you do to solve the problem?'

'I gathered stones from the river. They carry an important energy that I needed to expel this spirit. I placed the stones in the four corners of the house. Then I performed the egg ritual.'

'What is that?'

'You must understand that the ancestors always guide you and tell you what do. Anyhow, I poked a little hole in the egg with a

*Medicine.
†Evil spirit who appears in the guise of a small human being.

needle and then put in some *muti*. I didn't just want the house to be protected. I also wanted to be sure that the *tokoloshe* was driven away so that it would never come back.'

'Has it ever returned?'

'For the last seven months I'm pleased to say that the house has been clear. But I also wanted to be sure that the people who lived in the house were free of any evil influence. So I took them to the mountains and made them cut small incisions in their joints. Then I placed specially prepared *muti* in the cuts.'

'Do your mother's friends respect your skill as a *sangoma?*'

Mpumi reflects for a moment. 'Yeah. Now when they're discussing "adult" things, they no longer send me from the room. They accept me as an equal. You know what? I think that's cool.'

With a laugh, Mpumi grabs her cellphone and, taking her leave, she climbs into her BMW. Revving the engine, she departs in a blaze of glory and a trail of smoke.

Dr Mark Harman – Psychic, Parapsychologist & Strega Witch

Banishing the dark forces with love and light

'I believe that there is Divinity in everything on this earth. From the smallest seashell to the largest whale; from an inanimate rock to a darting rock leopard; from a newborn babe to a dying old man. All this Divinity comes from one source – the Goddess who is Supreme. For me, being a Strega witch, the name of this almighty Goddess is Diana.'

Dr Mark Harman

Photographed by Francki Burger

The man's voice at the other end of the telephone line was alive with excitement and enthusiasm.

'Hi. My name is Dries. I believe that you want to know about Dr Mark.'

'Yes,' I said.

'Well, let me tell you, that man is a miracle. I was desperate, truly desperate. I couldn't pay my bills and I couldn't get any work. I work as a bricklayer, you know. It was so bad that one month my neighbour had to pay my lights and water bill. I knew that my house was possessed by an evil spirit. Actually, I think it was my brother-in-law who was responsible for the curse that had been laid upon us. At night my wife and I were unable to sleep. The house used to shake and it sounded as though rocks were falling all around us.'

'How did you come to Dr Mark?'

'You know the Afrikaans TV programme *Voorblad?** I had seen Dr Mark on this programme – you know he's on TV quite often – and I was so desperate that I phoned the show's producer and asked for Dr Mark's number . . .'

'What did Dr Mark do when he came to your house?'

'He walked all around the place. Then he finally stopped at a specific point and he began to "cut" the air with a dagger. He said that he was removing the curse.'

'Was he successful?'

'Yes. Not only did the night noises stop, but he did other remarkable things as well.'

'Such as?'

'My wife used to suffer from terrible headaches. Dr Mark walked up to her and laid his right hand on her forehead. Now her headaches have gone. Another thing. When Dr Mark walked into our lounge he said that our TV set, which was switched off, was broken. This was true. It used to flicker horribly. Only I didn't have

the money to fix it. Dr Mark sort of moved his hands over it and you know what? Today our TV set is as good as new!'

'How about your work situation?'

'Within twenty-four hours of Dr Mark's visit I was offered three big jobs. Not only that. I had no trouble getting paid for them. Before Dr Mark came to our house, even if I had work I used to *sukkel*† to get my money from people. Do you know what else?'

'What?'

'There were no flowers in our garden. We simply couldn't get anything to grow. Dr Mark walked around outside looking at the empty flowerbeds and he said that if we planted now within six months everything would be blooming. If you like I'll take a picture of our garden as it is today and then I'll take another picture in six months' time and bring it to you. Would you like that?'

'Yes, thank you, Dries. I'd like that very much.'

'Heck. Dr Mark . . . he's not an ordinary man. He's a magician. A real magician. Not like those phoney con artists who promise you the earth and all you get from them is dust.

Mark Harman was born in Camberwell in England, the eldest child of a family of four children. Both his mother Freda and his late father Joseph worked in the police force, although his mother became a full-time housewife after her oldest son's birth.

From an early age, probably when he was as young as three, Mark began 'seeing' things – shapes and shadows and occasional clear figures. These apparitions terrified the young boy although his father, who also had strongly developed psychic gifts, was able to comfort him and tell him that he must not be afraid.

In addition, since Camberwell is an area well known for its haunted houses and its ghost sightings, no one seemed unduly perturbed by Mark's ability to see things from the spirit world.

During the years of the Second World War, tragedy struck the

*Front Page.
†Afrikaans word meaning 'struggle'.

family. No one is quite sure exactly what happened, but it appears that the blast of a falling bomb during the Blitz did irreparable damage to five-year-old Mark.

The small boy was in a coma for about six months and when he regained consciousness, it was discovered that there was neurological damage to the right side of the brain. Mark's left arm and leg remained permanently paralysed.

Faced with the dilemma of whether to send Mark to a special school or to allow him to continue his schooling in the mainstream, his parents chose the latter option. It was a wise decision for although Mark may have been physically challenged, academically he remained extremely bright.

Mark spent his high school years at Wilson's Grammar, a public school that dates back to 1615 and has seen a number of famous pupils, including the actor Michael Caine, pass through its portals.

For Mark, an essentially gentle person who abhors violence, his schooldays were something of a trial, although he did ultimately learn how to defend himself when other boys bullied and mocked him.

After leaving school, Mark received a scholarship to London University where he studied medieval and modern history. However, he soon found himself disenchanted with the course. His real interest lay in Egyptology.

The ancient Egyptian gods and goddesses fascinated him. He read all he could about deities like Osiris, Horus, Seth and Hathor, the goddess who wore a crown composed of a sun disk surrounded by a pair of cow horns. Unfortunately for Mark, while his school marks were good, they were not good enough to gain him admission to the Egyptology course.

Disillusioned, he abandoned his degree at London University and went to Oxford where he worked in a library. He was later to become a chartered librarian and he then completed a degree in social studies, majoring in psychology.

After working in the field of childcare for approximately seven years, Mark met his late wife, South African-born artist Lila Nicolson. Lila persuaded Mark to come to South Africa and it was in this country that his only child, his daughter Elaine, was born.

While the marriage bonds proved strong, there was one area of Mark's life that Lila could not share. The idea of the supernatural made her distinctly uneasy. Consequently, Mark repressed his natural psychic abilities and his desire to work with mysticism and the occult.

It was only when Lila, a diabetic, died some eleven years ago that Mark felt he was able truly to develop his spirituality. 'You see, Lila appeared to me from the other side, not once but twice, and said that it was all right. Finally she understood and was no longer afraid.'

The obstacles blocking Mark's path to his true vocation had been removed. He could give full rein to his extraordinary psychic abilities.

His second wife Fiona, a nursing sister, taught Mark how to read the Tarot and he found that this skill heightened his psychic powers and gave a new accuracy to his readings. This, coupled with the fact that he also began to incorporate the things he saw in his crystal ball into his work, gave additional credibility to his predictions.

Yet Mark still felt that something was missing from his life. He had been practising humanism, the belief that all people are divine, but found that this did not satisfy the spiritual longing in his heart. For where, he wondered, was Nature in this equation?

Nor did he find comfort in the Anglican religion of his mother. 'The devil is a creation of the Christian Church sent to instil fear. This cannot be right. For religion should be about loving. About doing right, not about doing wrong.'

Still searching, Mark became interested in Paganism and Wicca.

When fellow witch and founder of the Pagan Federation in South Africa Donna Darkwolf Vos mentioned to Mark that he was possibly a more traditional witch, a Strega, he was intrigued. By chance he stumbled upon the well-known book *Ride a Silver Broomstick* by Silver Ravenwood, a renowned Pow-wow witch of German American and Indian extraction, which confirmed Donna's view.

Henceforth, Mark would follow the centuries-old rituals and practices of Italian Strega witchcraft.

In his book *Ways of the Strega*, Ravan Grimassi explains that there are three separate traditions which are followed by the Strega witches of Italy: *Famarra*, *Jamarra* and *Tamarra*.

These Triad Traditions may be roughly divided as follows: The Famarra coven is known as the Keepers of the Earth Mysteries; the Jamarra are Keepers of the Lunar Mysteries; while the Tamarra are regarded as the Keepers of the Stellar Mysteries. Common to all three systems are the arts of herbalism, divination, magic and ritual.

There are possibly only a dozen or so Strega witches in South Africa and most of them have studied under Dr Mark. While all aspects of nature are important to this select band of witches, none is more vital to their work than the moon in all its phases.

For it was Aradia, the Holy Strega who brought about a revival of the old religion, *La Vecchia Religione*, in the fourteenth century, who urged her followers to 'Seek the Moon above all others for the purpose of Magick'.

Dr Mark explained to me that the moon is the focal point of power upon the earth, absorbing, condensing and channelling all forces that are received by our planet.

Bearing this in mind, rituals or spells which involve a new beginning are performed during the new moon. Spells designed to influence something already in progress are performed at the half moon, while the full moon is for workings that require the greatest force. Magical herbs for use in spells are usually planted at the New Moon to ensure the waxing of their powers; they are then harvested at the Full Moon when they are at their most potent.

'I cannot emphasise sufficiently the power of the moon in all events that shape the destiny of man,' said Dr Mark with fervour. 'Man has worshipped the moon in all its phases since the beginning of time. Why, it is even written in The Old Testament, Jeremiah, Chapter 7, Verse 18: *The children gather wood and the fathers kindle the fire and the woman knead their dough to make cakes to the queen of heaven.*'

'Could you explain exactly what you hope to achieve with your rituals and spells?' I asked.

'Magic is used mainly for healing purposes,' replied Dr Mark. 'To heal troubled relationships, to bring people together, to help them find love. Magic can also be used to help people suffering from anger to turn their negativity to positive energy. I also help people transform poverty into prosperity.'

'Do Strega witches, like the Wiccan and Pagan covens, have a close relationship with nature?'

'Indeed we do,' replied Dr Mark. 'The Earth is a living organism, a direct gift from the Goddess and God. Because nature and our planet are directly linked to the deities, they are both sacred; both holy.'

I received an amusing testimony to Dr Mark's magical powers from a friend of his who sent me the following letter:

Dr Mark Harman and I went down to Amanzimtoti in Natal. The journey there was very pleasant. On the way back to Gauteng, however, as we neared Mooi River, I noticed that Dr Mark appeared to be uncomfortable and in great pain.

I was driving at around 130 kilometres an hour but I decided to increase my speed to 180-190 kilometres an hour. Not long after we had passed the Mooi River tollgate, with me continuing to drive at speed, I observed Dr Mark looking somewhat apprehensively at the speedometer for the first time.

When he commented on the high speed at which I was travelling, I slowed down slightly and told him that the speedometer reading was inaccurate. We shared a chuckle for a moment or two, and then all of a sudden a traffic officer appeared and ordered me to stop.

I immediately complied with this command, but as I was travelling so fast I had to reverse back in order to meet the officer. As I was reversing Dr Mark told me not to laugh, as I have a habit of giggling nervously when I know I'm in deep trouble.

I rolled down my window and greeted the officer who immediately asked me whether I had a driver's licence. Without thinking, I replied 'No.' He stared at me in utter shock and disbelief, until I explained to him that both my driver's licence and my ID book had been stolen during a recent hijacking. I went on to inform him that I did have a copy of my ID book in my bag on the back seat of the car.

The traffic officer looked at me with a mixture of anger and irritation. In a cross voice he told me that he had clocked me at the speed of 179 kilometres per hour. 'If you'd been going 180 I'd have had to instigate criminal charges against you and lock you up at

the Estcourt police station,' he growled.

With my knees knocking, I climbed out of the car and began going through the contents of my capacious bag in order to find the copy of my ID book. After about ten minutes I reluctantly had to explain to him that I was extremely sorry but I couldn't find it.

Imagine my surprise when I saw that the burly officer was standing in a cloud of bright white light. With a smile, he said that we could proceed on our journey.

'Aren't you going to fine me?' I asked. When he replied in the negative, I almost wanted to grab hold of him and kiss him. Realising that it was best not to push my luck, I thanked him politely and,

shaking his hand, I wished him a lovely day. In my rear view mirror I watched as he returned to his fellow traffic officers, who regarded him with utter bewilderment.

Turning to look at Dr Mark, I saw a quiet smile on his face. To my undying gratitude, although he did not say a word, I knew he had saved the day by sending out his miraculous energy which had been powerful enough to mellow the heart of this angry officer.

Regards,
Di

Despite international recognition for his extraordinary psychic abilities and his gift of healing magic, life has not been easy for Dr Mark. His physical limitations, the untimely death of his beloved first wife, coming to grips with his divorce from his second wife, have all left him saddened and lonely.

However, as proof that the Wheel of Fortune does indeed turn, Dr Mark's recent marriage to his beautiful new wife, Jean, has lightened his heart and filled him with renewed hope and optimism. A deep vein of amazing courage is embedded in the soul of this learned and gentle man.

In a recent television interview he spoke of Nelson Mandela and how he views him, along with Mother Teresa, as one of the greatest figures of recent centuries – a living saint.

Dr Mark also spoke about South Africa. He said that despite many difficulties, the ANC had achieved a great deal – more than most people credit them with. He talked of the miracle of the healing spirit of understanding and reconciliation that existed between the various cultures and races. He pointed out that every day, despite the fact that progress sometimes seemed slow, more and more people were enjoying the benefits of education, electrical power, clean water.

He concluded our interview with these memorable words: 'I predict that by the year 2003 this country will be the most wonderful place to be. The economy will have straightened out and the crime levels will have dropped substantially. The gold price will have risen to $300 an ounce. Thousands of people who have left this country will be clamouring to return. This is the beginning of our Golden Age . . .'

Please God, your prognostications are correct and our troubled land will indeed be healed and whole, dear Dr Mark!

Dr Melanie Polatinsky – Spiritual Philosopher, Grief Counsellor, Inner Child Therapist

From trauma to tranquillity

'I believe that human beings have lost their direction and are using their God-given energy extremely negatively. When it returns to them in pain they can't understand why. My role is to show them that there is life beyond their pain.'

Dr Melanie Polatinsky

Photographed by Francki Burger

On a stormy Friday afternoon in mid-September I interviewed well-known psychotherapist Dr Melanie Polatinsky in her warm and inviting consulting rooms in Johannesburg's northern suburbs.

It was Rosh Hashanah, the Jewish New Year, and the room was overflowing with floral bouquets – tributes from those whom she has helped through the dark tunnel of pain into acceptance, understanding and spiritual growth.

Melanie believes that each one of us must face the burdens and lessons specifically designed for our soul's unique personal development.

In her acclaimed book *Life Beyond Your Pain – The Pathway from Anguish to Eden*, she writes: 'Whatever the soul/inner child does not complete in a lifetime of psychological or spiritual lessons she* must return to the classroom on earth to redo those lessons. There is simply no escape. For this reason I always implore people to face their pain, their childhood abuses, their traumas, their psychology, their grudges, their inability to relate intimately and their lack of forgiveness, and work them through to the very end.'

As a child growing up in a middle-class Orthodox Jewish home in Saxonwold in Johannesburg, the middle child in a family of three siblings, Melanie displayed little sign that she would grow up into a respected academic – she completed her PhD in social work in 1984 – and a psychotherapist, lecturer and teacher of note.

'While I got excellent marks in primary school, I couldn't make any sense of high school. I was disinterested and disconnected. My high school years were definitely my period of mediocrity. I enjoyed netball, but the sports teacher never even gave me a chance to try out for the A team, preferring to choose one of her favourite pupils. I guess there were important lessons for my soul even in small matters.'

Melanie collapses into giggles and I cannot help but observe

that despite the seriousness of the work she does – everything from conducting terminal illness and life-after-death groups, to inner child workshops, to bereavement counselling; to how to contact and work with Angels; to lectures on the teachings of the Ascended Masters – Melanie's contented inner child is much in evidence.

When her mother Sylvia asked her daughter what she intended to study Melanie, armed with a matriculation certificate and without any deliberation, decided to enrol at the University of the Witwatersrand for a BA Honours degree in social work.

'I knew that I had to do something that involved working with people and I believe that this was one of the typical incidents in the life of my soul being automatically steered in a particular direction.'

Her talent for handling group workshops and her extraordinary ability to handle the practical side of her new-found career immediately became apparent.

Aged only eighteen or nineteen, Melanie walked where angels might fear to tread. She went into prisons and worked with criminals and their families to try to restore some semblance of normality into their dysfunctional lives. At the other end of the spectrum, she worked with the aged, establishing social clubs to help them combat their loneliness and develop their own resources. She also worked with cerebral palsied children at the Hope Home in Johannesburg.

As a progression of her work with physically challenged children Melanie, who had recently married and had had only one of her four offspring, was asked to work with a group of young mothers who had recently experienced the anguish of having had their infants diagnosed with varying degrees of mental handicap. She realised that many of them felt that producing a handicapped child was a reflection of their own worthlessness.

Intuitively Melanie knew that she had transported the heavy

*Soul is spoken of in the feminine because the soul is the feminine polarity of soul and spirit. Spirit represents the masculine polarity.

hearts of mothers with their Down Syndrome babies away from their feelings of inadequacy, pain and hopelessness to a place where they could comprehend that they were privileged to be the mothers of these special children and to understand that their children, not burdened with the tasks of the human intellect, were able to live love. She explained to the parents that they needed to look beyond the physical body to see the spiritual beauty that these little messengers had brought with their omnipresent smiles, to appreciate every small milestone that they passed in order finally to come to the realisation that there is always something positive, no matter how small, in every painful situation.

Despite the demands of her growing family, Melanie completed her MA in social work in 1978 with a dissertation entitled *A Preventative Social Group Work Approach to Parent Education in Schools*.

In her school counselling career, which stretched over nine years, Melanie adopted the revolutionary approach of teaching not only the children but counselling the parents and teachers as well in how to handle their children, understand their emotions, and make negative and positive emotions a most natural part of life and living.

At this stage of our interview, I felt it necessary to ask Melanie a question that was perplexing me. 'You are known as a spiritual teacher. All your present counselling is conducted from a spiritual point of view. Yet at this time in your life your solutions could have been those of any empathetic and trained psychotherapist.'

'I believe that I was only ready to receive my spiritual awakening when I had established credibility in my profession. I needed to have reached a point when people no longer thought of me as a crank or weirdo. Although I had always been quite religious and had always prayed, although I never doubted the presence of God, I received my spirituality only when the time was right.'

'When was that?'

'The death of my mother-in-law at the age of sixty-two triggered a memory of everything spiritual, things that I knew I had learned in past lives. I was suddenly comforting people with words and I had no idea where they came from.'

Once her spirituality was awakened, and as a natural progression from her vast experience of counselling children and their parents, an important part of Melanie's current work deals with inner child therapy.

'For me, the inner child and the soul are synonymous,' Melanie explained. 'We experience the feelings of the inner child in the pit of the stomach, usually in the form of a "knot" or "butterflies".

'In contrast, we feel our adult feelings in our hearts. It is important to take cognisance of our inner child/soul feelings and to work with them to restore our psychological balance.'

'Could you give me an example of this?'

'Yes. Take this case. Twenty-five-year-old Colleen's mother had been chronically depressed all her life and Colleen had always felt responsible for her. In a regression, Colleen spontaneously went back into scenes from two previous lifetimes with her mother.

'In the first incarnation, Colleen was a young Indian boy who was murdered by her brother. Her mother survived the ordeal of losing her most beloved child with amazing strength.

'In the second incarnation, her mother was captured by soldiers and separated from her. Although she desperately needed her mother, she managed to survive the separation. Colleen felt that her mother's strength had waned over these painful incarnations, but that these regressed scenes revealed to them that they were both "survivors".'

'How is a person able to contact their inner child/soul?'

'Here is a meditation that will help lead you there,' said Melanie.

Meditation

Close your eyes. Relax your physical body and concentrate for a few moments on your breathing. Allow the meditation music to carry you along. Slowly journey into the secret chamber of your heart. You will enter through a door opened by your Higher Self, who tends the flame of the altar. Your threefold flame is blue, yellow and pink and represents your inner God qualities of power, wisdom and love.

You will notice three chairs in front of the screen.

Your spiritual parents embrace you and sit on either side of you facing the screen. You feel the safety of their presence and can even hold their hands. Kuthumi, the Ascended Master psychologist, projects the first learning from your childhood, from this or a previous lifetime.

Observe this scene and love your inner child.

Now pick up pen and paper and draw or write about your experiences with your non-dominant hand.' (Your inner child expresses herself with your non-dominant hand.)

'How should a person feel when they have done this meditation?'

'You may experience a feeling of sadness or aloneness,' replied Melanie gently. 'Allow this feeling to surface and see the entire scene flooded with scintillating white light. Ask the violet flame angels who bring a sense of joy, freedom and buoyancy, to lovingly comfort and bless your soul.'

One of the most important aspects of Melanie's work is bereavement counselling. With great love, nurturing and compassion, she leads the bereaved through the process of facing the dark tunnel of pain all the way to a triumphant transformation into the light.

'Throughout my career, in whatever field I was working, bereavement cases have always taken priority in my life. I felt that they were my definitive life assignments sent to me from the Heavens.

'Being grateful not to have suffered tragic loss in my life, I feel immensely privileged to have been selected to "be there" for so many people going through heart-rending tragedies. I know that my knowledge of bereavement and the grief surrounding it is something I carry deep within my heart and the wisdom to deal with it definitely comes from the experience I have gained in previous lifetimes.'

Whether Melanie is lecturing, holding workshops or counselling, her stalwart assistant and soul friend Bernice Kaplan is there to assist her both with the administrative work and the grief counselling.

Bernice came to see Melanie after the tragic death of her forty-eight year old husband, a healthy man in the prime of his life. After being startled by an unexpected noise in their house one evening, her husband was carrying a gun in his bag. He accidentally dropped the bag, the gun went off and the bullet hit him in the aorta, severing it from the heart.

Her two young children were alone at home at the time of the accident. Bernice returned home to find her husband being taken by helicopter to an emergency hospital centre. Needless to say, she and her children were totally devastated.

As is the wont of so many psychiatrists dealing with people in intense emotional pain, the distraught widow was immediately put on heavy medication for depression.

An assorted array of mind-numbing drugs was prescribed in increasingly heavy doses, as a result of which Bernice was unable to remember either her husband's funeral or anything that happened immediately afterwards.

When Melanie saw Bernice she told her that she was suppressing all the emotions that needed to be brought out of her system. 'I explained to her that bringing all her bottled-up grief into the open would be part of the very necessary healing process. If she suppressed it, it would only resurface at a later stage,' Melanie told me. 'In order to emerge from her anguish, she needed to go through Nigredo.'

'Nigredo?'

'So often when individuals go through what they term their "darkest hour" they feel every negative emotion such as extreme sadness, abandonment, fear, guilt and worthlessness,' Melanie replied. 'This darkness is a death, but not of the physical body. It is the death of the old self, out of which the soul can be released.'

At first Melanie's counselling, with its emphasis on spirituality, was difficult for Bernice to accept. She was angry because her near perfect life had been so abruptly destroyed.

However, she persevered with Melanie's highly individual method of bereavement counselling, attending both bereavement groups and later many inner child groups. Within a few weeks Bernice had come off all medication and, finally, she was able to assist Melanie in counselling those in deep grief.

To these people Bernice says simply: 'I know what you are feeling. Believe me, I thought I could never ever see a reason for my husband being taken. But now that I view it all from a higher level of consciousness, I understand that to have stayed where I was, as comfortable as it was, would have been a waste of this lifetime.'

It is surprising that Melanie with her compassion for people in pain, with her gentle yet humorous way of counselling, is seen by some members of the Orthodox Jewish religion as a somewhat controversial figure.

When I asked Melanie about this, she replied: 'All orthodox religions have a mystical path which once constituted a large part of these religions when they were first put into practice. Later in the evolution of many orthodox religions, this mystical path became separated from the mainstream of the rituals of the religion.

'I believe that individuals lost the ability to communicate with God and so relied on leaders of religion to intercede for them. Now we have reached the Aquarian Age, people are once again becoming motivated to find God and their own individualised God-self.'

'In your lectures you say that the aim of the mystical path is for the soul to attain union with God. What, for you, constitutes soul?'

'I believe that God created man's soul with the potential of his likeness and image; whereas He created the Spirit in His likeness and image. Thus Spirit is the permanent part of us, whereas soul is impermanent and must be made permanent. This can only be achieved through various incarnations whereby we come to learn our lessons in Earth's schoolroom.'

'Do you believe that there are perfect souls who no longer have to reincarnate because they have learned all their earthly lessons?'

'Yes. The Great White Brotherhood is a Spiritual Order of Ascended Masters who have risen in every age from every culture and religion, East and West. The term Ascended Masters refers to those beings whose souls have completed their earthly incarnations, have graduated from earth's schoolroom and have reunited with God.'

'How do these Ascended Masters bring their teachings to the earth plane?'

'They survey mankind, assessing those souls that are ready and receptive to their teachings and those that have already known their teachings in previous embodiments, although they may not be consciously aware of this. The Masters use many organisations as well as individuals to bring their teachings to the world.'

'Such as?'

'The Theosophical Society, founded by Madame Blavatsky in 1875 and continued into the present century. The original I AM Movement which was begun by Guy and Edna Ballard at the beginning of the twentieth century and continued until 1931. Currently, the teachings of The Summit Lighthouse which was formed in 1958 by messengers Mark Prophet and Elizabeth Clare Prophet.'

It is Melanie's philosophy that our lives, should we so wish it, are intimately bound up with the teachings of the Ascended Masters, the belief that death is not the end, but rather the beginning of a new chapter in our many lives, that makes her unique as a bereavement counsellor.

Take for example this moving story of Tessa, a thirty-three-year-old woman with breast cancer who underwent a mastectomy. After the operation, her spirituality awakened, Tessa began attending Melanie's classes. Her fear was not of death, but rather of abandoning her two young children.

When Tessa's period of remission from her illness ended and she faced death, Melanie sat with her and answered her grief-stricken children's many questions. The oldest child wanted to know whether Mommy would still be able to see him when he went to school and university? Would he still he able to 'see' his mommy?

Tessa and Melanie both comforted the child by assuring him that there would never be a separation of their love and that if he needed her, his mother's love would always be carried in his heart.

In answer to the second question, Melanie, a firm believer in dream therapy, assured the anxious boy that he would always be able to see his mother in his dreams. In this way he could meet with her in his 'higher consciousness' and this would not disrupt her progress in the other dimensions.

After this session, Tessa, feeling that her earthly work was done and that she had no more unfinished business, asked impatiently when the angels would be coming to take her, for she had had enough!

In her final hours, when Tessa had asked to be moved to hospital to make the transition easier for her, Melanie remained with her, praying with her and singing Psalm 23 to her.

> 'Yea, though I walk through the valley
> of the shadow of death,
> I will fear no evil: for thou art with me.'

Dr Melanie Polatinsky. A controversial figure to some, but to a growing body of believers, a shining beacon of hope through life's darkest hours.

Jayshree & Mellissa Mallaya – The Mystic Sisters – Intuitive Palmacologists

Power in the palm of your hand

'We have discovered that the lines on your palm symbolise the amount of karmic lessons that your soul has to undertake in this lifetime. We believe that you need to face these lessons in order to help your soul to make its journey easier.'

Jayshree and Mellissa

Photographed by Terence Hogben

On the second floor of the sprawling Gateway Shopping Centre in KwaZulu-Natal is a tastefully designed shop called The Mystic Sisters, Gateway to Your Destiny.

A far cry from a mere stall at an esoteric fair or a little tucked-away fortune telling cubicle in a larger department store, this emporium with its impressive outside signage, complete with an outsize photograph of the sisters, Jayshree and Mellissa, spells out the fact that predictions and palm reading have moved from fringe entertainment to serious business. Or, as Mellissa so succinctly puts it: 'Money doesn't make you, you make it.' An upmarket range of New Age products is on sale in the stylish reception area, there are two discreet consulting rooms, a healing massage centre and a coffee shop area.

Enterprising entrepreneurs, these determined young women are continually searching for new ways to expand their burgeoning esoteric empire. They are both involved with designing a fountain for the shopping centre that will feature a statue of a sexy sari-clad woman, Nasthasi, which will be sculpted to resemble a composite of the two of them.

The purpose this statue is not sheer vanity; rather, the emphasis is on using the eye-catching edifice as a means of raising money to help the less privileged members of the community – particularly abused women and children.

Well-known throughout South Africa, and particularly in their home base of KwaZulu-Natal, the Mallaya sisters are tireless – and extremely inventive – fundraisers. As part of their charity drive, Jayshree and Mellissa are proud sponsors of a horse race known as The Mystic Sisters, the proceeds of which go to help blind and deaf members of the community.

The desire to help the less fortunate was instilled in them by their late and much-lamented father, Rejji. Mellissa tells me: 'Our father used often to remind us of the saying "I cried because I had no shoes, until I met a man who had no feet." '

Rejji Mallaya was, from his daughters' account, an altogether remarkable man. It was from Rejji's father, Mallaya Rapeti, a learned and cultured scholar who had a certain psychic ability as well as an aptitude for reading palms, that his granddaughters inherited their clairvoyant gifts.

Mallaya Rapeti died when Jayshree was only one month old. However, there is a story about her late grandfather that she relates with fondness.

'When I was just a couple of weeks, granddad held my hand and read my palm. "This girl is going to have more clothes than she knows what to do with," he declared.'

'Is this correct?' I ask.

Jayshree nods her head. 'I love fashion. You can ask Mellissa. I have clothes stored everywhere. And as for shoes . . .'

Following their father Rejji's marriage to Treasa – a noted exponent of traditional Indian food – four children were born: Jayshree, Jayson, Mellissa and Kuben.

While Rejji was a dedicated father to all his children, his two daughters held a special place in his heart. 'We were his princesses. He was devoted to us and we to him. While he was alive we had no need of boyfriends . . . he was the special man in our lives,' declare Jayshree and Mellissa.

Thus when Rejji died unexpectedly in the intensive care unit of Durban's St Augustine Hospital after a massive heart attack, it was a turning point in the lives of the distraught girls.

Jayshree, who was in her third year of legal studies at the University of Durban-Westville, felt almost as if her life had ended. 'What am I going to without my father's powerful influence in my life?' she wondered.

Firmly believing that out of every negative situation there must be something positive, Jayshree realised that she now had to take control of her own life; to be master of her own destiny.

After much soul searching, she decided that instead of furthering her legal education, she would rather concentrate on developing her mystic abilities – a gift that, at that stage, she and Mellissa had been using simply to keep family and friends entertained with palm readings at family gatherings, school, university or at their dad's shops.

For Mellissa, four years younger and just out of school, her father's death was equally traumatic. She was immediately thrust into the business world and the enormous responsibility of the management of one of her father's stores.

It was only after her grief had abated somewhat and suitable people had been found to take care of her late father's business that Mellissa was able to decide where her career path lay. Like her older sister Jayshree she, too, resolved to concentrate on perfecting her psychic gifts.

Both girls instinctively knew that in the field that they had chosen they had one devoted guide who would be with them throughout their lives. Their father Rejji would, they felt, continue to watch over and support them, albeit from a different dimension.

Thus his daughters still talk to their departed father on a daily basis, seeking his wisdom and his blessing in all that they do.

'Do you have any other guides besides your father?'

'No,' replied Mellissa shaking her head emphatically. 'Our dad continues to give us all the guidance that we could ever need.'

With their exuberant personalities and trendy dress code, in next to no time The Mystic Sisters, aided by the media who supported them from the very beginning, attracted a cosmopolitan clientele that included many celebrities.

They told a rather surprised Amichand Rajbansi, Minority Front Leader, nine years ago that he would be getting divorced. Sure enough, some years later his high profile divorce made headlines.

The girls also made an accurate prediction about beauty queen Kerishnie Naicker's chances in the Miss World competition. 'We would have loved her to win, although we "saw" that this was not possible. We did however state that she would make it to the final ten.'

When the girls first opened their offices in Durban's upmarket Florida Road they required the services of a receptionist. One of the girls who applied for the post appeared quiet and shy, but Mellissa instinctively felt that she was the candidate best suited for the job.

Once again, her intuition proved right. In due course, the receptionist, Adele, became their older brother Jayson's wife as well as the proud mother of a beautiful baby girl, Priyanka. Needless to say, this receptionist still works for her two sisters-in-law.

Soon top businessmen (all of whom wish to remain anonymous) started visiting The Mystic Sisters in search of financial advice.

'Didn't this intimidate you?' I ask.

'At first,' said Mellissa, 'I used to feel nervous when I was advising a businessman about a big business deal. But I soon gained confidence. Because of my intuitive knowledge, I've never yet given the wrong advice. My job is not to predict. All I do is see what's in the palm and then I give the client the options that will work best for them.'

'How do you feel about this country?'

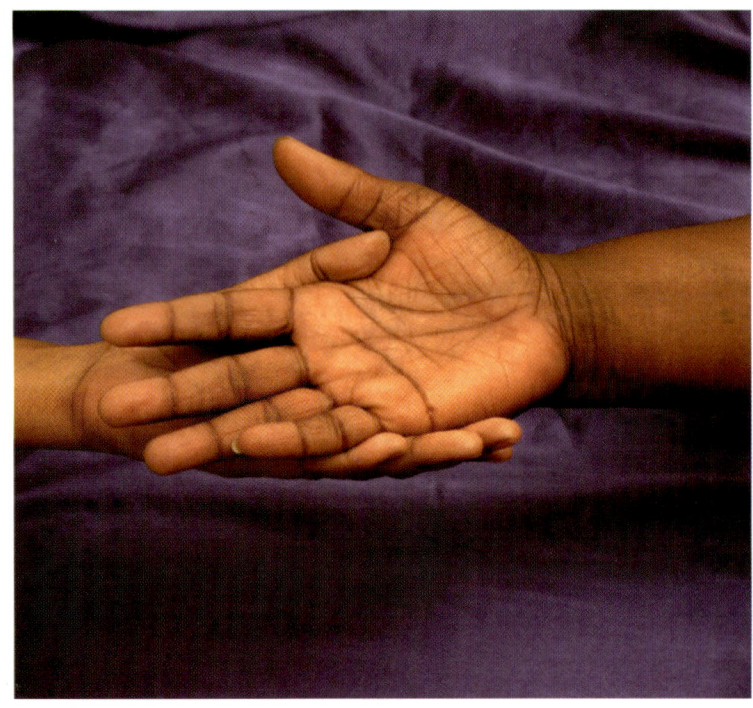

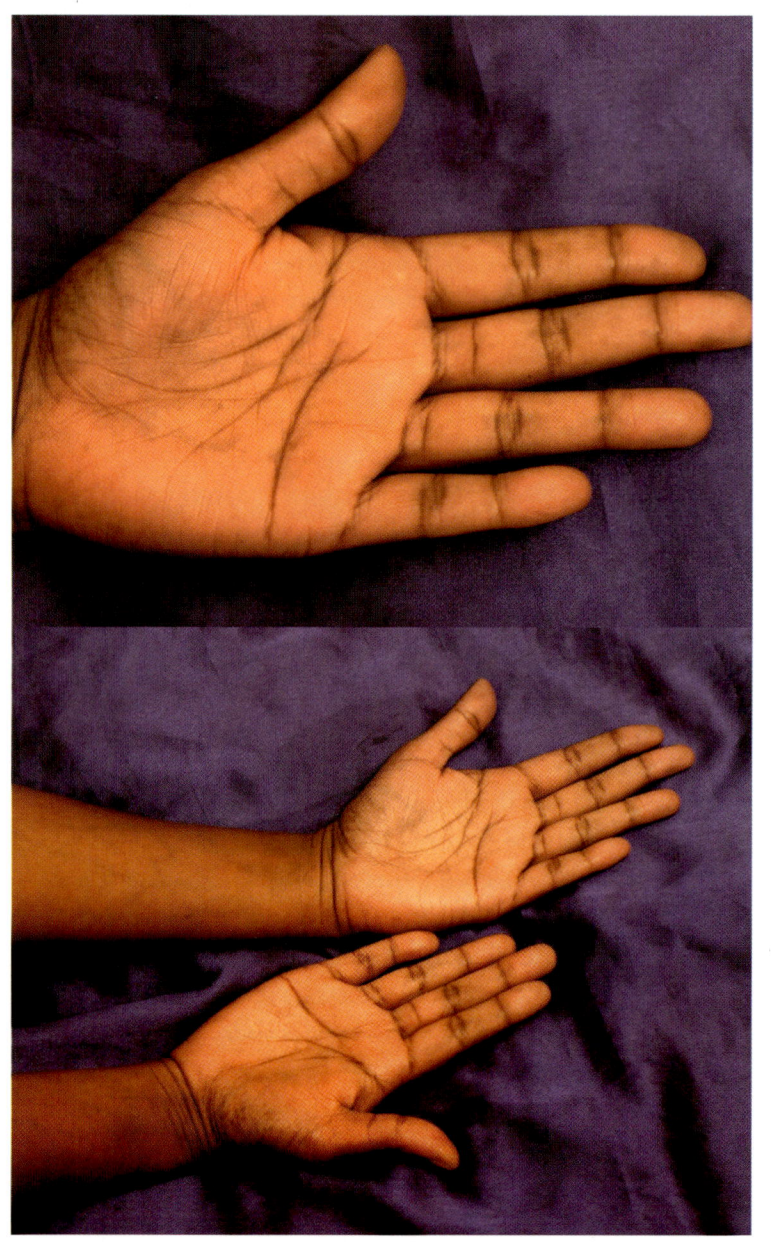

'South Africa is a wonderful place. Why do people want to leave? A woman came to see us to ask if she should emigrate to Australia. We advised her against it. Still, she went. She'd barely set foot in the place when she was robbed. The thieves took everything. The grass definitely isn't always greener on the other side! Having said that, we have also predicted many successful emigrations for our clients.'

A reading with Jayshree and Mellissa will consist of a palm reading of both hands. A follow-up reading gives additional insight from the Tarot cards. Where The Mystic Sisters' reading differs from many others is that they will also provide intuitive advice on how to transform your life by combining each palm reading session with some motivational positive thinking. Or, as Jayshree and Mellissa call it, 'Palmacology'.

'Why do you read the palm of both hands?' I want to know.

'What can appear on one palm may not appear on the other. If something appears on the passive palm i.e. the left palm, you can't use this knowledge until you become aware of it.

'The left palm contains inherited traits and the path that you were born with. The right palm is the active palm which contains future, past, present and personal information that has been shaped or reinforced by you, other people, education and even environmental influences.'

'Can the markings on your palm change?'

'Your lines will change to accommodate any difference in your proposed future to that which you shape yourself. Negative thoughts and actions can have detrimental repercussions.'

'How do positive thoughts alter a person's palm?'

'Your thought patterns are filtered through to your brain. If these thoughts are consistent and strong, they will stimulate, alter and even replace your previous thought patterns. This will create new brain impulses. These new brain impulses will begin the cycle again. New information will now be relayed to your palm. It will emerge on the surface of your palm changing and altering the affected lines.'

'You call yourselves The Mystic Sisters. Explain the link between Mysticism and palm reading.'

'Many people are probably unaware that you can count the number of karmic lessons that you will experience in this lifetime on your palm and even the reasons why we are here. Through our many readings we have been able to discover that you hold the secrets of your karma in the palm of your hand.'

'How do you read this?'

'The Mystic Eye is the semicircular line running from the outer edge of the first finger which ends between the first and second fingers. If you have this sign on your palm then you possess a high level of intuition and perception.

'Within this Mystic Eye formation lie the karmic lines. If they are well marked on your right palm, you have managed to overcome your karmic lessons. If the lines are faint, you have somehow failed to learn your lessons.'

'Could you explain the difference between karmic lessons and karmic cycles?'

'Your karmic lessons are unavoidable. They are part of the divine plan that we are all powerless to change. Karmic lessons are laid down for your soul to overcome.

'Karmic cycles, however, are created by the decisions you make and what you do. If you do harm to other people, you must be prepared to endure a cycle that will send harm back to you. If, on the other hand, you surround others with positive energy and kindness, you will be rewarded with positive energy and kindness. We believe in the saying "As you sow, so shall you reap".'

When one spends time with the Mallaya sisters, one cannot help being struck by the extremely close bond between them. If Jayshree starts a sentence it could well be that Mellissa will finish it. When they go shopping separately, they are both likely to pick out the same items. Their generosity of spirit that reaches out to help less fortunate members of the community, also extends to their magnanimity to each other.

When Mellissa turned twenty-one, at her lavish party on board the luxury yacht *The Isle of Capri*, Jayshree handed her sister the keys to a brand new BMW 525.

However, because Jayshree had a 'feeling' about the gift, she warned Mellissa not to drive the car on certain days or at certain times. Her younger sister chose to ignore Jayshree's warnings – at her peril. Three weeks later, the new driver, out joyriding with her friends, skidded in a puddle of oil. Fortunately, no one was harmed, although the car was a write-off. 'From that moment on, people began to take our predictions seriously.'

Whether it's palm readings, writing astro columns for newspapers, broadcasting on radio or appearing on television, there is a common thread that runs through all the sisters' endeavours – positivity.

As they wrote in their best-selling book *Palm Reading & Positive Thinking*:

'Believe in the positive power of your mind. Don't build a retaining wall of fear around yourself. Build a wall of positive strength around you. Before you believe in anything, believe in yourself. You are as special and talented as the next person.

God doesn't make rejects. You do. Your mind does. What gives you the authority to judge yourself or the next person? By doing this you have already assumed negativity. Practise your belief in yourself. Practise your belief that you can do it. Go out there and live your life.'

As the sisters take their leave, full of affection and giggles and the promise of a gift of samoosas made by their mother for my journey home, I think to myself that, yes, these girls certainly are out there living their lives to the full and filling the lives of many others with faith, hope and charity.

Chris Tokalon – Sound Healer

In tune with the Universe

Photographed by Francki Burger

'Harmonious sound waves wash through our bodies on a cellular level and have the capacity to shake loose stress and trauma, thereby restoring a balanced, even energy flow. Music created with such intent is the perfect stress reliever, revitalising body, mind and spirit.'

Chris Tokalon

I do not believe that it was coincidence that shortly after I visited sound therapist Chris Tokalon in the tucked-away Hansel and Gretel-type thatched cottage near Fourways where he was living at the time, I received the following e-mail:

Dear Friends,
We are asking for everyone's assistance in getting this message circulated worldwide ASAP so that all who choose will be able to participate on Nov. 11th at 11.00 am [2001].

A friend of a trusted friend and fellow Light Worker, Jahn Starr, has been guided by Spirit to have the vibration of SOUND go around the Planet to break away the last pieces of the old vibration of discord and separation and to bring in more fully and to activate more completely the frequencies for LOVE, PEACE and BALANCE.

She was given a vision of a huge group of Angels over Afghanistan assisting everyone to Love and Peace, and then the same vision was repeated for the USA and then again for the whole world. Just as we lit candles for all those who gave their lives and their loved ones and their service on September 11th, we are now being asked to bring in the vibration of sound, for it is the vibration of sound (the Word) and Light (the Creator energies, the Christ energies), that will help heal the Planet and all beings on her.

Wherever you are on Nov. 11th at 11:00 am (11-11-11) please ring a bell, sound sacred tones with your voice, use whatever sound/instrument you are guided to do. The important thing is that we now need SOUND to help the restoration of BALANCE on the planet.

This date is very important in world peace and carries a very high Spiritual energy. If you are called to join us, please make your Sacred Tones on this day and help us to get this information out by sharing it with all you know as soon as possible.

I would like to suggest that for the 11.11 event, you have people use the 'AH' Sound, in whatever key or tone feels comfortable for them. This is an extremely powerful sound – particularly useful for generating compassion. I know you will agree that compassion is truly a key to transformation of consciousness on this planet.

As you may know, the 'AH' sound is a sacred seed syllable. It is found in most of the God and Goddess names on the planet (Tara, Buddha, Krishna, Yah), as well as many of the sacred words (Amen, Alleluia, Aum). Most mystical traditions worldwide also find it to be the sound of the heart chakra. Yet, as a vowel sound, it defies denomination or description as a mantra and it is acceptable by everyone.

Like Jahn Starr, Chris Tokalon, who describes himself as a 'detribalised Cypriot', is well aware of the importance of sound, both for balancing the vibrations of the universe and for 'toning' the individual in order to restore balance, joy and well-being.

Chris describes the process of toning simply as a vocalised meditation using vowel sounds as mantras. He believes that when colour visualisation and focused intent are included in the process we have a powerful, readily available tool that is capable of dislodging dense stagnating energy (i.e. fear) and releasing it from our body.

For Chris, a being is a perfect musical instrument designed to receive and transmit energy vibrations, literally an orchestra of frequencies. He believes that an electromagnetic field surrounding our every cell transmits a frequency particular to that cell's energetic composition. To illustrate this point, Chris explains that our spleen has a different frequency to the vibration of our heart cells.

According to Chris, when the different frequencies of body, mind and spirit are resonating at optimum level and in harmony, we are a symphony of consciousness.

In his opinion many of us seldom experience life as it happens because we are holding on to and clinging to the resonance of past happenings, while anticipating what the future might hold. We therefore feel soul loss by not being in the music that every moment of our lives has to offer.

Synchronicity and harmony with the rhythms and melodies in the dance of life allow us to experience the frequency of divine consciousness, i.e. the vibrations of joy and peace that allow us to truly be human beings, having a divine experience on earth.

'We create heaven or hell on earth by exercising the dynamic of choice. The effect of dissonant frequencies such as negative thoughts, words or even loud noises is an imbalance and causes a blockage or depletion of energy. Holding these energies in our body eventually causes cell mutation and, ultimately, disease,' declared Chris.

'However, I believe that negative or dense energy can be unblocked by the use of sound in the form of music or our own voice creating a massage on a cellular level. After all, our body is largely composed of water and sound travels through water five and a half times faster than it does through air.

'Water amplifies sound. When we combine our breath, voice and body, we become the musician and the instrument. Through regular toning sessions, we can restore balance to our bodies, using sound for cleansing and release just like medicine.'

'What happens at a toning session?' I asked.

'The toning process I follow is focused on our seven main energy centres or chakras. Starting from the bottom, I use the notes C, D, E, F, G, A, B and the colours red, orange, yellow, green, blue, indigo and violet.

'The vowels I use are uh (herd), oh (phone), oo (who), ah (fun), i (high), ay (hay), ee (he). There are varied opinions as to what works and I recommend that you use your intuition as a guide as to what works for you. Simply be curious, explore and experiment.'

'Where does one begin?'

'I tell everyone to be relaxed and grounded and to sit with a straight spine. To breathe evenly and deeply. Each participant is required to do anything from three to seven repetitions per chakra and visualise the colours with their eyes closed. If they don't have an instrument at home, then they can choose any low note and start from there, singing a scale.'

'What if you're not musical?'

With a smile, Chris suggests that I contact one of his clients, Mark.

From Mark I received the following testimony:

'I have never had an ear for music, I couldn't put one and a half steps together on a dance floor or ever attempted to sing a note.

'Yet after a couple of sessions with Chris – I consulted him because I was suffering from difficulties in my relationship and extreme financial burdens – for the first time that I can remember, I started to hear music and sound through my body.

The rain stick, the flute, the shakers and especially the overtone singing* touched parts of me that had long ago fallen asleep or perhaps died. I felt energy stirring within, colours and shapes played behind my closed eyes, images of my life replayed before me.

A recurring pain in my lower back seemed to react to Chris' sound – it eventually released itself and disappeared. Thankfully, I experienced no further discomfort.

I still have problems – those have not left me and I expect that

*Singing which creates two or more notes in harmony simultaneously. The first note, called the fundamental, is held while the harmonic overtone scale is sung over it. This extraordinary and mesmerising resonance sets up vibratory patterns that are at once soothing and uplifting to the spirit.

they never will. However, I feel a lightness of being that flows more easily around these obstacles and finds new ways of living.

For me, the beauty of Chris' method of working is that there are no lengthy explanations needed to satisfy our curiosity and our intellect. There is just a very real experience combined with definite results!

Chris' journey to the path on which he now finds himself was not always harmonious. The eldest child in a family of three siblings, Chris was overweight and lonely throughout his primary school years, seeking refuge in reading.

Tired of the unkind taunting of his peers, Chris put himself on a massive diet in high school, an institution that he saw as steeped in tradition, rules, morals and haircuts.

Desperate for acceptance amongst the other boys, he took refuge in humour. His ability to mimic sounds – he can still imitate a saxophone to perfection – and people brought him some much sought after popularity but, in truth, school bored him.

It was only when he could escape to his room and his music – a particular favourite of the young teenage boy was the music of Jesus Christ Superstar, an LP that was subsequently banned for being too controversial – that he felt alive. 'I felt a deep empathy for Christ. I was so sorry that he had been betrayed.'

If school was difficult, religion, too, held little charm for him. Forced from an early age to attend the Greek Orthodox Church, Chris battled to understand the services that were conducted in High Greek. The only salvation for him was the lavish meal served by family and friends at the conclusion of the service.

After a mediocre school career – 'I always saw that I did enough work just to pass' – Chris could find little satisfaction in the various job paths he attempted in an effort to appease his father who insisted that his only son have a 'proper' career.

He tried law, then he worked in construction, but nothing that he did lasted longer than six months. Finally, when he turned twenty-one Chris, with no musical training, saw the light. He knew that he must become a musician.

'Once I'd made the decision, everything seemed easy. I loved all types of music – jazz, folk, rock, underground, Elvis. I played the saxophone and the flute. I was entirely self-taught.'

With Chris as leader, a band named 'Spice' was formed. In the following years Chris played in clubs and shows, at weddings and barmitzvahs – anywhere, in fact, where he could get a gig.

Chris found his love of music all-encompassing. 'I found romantic relationships with the opposite sex painful. About five years ago, I finally entered into a relationship that was both meaningful and spiritual to me. At the prompting of my partner, who encouraged me to use music and sound as a spiritual tool for healing, I began to explore new avenues. I gave my girlfriend my heart and soul on the false assumption that she could heal my pain.'

When the relationship ended, leaving Chris desolate, he began to look to the fundamentals of using sound as a means of healing himself. Out of his despair his destiny had finally manifested itself.

In the fullness of time, Chris formed an attachment that also had a profound spiritual significance for him. His friendship with Nelia Spies of Halo Gaia Holistic Journeys resulted in his becoming a facilitator on dolphin trips to Mozambique.

'Dolphins,' says Chris, 'are magical, mystical creatures and their ability to uplift and transform the human psyche is known and documented worldwide. I believe that the way dolphins use sound and transmit their joyful and peaceful energy to humans is based on the same principles as fundamental sound therapy.'

Thus it was with the greatest joy that Chris was able to add the soothing song of the gentle dolphins to his list of healing instruments.

One of the most inspiring testimonials on Chris' sound journey into the soul came from one of his clients, Hanneke.

From the age of ten, Hanneke had suffered from temporal lobe epilepsy that led to debilitating seizures with resulting confusion and depression.

So great was her unhappiness that she attempted suicide in 1993. All she desired was to return 'home'. During her near-death experience, Hanneke's heart stopped and she saw herself outside her body.

Suddenly she heard, clear as a bell, the sound of the Tibetan Bowl* vibrating with clear resonance. The sound was turning her back – clearly it wasn't her time to leave this planet.

In an effort to control her epilepsy, Hanneke was put on heavy medication. She knew when she was about to suffer an attack because she always 'saw' the aura of it and spots danced before her eyes. Yet she resented the heavy medication that periodically robbed her of two or three days of her life as she lay in a drug-induced stupor in an effort to deal with the pain of her physical condition.

As an intelligent and well-informed woman, Hanneke was aware of the astonishing power of music that could induce alpha waves that had a relaxing impact on the brain.

She knew that it was well documented that Baroque music had a calming effect on the psyche, instilling a feeling of calmness and serenity. More importantly, unlike her medication, music had no side effects.

With this in mind, she decided to consult Chris. 'I have been seeing Chris for about two years,' said Hanneke. 'He has been an integral part of my transformation. From the outset, it was clear that he understood my pain and my struggle.

'When I started seeing him, I was not in a good space. I couldn't stop talking throughout our sessions. Yet Chris remained calm,

professional and empathetic. At the same time his wonderful sense of humour shone through. He was always light-hearted and ready to have fun . . . which is so important for healing.'

'What exactly did Chris do?'

'First, he consulted his spirit guides through intuition and kinesiology† to find out exactly what sounds I needed to hear in order to restore calm and balance within me. Then he proceeded to take me on this magical sound journey – everyone who goes on this path comes out deeply relaxed and energised. Plus it's so much fun.'

'Is your epilepsy under control?'

'I still consult a neurologist and when I feel a seizure coming on, I take a combination of Tegretol and Epilim to prevent the

* Bowl used by Tibetan monks. Made of an alloy of seven different metals, the bowl resonates with a vibratiion rich in overtones when struck with its specially fashioned wooden stick.
† Kinesiology is the use of muscle testing to locate where the body, mind or spirit is holding negative energy.

attacks. This, together with the tuning and toning of my chakras as done by Chris, means that I no longer have to take such heavy medication. I believe that it's perfectly possible to combine conventional treatment with alternative therapy. Today, thanks to Chris, I'm in a much happier space.'

So convinced is Hanneke of the power of sound therapy, that in her work as a rei-flexologist* carefully chosen music plays an integral part in her clients' healing process. Moreover she, with her husband and her two children, has started drumming sessions with musician Vaughan Harris, sessions that she describes as both 'grounding and empowering'.

In conclusion, Hanneke told me: 'A lifelong struggle to remain in my body is over. I am learning to move in and out of body as a matter of free choice, as appropriate for each situation.

'I am experiencing the joy of being in this female body. This embodiment was and is facilitated by remaining Aware in the Present Moment during energy work, art-making, story telling, sound energy, sharing, drumming, singing, mothering, love-making, gardening, renovating, eating, drinking, swimming, rafting, hiking and rock climbing.'

As I was taking my leave of Chris, with his enormous generosity of spirit, he insisted on presenting me with a copy of his magical self-produced CD *Dance in De Light*, subtitled *Music for our Chakras*.

This CD consists of seven tunes, each designed in pitching, rhythm, music and intention to tune the chakras in ascending order.

On one level this CD functions purely as music, albeit that it is filled with natural sounds such as water and bird calls. After listening to it, I found that I was filled with a great sense of peace and energy was pulsating through my body like a drum.

Chris Tokalon – musician, healer, master of sound. Of all the instruments I heard during the time I spent with him – he took me briefly on a musical exploration – what I will remember best about him is the joyous sound of his laughter. A deep chuckle that serves to accompany his belief that a sound journey should be fun and the noise which one makes, should, above all, be joyful!

*The practitioner combines Reiki with reflexology.

Nandiva (Wendy) Wood – Yoga Teacher & Natural Healer

The perfect balance of body,
mind and spirit

'I believe that yoga is a way that we can find
our true essence. Yoga gives us strength on
every level as well as providing us with the
ability to detach ourselves from physical
energy and to connect with a Higher Source
of life.'

Nandiva

Photographed by Francki Burger

Nandiva (known to most of her pupils simply as Wendy) sits cross-legged on the teachers' podium at Ishta, the magnificent yoga centre she has created in the heart of the Johannesburg suburb of Atholl.

The octagonal soft yellow studio, hidden by its high surrounding walls the colour of newly turned earth, is tastefully adorned with pictures of the great swamis and gurus, together with artistic representations of the chakras and various charts. Skilfully scattered Moroccan-style cushions and large coloured candles are much in evidence in this stylish sanctuary. The vases are always filled with fresh flowers.

The studio's glass doors open out on to a carefully tended garden. Here, in a pond with water falling gently from a rock waterfall, assorted fish, including some magnificent koi, swim in crystal-clear water. Bird life abounds and the sound of wind chimes fills the air.

The lush garden contains an eclectic mix of objects – crystals, Tiger's Eye and other semi-precious stones, a depiction of the Buddha, small statues of frogs and tortoises, witches, gnomes, elves and fairies. Ishta is indeed an enchanted place.

Consequently it comes as no surprise that its owner Nandiva herself, with her enviably slim figure, her gentle manner, her large blue eyes, long blonde hair and snow white clothes, very much resembles the archetypal fairy princess.

When I mention this analogy to her, she dismisses it with a shy laugh and the wave of a well-manicured hand. For Nandiva – the name she was given by her guru and mentor, the late and much revered Kavi Yogiraj Mani Finger – is modest in the extreme.

Ishta* Yoga which is taught at the centre, together with various breathing techniques, mantras and meditation, was developed by Mani Finger, original founder of the Yoga Teachers Fellowship of Southern Africa.

Her guru Mani gave her the name Nandiva. Her parents, her Afrikaans mother Catharine Gertrude, and her Russian Jewish father Nathan Breslawsky, christened her Deborah. Her brothers soon tagged her with the affectionate nickname 'Deborkah'.

While she might have been a child of few words, Deborah had a strong will of her own. At a very early age, she decided to use only the second name with which she had been christened. 'From now on,' she told her surprised family, 'my name is no longer Deborah. I am Wendy.'

She paused for a moment. 'You know, your name is your mantra.[†] So it's no surprise really that I was christened Nandiva by Mani – a name most probably derived from the Bilaspur goddess Naina Devi who, being the goddess of eyes, saw things that most others could not.'

'Such as?'

'Well, I am able to see the elementals of the water, the spirits of the trees, the spirits of the plants, gnomes and fairies. It was only when my perceptions deepened as a yoga teacher, that I realised that I do indeed have a connection with these elements.'

'Do you see these elementals as beams of light?'

'Some are of the earth, some are of the light. They are simply energy of a different vibration.'

'Can you talk to these spirits?'

'In words, no. Although I can definitely communicate my feelings to them . . . and I know how they feel as well.'

Nandiva pauses in slight embarrassment. 'Should I be telling you all this?' she ponders.

Nandiva's grandfather was a religious man and it was from him that she learned to pray. Not that she went with him to church, though – prayer for the little girl was a personal and private matter. When she was only seven or eight years old, her mother Catharine, aware that her husband would like each of their three sons to have

*Integral science of Yoga.
†Verbal incantation or mystic formula used devotionally.

a barmitzvah, converted to the Jewish faith.

Her small daughter was also taken to the *mikveh* or special baths for ritual immersions. Officially the little girl was now Jewish, although Nandiva has always preferred to follow her own spiritual path.

Noting that her daughter displayed no particular interest in sport, Catharine decided to take her to ballet lessons. These progressed satisfactorily, until it reached the stage when *pointe* work caused Nandiva's toes to bleed. 'Ouch!' she cried. 'This is definitely not for me!'

At this time, Mani Finger had a column in the local newspaper, the now defunct *Rand Daily Mail*, in which he demonstrated yoga postures and wrote briefly on the philosophy of yoga.

In essence, the Hatha yoga of which Mani wrote comprises postures (*asanas*) and breath control (*pranayama*). 'Ha' means sun and 'tha' means moon, therefore hatha yoga means balancing opposites.

Hatha links the movement of the body with breathing, bringing about a centred, harmonious feeling. The mind, body and breath are all in harmony. Yoga balances forward bends with backward bends, standing poses with inverted poses and inhalation with exhalation. It is designed for relaxing and releasing deep body tension, balancing the nervous system and stimulating the internal organ functions.

Fascinated by what she read, Nandiva tried to do the postures herself and was delighted by the ease with which her naturally supple body could do even the most complicated *asana*.

Inspired, she began studying yoga. She noted that her teacher, who was named Joy, did indeed seem to possess an outer radiance combined with an inner tranquillity. This impressed her so much that from her second lesson, Nandiva knew that she too would become a yoga teacher.

When Joy retired, Nandiva made her way to the studio of the man who was to become her beloved friend and mentor, Kavi Yogiraj Mani Finger himself.

Their close association, which developed over many years, was not severed by Mani and his family's relocation to the USA and ended only in 2001 with the great guru's death at the ripe old age of ninety-three.

It was from Mani that Nandiva learned much of her philosophy of life. 'Why do people find it so easy to believe in coincidences and so hard to believe in miracles? Expect a miracle every day,' he told Nandiva.

Sitting on her mat in one of Nandiva's popular yoga classes, I notice a woman doing the postures although she is well into her eighth month of pregnancy. Intrigued as to the reason this expectant mother chose to come to yoga rather than attend conventional prenatal classes, I talked to her after the lesson.

'Mandy, how do you feel yoga benefits an expectant mother?'

'I did yoga exercises before the birth of my other two children. I find that it gives the unborn foetus a wonderful introduction to the spiritual aspect of life. Also, because of the spiritual nature of the class, creative forces surround one. This, for me, makes the process of creation tangible.

'The birth of my son Alessandro was a difficult hospital birth and so, to be truthful, the yoga I had done was not all that beneficial. However, my second child is a girl called Arielle – which means God's Lioness. Arielle was born at home. While I was in labour I did the yoga breathing and it made me so relaxed that I hardly felt any pain or discomfort.

'Also, doing the yoga postures regularly for nine months helped my body do what it had to do. I didn't resist at all. Arielle was born in an atmosphere of great calmness which I like to think contributes to the fact that she is such a happy child . . . she simply adores being on this earth!'

For Nandiva the teaching ray and the healing ray are symbiotic, both coming from the same blue light. Consequently, it seemed natural to her that once she was a teacher, she would also become a healer.

Healing for Nandiva began many years before in her little greenhouse. With a shy smile she tells me that she used to spend Saturday afternoons there healing her plants, tending them and talking to them, taking cuttings and potting them in soil so that they would grow.

'It was not an effort to get my hands wet, to feel my fingers in the sand. I always felt as though I was planting seeds in the soil of the subconscious mind, so that my thoughts could grow and flourish.'

During an open day at Mani's studio, a Reiki healer was speaking. The weather was hot and Nandiva was getting agitated. She knew that she should return home to her husband and two daughters. Yet she stayed and allowed the healer to perform Reiki on her.

'At the time I had some discomfort – I wouldn't actually call it pain – in my back. When the healer worked on my shoulders I felt a slight tingle, but then I forgot about it. A couple of days later, I noticed that the discomfort in my back had vanished. It never came back and I attributed this to the power of Reiki.

'As a result of this, and encouraged by Mani, I went on to become a Reiki Master, following the Usui system of natural healing.'

'I am sure you have helped many people . . .'

Ever modest, Nandiva declines to talk about this

although she tells me with a deprecating grin, 'Well, I know that I definitely cured a dog, an SPCA special who was limping badly.'

For pupils seeking meditation classes, the Ishta Centre offers group meditation. This incorporates the Himalayan tradition of yoga meditation, combined with the wisdom of Patanjalis Yoga Sutas, the philosophy and practice of the Tantras and the specific oral instructions and initiatory experiences passed on by a long line of saints and yoga masters.

'What are the benefits of meditation, Nandiva?' I asked.

'Meditation leads to inner peace. It helps to relieve tension by balancing the emotions. It revives energy and stimulates creativity. In essence, it helps you realise your full potential.'

For Nandiva, the new millennium has been filled with challenges. 'The wise person will actually embrace challenge for in order to overcome difficulties, we need to use our inner resources. It is how we handle our problems that gives us our personality.'

'Some people might not have handled their problems with your apparent acceptance and calm,' I remark.

'We are all placed on this earth to learn lessons,' she replied. 'Yet the Divine never gives us more than we can handle. If our lives were too easy, too cushy, we would learn nothing. The true yogi is not concerned with his or her dislikes and is able to thank the Divine for their adversity. For without adversity, there can be no growth.'

As I was taking my leave, Nandiva left me with the following thought: 'Mani used to say that yoga is like sugar. You can't explain the taste of it. You've just got to try it for yourself.'

The hard path from drugs to the Divine

Photographed by Francki Burger

'My belief is that all physical illness originates in the head from past traumatic experiences that have not been processed. This goes for previous lives as well. I work with the chakras and with ghosts and angels, if necessary. Naturally, all this makes me very tired.'

Durgana

On a warm Saturday afternoon in mid-November the head of the Yoga Teachers Fellowship, Durgana, alias Magda Inglethorpe, is sitting on the podium of the Ishta Yoga Centre conducting a workshop with fellow yoga teachers, many of whom have come great distances to attend this Fellowship day.

With her short grey hair and glasses, the frail frame of this mother of eight, grandmother and great-grandmother, belies her inner core of steel that has helped her conquer the many obstacles that have afflicted her life. With Herculean strength, she has overcome drug addiction, cancer and debilitating deafness.

Today Durgana, inspired by a book she read many years ago, *Kahuna,* which dealt with the work of the natural healers in the Philippines, is attempting put into practice the Kahuna principle of *Cutting the Ties* by means of which psychic threads, the bonds of relationships that are painful, harmful or obsolete, are severed.

Always willing to experiment – 'I will use anything that works' – Durgana came to the conclusion that these ties of which the healers wrote were linked to the Yoga chakras and thereby to the Yogic doctrine of non-attachment or *Vairagya*.

Thus the workshop she is conducting with the teachers is not pure yoga. Rather, it is her own recipe – a dash of Kahuna combined with a dollop of kinesiology mixed with a healthy portion of yoga philosophy. She tells me that she has had great success with this therapy with individuals – she now wishes to see if *Cutting the Ties* will work with larger groups.

She is tackling this experiment with her usual mix of forthrightness, candour and humour. 'God in his wisdom put you with someone. Problem is, how do you live with someone who bugs the hell out of you?' she asks the class.

The lesson she delivers in colloquial, conversational fashion – 'One must learn to accept people as they are – not to get into a tizz when somebody doesn't put the lid on the toothpaste' – is so full of practical common sense and humour that one almost misses her extraordinary grasp of things esoteric. 'I had terrible in-law problems. When I looked at my astrological chart I saw Saturn in the seventh house of relationships ruling the tenth house of in-laws. What chance did my marriage have?'

Not only does Durgana have a sound knowledge of the practicalities and philosophy of yoga, she also has an innate understanding of life and after life; of devils and angels; astrology; kinesiology and reflexology. So wide is her knowledge that she is currently writing a training manual for yoga teachers – bending all the old rules, as it were.

'Go into a relaxed state. Let your hair down,' Durgana tells the class. 'Today we are going to cut the ties . . . remove layers of irritation that were never processed. I do not wish to make enemies of people. Rather, I am making you into friends or even making you into friends with yourself.

'When you approach the other person it must not be with jealousy or hate. In a sense, I want you to sort out your differences. I want you to have a conversation at an astral level. Invite the person into a safe place and talk to them. At that level there are no lies. Try to be tranquil. Don't dump your emotions on the other person. Listen to the other person. Tune into his or her emotions.'

The silence in the room is palpable. Durgana continues: 'Look at the person or "partner" to whom threads are linked. By what chakras are you linked? Is it at the sacral level? The navel? The heart? The throat? The brow?

'It is your secret where this link is. Now take out the thread. That's right. Pull it out. Once you've cleared it out, imagine a blue light shining into the chakra. Then seal it so that there can be no reconnection. Now look again. Are there any more links which need to be severed?'

Once the exercise has been completed, Durgana gently goes

around the class and asks each member whether the experiment has worked for them.

One woman burst into tears. 'I could never get on with my mother. She didn't want me to grow up. She almost kept a stranglehold on me. Today, I feel that I have finally broken loose . . .'

Durgana smiles broadly. 'That's the best news I could possibly have. The trouble is we do not know how to voice our feelings in a way that is acceptable to people. Thus we either scream or shout or shut up.'

As Durgana goes around the class, the pupils talk of the success – or failure – of Durgana's experiment. She listens attentively and in conclusion she says, 'Thanks, folks, for letting me do this. You've been the guinea pigs . . . and I've learned so much!'

Cutting the ties of unsuccessful relationships is something that Durgana has had to learn the hard way. Born in Queenstown in the Eastern Cape in 1927, her father was a schoolteacher and vice-principal of a boarding school. Her mother was passive, submitting meekly to the authoritarian rule of her husband.

'I was terrified of my father. He was dominant and brutal. I only remember him giving me one hiding. It was pretty savage. I had stripes on my back for three weeks. When I was twelve, he raped me. This experience scarred me for life. I thought he was punishing me somehow. I didn't realise that what he was doing was sexual . . . the first time I became aware of this was in 1987.'

'What happened then?' I ask.

'I went to a woman who did the metamorphic technique. This was prior to reflexology. While she was massaging my feet, as I lay in a semi-trancelike state I suddenly had a vision of my father raping me. I didn't know whether to believe it or not . . .'

It was only many years later when Durgana, who had herself evolved spiritually to a much higher level, was in therapy with Jane Blecher/Mirabai Devi, the renowned spiritual teacher, that she was able to come to terms with this traumatic event.

'I read *The Journey* by Brandon Bays. I then used the technique in the book and, working by myself, I went back to the experience of the rape. I realised that my father must have been a deeply unhappy man, forced to suppress his homosexuality, living as he did in a small town where this sort of behaviour was totally unacceptable,' Durgana said softly. 'I knew that I had to resolve this event if I wished to have a healthy relationship with a male partner.'

She reflects for a moment before adding, 'I subsequently realised that I had been a rapist in a past life. In order to redress the suffering that I had inflicted, I understood that I had to go through this trauma in this life.'

Her marriage at nineteen to a medical doctor, nine years her senior, in the 1940s, brought even more hardship to her young life. 'I was very green. It took me a full year of marriage to realise the enormity of my husband's drug problem. When he took drugs, his personality changed. He was careless with money. He didn't work. His mother helped him financially. He used to put drugs in my tea.

'He was so angry with me when I said that perhaps he should see a psychologist about his problem, that he said, "Here's a vitamin for you." To justify his own guilt, he gave me a drug-filled injection. My husband turned me into a drug addict . . .'

Eight progeny were born of this unhappy union, four girls and four boys. Shortage of money was a constant factor in the marriage.

Although her husband continued to practise medicine, his increasingly expensive drug habit took large chunks out of the family's income. To add to her woes, Durgana was obliged to look

after her mother, who was now senile.

To her credit, before her fourth child John, a deeply spiritual soul, was born, Durgana had freed herself of her drug habit.

'When John was born at home, I went into labour early in the morning. I woke my husband up . . . he just went back to sleep. I said to myself: Magda, you're just going to have to do this on your own. The midwife didn't pitch and finally I was able to arouse my sleeping husband who delivered the baby.

'He also gave me an injection that contained a potent cocktail of powerful drugs. In my weakened state, I couldn't refuse. Once again, I was back on drugs and I was very angry with my husband. I was so unhappy. I thought to myself: "What the hell is life all about?" '

Years of unhappiness followed until one day Durgana's brother gave her a small book. Entitled *Fourteen Lessons in Yoga* by Ramacharaka, this book was to mark a new chapter in her life.

With her interest in yoga awakened, when the opportunity presented itself, Durgana gladly accompanied her niece Joy to a Sunday night meeting or Satsang at the home of the late Kavi Yogiraj Mani Finger. Within three months of meeting Mani, Durgana had cured herself of her drug addiction.

At last Durgana's life seemed to have purpose. Within five months of yoga with Mani, he told Durgana: 'You've got the strength. You must teach.'

'I started teaching yoga at Sam Busa's school. Lunch-hour classes and evening classes. This continued until the school closed because of financial difficulties.'

In the meantime, Durgana's husband's drug problems led to him having a stroke. 'Can I leave my husband?' she wondered, feeling trapped. However, she knew that as he was weak and ill, she had no choice but to stay with him.

One day, while they were on a trip to Krugersdorp, her husband started to breathe heavily. Alarmed, Durgana tapped him on the shoulder, but he was already dead. He left her with R14 000 and four children to educate.

'I don't know how, but we managed. We moved to an old house in Florida. I bought some camping equipment and I started going away on excursions with the family. I needed to recharge my batteries – looking after my senile mother was taking its toll on me. Still, we had a lot of fun.'

With a twinkle in her eye, Durgana tells me: 'My life began when my husband died.'

In 1975, Mani decided that, in order to create a sense of unity and discipline within the teaching community, it was time to establish a Yoga Fellowship. Far from the well-run organisation that it is today, the Yoga Fellowship had humble beginnings.

Durgana became the secretary. Realising that they needed something with which to print the newsletter, she managed to find an old roneo machine for R20. This was fixed up for a cost of R140 and the first newsletters of the Fellowship were printed at nominal cost.

Not that the early days of the Fellowship were all plain sailing: 'I resigned a couple of times, but somehow I always came back,' she says with the blunt honesty that is characteristic of her.

In the 1980s Durgana started working at the Aquarian Bookshop which specialises in books dealing with all manner of esoteric disciplines and is well known to people seeking enlightenment. Magda began to realise that, in her words, 'Yoga by itself is not enough. If I wanted to heal a person, I needed additional knowledge.'

Like a sponge, she began to absorb all she could, concentrating particularly on kinesiology and reflexology.

'What exactly is kinesiology?'

'Kinesiology is muscle testing. By exerting pressure, you are able to create the activation of a certain muscle that is linked to a meridian. There are twenty-six meridians. Two main ones, yin and yang, or male and female, and twelve pairs that relate to various organs such as the liver and the spleen.

'Through kinesiology one is able to establish whether the muscle is blocked or unblocked. If the muscle is blocked, then the meridian is not functioning properly. If, however, the meridian is clear it will indicate that that particular meridian is balanced.'

The people who discovered kinesiology call it the bio-computer of the body. Durgana prefers to link it to the Higher Self or Soul. 'I believe that with kinesiology one is able to establish everything that ever happened to the person, be it in this or in previous lives.'

Through her yoga, her studies and her meditation, Durgana was able to uncover her astonishing powers of healing. A testimonial from one of Durgana's clients, Adriane Ludwig, reads as follows:

In 1981 I got breast cancer and had to have a double mastectomy. The drug I was given to stop a recurrence of this cancer could cause other types of cancer. The doctor who was treating me did not tell me this. I only discovered it by chance through watching a television programme.

In 1983, I had to have a full hysterectomy. As I could not have hormone treatment, I started going into early menopause. I was a total wreck and fell into a state of deep depression.

132

It was at this stage that I met Durgana. I knew her then as Magda Inglethorpe.

I started going to her once a week for reflexology. Soon I was feeling much better. I decided to throw away my drugs. This made my doctor very angry. He said to me 'Let this be on your own head. You must not come crying to me if your cancer recurs.'

After a very short time, my hot flushes went away, the hair that was growing on my face fell out and, as if by magic, my depression lifted.

A few years later I had a very bad hip and could not walk up stairs. The doctor told me that I had rheumatoid arthritis and put me on a course of cortisone injections, which were very painful. Durgana did one session of kinesiology on me and I never limped again. When I went back to the doctor, he simply said that I had been misdiagnosed.

I still go to Durgana every second week and after twenty years I am hale and hearty. In fact the only medication I take is vitamins.

Is it any wonder that I regard her as a very special lady?

Durgana is nothing if not a survivor. She has had an enormously hard life, although she says that it was only recently that she realised this. She has endured many hardships, including a burst eardrum that resulted in acute hearing problems. 'There was a time when I was so deaf that I couldn't even answer the telephone. When I was driving to the hospital with my burst eardrum, I was dizzy, nauseous and vomiting. I looked up and I saw an angel. "Are you the Angel of Death?" I asked the vision.'

'What was the reply?'

'Silence,' replied Durgana with a grin.

However, with all the classes that she still has to conduct, the workshops that she still has to lead, and the instruction manuals she still has to write, it would seem that Durgana's earthly work is far from complete.

Although she is blunt, outspoken and forthright, throughout the course of her eventful life, Durgana has managed to garner many devoted disciples. I received the following testimonial from yoga teacher Sandra Faulkner of Randpark Ridge:

Everything I know has been taught to me by Durgana. So open is her mind that she has delved into all sorts of disciplines – everything from astrology, to karate to tai chi. Constantly keeping yoga as her base, she then delved into kinesiology. I gladly became her guinea pig, drawing inspiration from her incredible fount of knowledge.

From there, we evolved once more into healer and patient. With amazing insight and clarity, Durgana gently led me on, insisting that I do the healing, while she became the facilitator.

I am constantly amazed and in awe of my beloved teacher, mentor, friend and guru.

May the sun always shine on your face.

Sandra

The wisdom of Durgana's teaching, mixed with her down-to-earth approach to esoteric teachings, can perhaps be summarised by this extract from an article that she wrote for the magazine *Complete Yoga*.

Mani (Kavi Yogiraj Mani Finger) used to say that this universe would fall apart but for a pin, and it is held together by LOVE. Each of us is but a cell in the magnificence of the universe.

I exist, and I have to play a part in this whole galaxy. It is a frightening thought. Why am I fussing about the next meal and a good mattress or a proper toothbrush, if I have a duty to perform in holding this universe together?

How does each one of us do this? This is quite a question. I cannot answer this question, but I would say that being able to love would certainly be better than creating discord and conflict, which is created by fear.

It seems that in spite of the discord in many parts of our planet, the balance is still maintained. Brahma or God or the Divine is certainly a force that we are not able even to conceive of. Even to gaze at a flower and marvel at its individuality of shape and fragrance is enough to shake the foundations of our belief systems.

Love and Fear are two opposites. Not hate. We only hate that which we fear. If we are able to rid ourselves of fear then love would be there always!

Corina Loe – Natural Animal Healer

'I believe in God. I believe that we all have Guardian Angels that assist us in all our actions. I believe that I'm a channel for Unconditional Life Force energy. I believe that I've been chosen to be an animal healer. I believe that by working with the Angels of the Violet Flame – Raphael, the Angel of Healing, Gabriel and Michael – and by channelling the energy of Saint Germain, Master Alchemist and Hierarch of the Aquarian Age, and of Jesus himself, I am able to assist man and beast in healing themselves.'

Corina Loe

Photographed by Francki Burger

Even as a child, the eldest of three girls, Corina Loe felt a natural empathy with animals. Her father was an accountant for a mining company and consequently the family travelled around a good deal. No matter where they settled, Corina surrounded herself with pets – all manner of animals, everything from budgerigars to cockatiels to various types of dogs. However, because of her mother's allergy, cats were barred from the menagerie. It was only after leaving university that Corina was finally able to adopt a feisty feline to share her flat.

'I remember a dog we had in Middelburg. Her name was Tanya. She was a bullmastiff cross. She was pretty difficult, inclined to be very overbearing. Nobody could handle her, except me,' Corina recalled with a grin and a touch of pride.

No matter what the species of animal, Corina appears to be fearless. Apart from spiders, she will willingly handle any creature. Her arachnophobia occurred following an unpleasant incident during her childhood. When she was thirteen a particularly large and hairy (although dead) Rohman spider was unceremoniously thrown down the back of her dress. For years after this so-called prank, Corina could not overcome her fear of arachnids.

But she worked on the problem, and when confronted with a spider inside her home today, Corina is able to lift up the offending creature and place it outside. 'No, I'm no longer scared of spiders, but let's just say I have a healthy respect for them.'

With her obvious affinity for animals, it seemed natural that Corina should become a veterinary nurse. She studied at Onderstepoort in Pretoria, graduating in 1988, after winning the prize for the most academically improved student from first to second year.

Working at veterinary practices in Pretoria and Cape Town, it initially appeared that Corina would carve out an extremely successful niche for herself in a conventional veterinary set-up.

Extremely knowledgeable about subjects such as anatomy, physiology and nutrition, excellent with the animals, calm and comforting with even the most highly strung owners, she appeared to have found her career path.

Innovative and hard working, she started a popular Weight Watchers class for cats and dogs. Under her able guidance, the veterinary practice at which she worked had a Pet Slimmer of the Year finalist for two years in a row. Both these animals lost more than 20 per cent of their total body weight. It was small wonder that in 1999 she was one of the six finalists in the Veterinary Nurse of the Year competition.

It was almost by accident that Corina stumbled upon Reiki in 1998. A friend of hers offered to give her a Reiki massage. As she felt the energy channelled through the masseuse's hands coursing through her body, clearing her chakras and brightening her aura, Corina asked herself the question that was to change her life: 'If Reiki could do so much for humans, why shouldn't it work equally well on animals?'

Corina's husband Roger is a computer programmer by profession. He was responsible for designing the VetSoft computer program, which streamlines all aspects of the day-to-day running of a veterinary practice.

As a supportive wife, Corina helps him with this endeavour. When a new computer site is installed she goes to the practice and trains the staff members on the uses of the VetSoft program. She firmly believes that technology need not wipe out her ever-increasing spiritual knowledge.

In fact, if Corina is honest with herself, she was wrestling with her conscience on two fronts: Not only did watching the veterinarians with whom she worked prescribing medication fill her with dismay – it seemed to her that there were far too many prescriptions for cortisone and antibiotics – but she was also battling to come to terms with orthodox Christianity.

Her Afrikaans-speaking family are devout members of the Dutch Reformed Church, which she was obliged to join when she was living at home. Corina realised that as much as she was questioning the orthodox methods of veterinary science, so was she finding that the religion in which she had been brought up was no longer satisfying her spiritual needs.

Thus it came as a tremendous relief to her when her husband supported her in her quest to learn more about Reiki – the practice that Corina believed would not only help heal herself, but would also heal sick animals' bodies as well as their souls.

When Corina did her first course in Reiki, she immediately recognised that it was almost as if her destiny was calling her. She felt completely at ease with the Reiki energy. She believed that without knowing it, she had instinctively been giving this energy to all the animals that she had loved and calmed and comforted throughout her life.

While still working as a veterinary nurse, Corina went on to do the second course in Reiki, after which she felt her healing energy to be even more concentrated. With the support of her husband, she continued to Reiki III. From this point on, there was to be no turning back for Corina. At the start of the new millennium, she made the brave decision to go it alone – to leave the security of her job as a veterinary nurse and to become a natural animal healer.

This was a wise decision if the growing collection of glowing testimonials from grateful pet owners is anything to go by:

Bella-Donna, our 3-year old Vietnamese Pot Belly Pig, mysteriously became very ill last year. She was lifeless and threw up bile all day long. Finally, she stopped eating altogether.

Transporting Bella to and from the vet is no easy task – not only does it take four brave, strong men to lift her, she is far too large to be weighed on any normal scale within the vet's practice.

We were becoming seriously alarmed. Her problem seemed impossible to diagnose. An ultra-sound scan proved futile. Both my husband and I felt that an exploratory operation would be seriously undesirable – for both the pig and the vet.

As Bella's condition worsened, we became increasingly sure that she would die. Both her body and her spirit seemed to be fading away. In a state of despair and despondency, we contacted Corina.

With her illness, Bella had become increasingly unsociable, so we were amazed when she immediately allowed Corina to approach her. Once the pig had become acquainted with her, Corina began practising Reiki on Bella. This immediately had a very calming effect. After each session Bella would stop throwing up and would even start eating a little nourishment.

We were amazed when, by means of Reiki, Corina was able to locate Bella's problem area. With this information, we were eventually able to communicate with a 'pig specialist' over the phone who diagnosed that our pet had an acute ulcer. He was able to provide us with the necessary information for her to receive the treatment she required.

Bella is now in perfect health. We believe that without Corina's help Bella would not have survived to celebrate the New Year!

Sincerely,
Maureen, Bert and Bella-Donna Grobler

Corina's decision 'to go it alone' was greeted with both dismay and some derision in veterinary circles. Just as the homeopath, the kinesiologist, the iridologist and the acupuncturist are not necessarily

welcomed into the bosom of conventional medicine, so the majority of vets could not support the idea of alternative healing and/or homeopathic medicine being of any real benefit to their patients.

When I asked Corina what vets thought of the new service she was offering she replied, with a laugh and a shake of her head: 'Vets call me a witch. A white witch. They don't give me the support I need. I wish there were more practitioners like Barry Hindmarch. He's studied overseas and today he's a qualified vet, homeopath and acupuncturist. He is enlightened enough to understand that conventional veterinary science and holistic treatments can work in tandem' – a point well illustrated by the following testimonial Corina received from grateful pet owner Tania Bisset:

I offered a home to a very sick stray kitten and I called him Merlin (he needed some magic to make it!) According to the vet he was six weeks old, but he weighed only 300 grams (the weight of a newborn kitten). He had very little fur due to extreme ringworm, he was covered with paint, very badly malnourished and to add to all these problems, he had lungworm.

The vet treated him with antibiotics for the latter condition and Merlin improved marginally. Then his chest got worse and the vet diagnosed severe pneumonia. His lungs were two-thirds full of fluid. The vet hospitalised him, but told us that he did not expect Merlin to make it through the night.

At this time Corina Loe, who was working with the same vet who was treating Merlin, offered to give him some hands-on Reiki treatment. She sat with Merlin giving him Reiki for quite a few hours that day and that evening.

The next evening I phoned the vet expecting to be told the worst. Imagine my joy when I heard that 'It's unbelievable – he has pulled through and he's so much better.' The vet even said that it must be Corina's 'magic hands'. Merlin's condition had improved so much that I knew that such results would have been impossible with medication alone.

We took Merlin home after he had spent one further day in hospital and Corina continued to do Reiki treatments for a few more days at our house. When we took Merlin back to the vet for a follow-up X-ray, his lungs were completely clear. He had no further problems and he appears to be completely healed.

I believe without any doubt at all that it was Corina's healing that pulled Merlin through, not the medication.

After completing Reiki III, Corina felt not only an increase in her healing powers, she also experienced a surge in her spirituality. Her Third Eye was opened and while administering treatment she began to "see" that her Spiritual Guides and the Angels of the Violet Flame were helping and guiding her.

'How did you see these angels?' I asked. 'As winged creatures?'

'No. I see them not in their physical form, but rather as shafts of colour. When Archangel Michael is with me, I see a blue light; Raphael, who has been with me from the beginning, ever since I became a veterinary nurse, is green; Gabriel is white. God works alone. When he is with me I see a magnificent golden light.'

'How do you know who is assisting you?'

'I always ask who is present. Sometimes I know that Jesus himself is with me.'

'How do you know that?'

'Not only does he give me his name, Jesus, but while I am working, I can sense my hands growing bigger. It is awe-inspiring. It makes my hair stand on end!'

Once Corina had completed Reiki III, her thirst for increased knowledge on more of the healing disciplines could not be slaked. She began to study Seichem healing, believing that if Reiki is the earth ray, then Seichem, which is earth, fire, water and air must be more powerful. She began to work with all the elements together: *Reiki – earth; Sakara – fire; Sophi-el – water; angelic light – air.*

Corina explained to me that each of these energies works differently, adding that you come to know which energy you're working with through what you feel in your hands. The energy can feel warm, cold, tingling or pulsating. The healing always takes place on a physical, emotional or spiritual level.

Even before she knew of the healing energy of crystals, it was natural for Corina to fill her house with rocks and gems. An introductory course on crystals with leading international crystal expert Dr Jacqueline Schultze-Zurhausen opened her eyes to the amazing power of these stones and she now incorporates crystal healing into her sessions with animals.

Always eager to learn more, Corina has also completed a course in Animal Reflexology conducted by Shellie Earley, a reflexologist from America.

When a client phones Corina requesting a home visit, in her methodical manner gained from her years in veterinary practice, she will first request various details: 'What kind of animal is in need of treatment? What is the pet's name? Its age? Its ailment?'

Then, prior to the visit, she will glean all the esoteric knowledge that she can. Seichem uses a multitude of symbols that have a certain effect during healing. For example, there are symbols for releasing karmic issues, for clearing chakras, for mental clearing, for balancing male and female energy, for giving increased courage and for untapping viruses.

After careful deliberation, she will see which of these symbols can best help the distressed animal. The same applies to crystals – will the patient respond better to the healing power of jade or jasper, kyanite or quartz; amethyst or moonstone? Reading and meditation, with advice from her spirit guides, will further prepare her for the first visit to the animal's home.

'For the treatments to be of maximum benefit, I prefer them to take place within the home environment. I like to know how the owner interacts with the animal. Where does the animal sleep? Who is the vet? What medication is the pet on? Then I will let the vet know what I am doing, for I believe that it's only ethical to inform him of any alternative treatment that the pet may be receiving.'

'Are all animals afraid?'

'Not at all. Nine out of ten creatures go to sleep during the session. I will sit on my haunches, coming down to their level. Then I will let the animal relax and get used to my presence. I will always ask permission of the pet's Higher Self to allow the treatment. I will call in its spiritual guides. I will cleanse its aura and then I will wrap the animal in an imaginary blanket of gold. It's wonderful to see how peacefully the animal sleeps after a treatment.'

'Do you inform the owners what transpired during the treatment?'

'At first I didn't. Now, I have come to believe that it's important for the owner to know where the trauma happened. Was it in this or in a past lifetime? What is the animal's karma? Are there any psychic ties that need to be cut?'

'What if the animal is too ill to be healed?'

'Like us, animals have a spirit that decides what is going to happen. They will decide when it is their time to die. When death is imminent, I will be with the animal, if this is what the owner desires. I will treat it and comfort it and make its passing into the Other Realm easier.'

Although many vets are still reluctant to accept working with Corina in her present incarnation – a prejudice which Corina is determined to overcome – she has an ever thickening file of testimonials from owners who are delighted with the service she offers:

I have two female British Bulldogs. The younger of the two, Petal, has a very nervous temperament and refused to get out of my car for walks. I tried everything from animal behaviourists to vets with no success.

I contacted Corina and explained the problem. She started Petal on a series of Reiki treatments. They were so successful that I had her treat my other dog, Pie, whose behaviour with regard to Petal and myself is overtly dominant. Both dogs benefited enormously from the treatments. Their energy changed completely and they both slept incredibly soundly. Petal now climbs out of the car at walk times and participates in the walk with a great deal more confidence and calmness. Pie is also much calmer and much less aggressive.

Corina has a deep commitment to alternative healing and a great deal of experience and love of animals.

She is a natural healer and she has an intuitive understanding of the animal's problem areas and needs. She exudes a wonderful energy of healing and love, which communicates itself both to the animals and the people she is treating.

Corina's insight into the problems I have had with my dogs has been invaluable to me. She works with sincerity, compassion and sensitivity and her positive energy has had an enormously healing effect on both my dogs and myself.

Sincerely,
Barbara Friedman

Undoubtedly, however, the greatest praise for Corina's unorthodox healing methods would come from her patients – if only they could communicate with us as well as they make themselves understood to this angel of animal rights.

Bernie Rowen – Complementary Natural Healer

Photographed by Jaco Wolmarans

'I believe that our consciousness is where it is at the time of our death. Our happiness and our hang-ups will follow us to the next dimension. Therefore we have a responsibility as to how we live, for this will determine how we die.'

Bernie Rowen

There's something so warm and friendly about Bernie Rowen, with her alert green eyes twinkling behind her spectacles and her casually styled grey hair, that it's difficult to realise that the smiling woman sitting opposite me in her Durbanville consulting rooms has so many qualifications that she's likely to forget a couple of the disciplines she's qualified to practise.

An astounding number of certificates lining the walls inform me that Bernie specialises in Energy Healing and Counselling; Ayurvedic Primary Health Care; Aura Reading – Kirlionics; Remedial Yoga Therapy; Crystal Healing; Aromatherapy and Reflexology; Reiki; Iridology; Flower Healing and Acupuncture.

Interested in the healing methods of other races and cultures, Bernie began training as a *Thwasa* or apprentice *sangoma*. She was welcomed to the training sessions with open arms – 'We've been waiting for you, *Sisi*.* The ancestors want to talk to you' – and she was given the African name, Nkanyezi (Morning Star).

As impressive as these manifold qualifications are, Bernie has yet more strings to her bow. A prolific author of esoteric articles for New Age magazines, she has just published her first book on the subject of massage and she mentions in passing that her next book will be on the discipline that has become her passion – Ayurvedic Primary Health Care. A lecturer and teacher on many subjects, Bernie also gives lessons in Ayurvedic cooking.

Constantly studying and travelling to places as remote as Kathmandu in Nepal and Tibet in order to further her insatiable quest for esoteric knowledge, Bernie recently received her diploma in education from the University of Cape Town. She dismisses this achievement with a wave or her hand, saying: 'Since I'm always teaching adults, I thought that I might as well know exactly how to teach them.'

Despite this, when I phoned Bernie to request an interview for this book, her reply was: 'Are you sure that you want to interview me? I'm so normal, so ordinary.'

True enlightenment begins only when one is able to quell the powerful monster known as ego.

There was little in Bernie's early childhood to suggest that she would become a lifelong scholar, teacher and healer. Born in Zimbabwe – her mother was the daughter of a Dutch Reformed minister and her Afrikaans speaking father came from a farming community – the family moved to England when Bernie was a mere eighteen months old.

Her only sibling is her sister, entertainer Marloe Scott Wilson who became known as *The Pink Lady* – an entertainer as famous for her shocking-pink dyed hair as for her glorious singing voice.

If Marloe gave their mother her fair share of headaches, Bernie too proved a real handful. As a child she was very different from her peers – a loner, a solitary soul.

During her wild, turbulent teenage years she was almost expelled from school for riding on the back of a motorcycle with a male friend. In the late 1960s the family was back in South Africa and it didn't take Bernie – with her bellbottoms and flowers in her hair, a self-styled pacifist and freedom fighter – much time to get herself christened *The Hippy Queen of Cape Town* by the media.

Her mother was so angry with her that Bernie was threatened with reform school. The final straw came when Bernie, like the Beatles, sought spiritual enlightenment from an Eastern guru.

'What did your mother do?' I asked.

'She disowned me,' replied Bernie with a smile.

'Have you succeeded in healing the rift?'

'Naturally. In fact, she lives a couple of blocks away. Parents invariably accept you back into the fold when you have your first child.'

*The Zulu word for sister.

While her mother was struggling to come to grips with her daughter's unconventional behaviour, Bernie herself was having difficulty in accepting her first knowledge of her burgeoning spirituality. When she was just sixteen she saw an auric field around a tree, although she failed to comprehend its exact meaning at the time.

Bernie recalls an incident during her youth when her mother was suffering from sinusitis. She knew instinctively that she could cure the problem simply by moving her hands across her mother's nasal passages.

Her mother, relieved of her head congestion but troubled by the manner in which Bernie had accomplished it, urged her daughter not to tell anyone.

'I won't,' promised Bernie and promptly decided to attend the well-known Rita Maas School of Drama in Cape Town. Following her graduation from drama school, and reading all the esoteric literature she could lay her hands on, Bernie decided that she'd better get herself a 'real' job.

She became an industrial relations and training manager for a large company. Married for the second time and with three children in tow, Bernie, now in her early thirties, seemed destined to lead a 'normal' life. Her spirit guides, however, had an entirely different path mapped out for her.

Despite her conventional nine to five job, Bernie's interest in New Age matters continued to grow. Having been initiated into the methods of Transcendental Meditation at the age of twenty, she sought further knowledge and became an initiate Satsangi.*

As she became more familiar with the techniques of meditation, Bernie began having visions of beings from another world.

'What exactly were you seeing?' I asked.

'Someone appeared to me in spirit form. I could clearly see the colours of his robes. It was like seeing somebody through a film of thick plastic. I questioned this entity about his appearance and was told that this is the nature of spiritual life.

'We basically live in different dimensions. Our consciousness just happens to be in this one right now. Past life, I think, is experiencing time in a different dimension. Some of us are fortunate enough to be able to connect to the energy in these different dimensions and that is where the energy healing I do comes in.'

'How exactly does energy healing work?'

'I work on people's auric fields. I have an aura reading machine, a GDV (Gas Discharge Visualisation) that is of tremendous benefit in helping my clients see their auras for themselves. They are able to see where their energy is operating under par or where it is overcompensating.'

'How does the machine work?'

'The GDV was developed by Professor Constantine Korotov of the University of St Petersburg.† The machine, when plugged into a computer, reads an aura by picking up the Su jock acupuncture points from fingertips. The method it uses is the very well-known Kirlian Photography process.

'Let us take an example. I took an aura reading of someone who was feeling kind of offish, but who could not really describe the problem. We scanned the aura and saw inactivity in the solar plexus chakra. On a physical level this would indicate a digestive problem . . . so we changed her diet.

'To add to the treatment I taught her to meditate on her solar plexus area and to use the colour pertaining to that area. This activity will continue until there is an improvement in the aura. When I say that I am a complementary healer, I mean that I will use various techniques such as energy healing or Reiki, massage, aromatherapy and various Ayurvedic therapies in order to achieve the best possible result.

'I am so excited by the possibilities of this method of diagnosis. Personally, I believe that it is the ultimate in preventative medicine.'

*A path of strict discipline that involves studying the teachings of The Masters, total vegetarianism and a great deal of meditation.

†Bernie is a member of the international research team under the leadership of Professor C Korotov of St Petersburg Technical University in Russia.

'I understand that you also teach energy healing.'

'Yes. The course is given over a period of four to six weekends. It works very simply. I believe that everybody has the capacity to be focused. For example, if you walk into a room and the atmosphere is unpleasant, you will pick up this negative energy. I start from that premise and I build from there.'

If I needed any proof of the efficacy of Bernie's alternative approach to healing the physically and emotionally unwell, I got it in glowing testimonials from her clients.

I first met Bernie six years ago. I was on the verge of a nervous breakdown and I was sent her for aromatherapy – healing by means of essential oils that pass easily through the epithelial tissue of the skin and then into the bloodstream to help rectify problem areas.

Right from the start Bernie introduced me into this wonderful world of light and love and happiness. Through the abundance of her own self-love and healing she taught me to live again. When she first did Reiki healing on me I was very afraid of the energy that I was experiencing. I am something of a sceptic and all this voodoo stuff was not exactly my scene.

Little did I know. Bernie taught me through meditation, Reiki and by helping me to experience the greatest love of all, Love of Self, to be non-judgemental and to live every moment to the fullest.

Light years away from the depression which almost caused my breakdown, I know that I am giving back to this world much love and happiness. Joyous sentiments that in return come back to me in abundance.

Pat

The Vedas are ancient Hindu scriptures which include the Rig-Veda, Atharva-Veda, Sama-Veda and Yajur-Veda. The Atharva-Veda is the particular work that encompasses the writing of

Ayurveda. The texts are about our mind/body connection and about how to live. Ayus means life and Veda means science. Thus Ayurveda is the science of life.

It is rare to find balance in the stressful lifestyles most of us lead today. The primary purpose of Ayurveda is to help alleviate stress by creating a perfect balance between our lifestyle and our true personality. Ayurveda includes many healing modalities such as lifestyle counselling and diet according to specific body type, aromatherapy, massage and yoga therapy.

A phone call from a total stranger was to prove a turning point in Bernie's life and a most unexpected introduction to Ayurveda.

'I was asked if I was prepared to meet with a Tibetan lama, Akong Rinmpoché, to work on his feet. I agreed and while he was in Cape Town, I worked on his feet every day. During one of our sessions he turned to me and said: "You will come to Tibet."

'At this stage, travelling to Tibet was a vague idea, rather than a lifelong dream. Still, I agreed to go. Next thing I knew, three months later, I found myself with a group of South Africans at the twelfth birthday party of the Karmapas, a high lama – the boy was probably next in line to the Dalai Lama.

'While I was there I met a very old Tibetan doctor who couldn't speak any English. Nevertheless, we were somehow able to communicate. Walking along the high mountains hand in hand, he pointed out some medicinal herbs to me. I realised that I wanted to know more about these herbs – there were great holes in my knowledge.

'When I came down from the mountains, I met a Nepalese person and asked him if he knew where I could study Ayurveda. At this time he wasn't sure, but three months later I received a fax inviting me to study at the Ayurveda Research Institute in Nepal. The invitation came at a difficult time . . .'

'Why was that?' I asked.

'The year was 1990 and my daughter was in matric. Nevertheless, she insisted that I go. In her typically unselfish manner, she assured me that she would be OK. After all, I wasn't the one who had to write the exams.

'So, once again I set off with my backpack. I learned Ayurveda the traditional way. I sat at the feet of the Vaidya – a learned doctor in Ayuvedic medicine. He would lecture me for half the day, after which I would work at the clinic, making medicines. I loved it. I made such fabulous friends. I loved walking up the dusty roads, living in a funny hovel . . . I was even adopted by a Nepalese family . . .'

'Was Nepal the only place you studied Ayurveda?'

'No. Later I went to England and studied pulse diagnosis with a famous exponent of Ayurvedic medicine.'

Putting this specialised knowledge of hers into practice has resulted in many of Bernie's patients experiencing new levels of healing, as borne out by this glowing testimony from one of her clients:

The motor accident on 26 April 1971 caused a triple fracture through vertebrae 5,6 and 7 and left me with chronic pain, even after three cervical fusions and other surgery.

I first met Bernie Rowen in March 1994 and she has treated me ever since. Her rooms are an oasis of peace and tranquillity, with gentle, healing spiritual music which envelops and revives one – so different from cold conventional doctors' rooms.

Working with Ayurvedic techniques and other treatments such as aromatherapy and acupuncture, she has brought me immense relief. She knows just where the painful knots are in my neck, shoulders and back, which are massaged into relief, but the treatment is both external and internal. I feel better without and within, for she has kindled an awareness of the wholeness of my being and its welfare, not just of my needful body which has dominated my life for so many years.

Bernie possesses a quality of spirit that inspires, lifts and fortifies one above and beyond oneself, above the debilitating fatigue, numbing pain and ebbing of energy and interest in life. Sometimes we speak. Then there are also the long silences and the meditation, the total relaxation within with which to recoup body, mind and spirit and so to regain that precious wholeness.

She has built me up and reaffirmed my self-worth as a human being who still has something to offer in spite of constant and intrusive pain.

Marie Braam

Today, as a registered member of the Allied Health Professions Council, Bernie Rowen is well satisfied with her lot in life. Despite periods of financial hardship – 'We were once so poor that I had to grow vegetables in my garden and water them with recyled bath water' – and two failed marriages (her current marriage is extremely happy), Bernie believes that she is greatly blessed.

'I look in my diary each day and I am delighted by what I find there. I relate to my patients; I love the work that I do. You know, my life is truly divine!'

Irma Bellingan – Clairvoyant, Clairaudient, Astrologer

Seeing and hearing is believing

Photographed by Francki Burger

'I believe that there is a God and it was this Divine
Being who created us. There are no accidents.
God knows exactly what He is doing. That's why
you can mix water and water forever and never
make whisky and why Rolex watches do not grow
on trees.'

Irma Bellingan

The five-year-old child with the large brown eyes and mass of brown curls knelt by the side of her bed and said her prayers. She spoke in Afrikaans, her home tongue. Her mother, Magdalena Rautenbach, could hardly believe the words that came from her small daughter's mouth:

'Please, dear God,' prayed the child, 'send me a husband who drinks a lot and who has money and who will give me children. By the way, God, he mustn't be a drunk.'

The adult Irma remembered those words when she met her husband, Bobby Bellingan. He was the bank manager and she worked in the bank. Attractive, as well as having a good head for figures, Irma was not likely to pass unnoticed: 'I was very clever at school. Not interested, but very clever, nevertheless.'

Irma married her boss when she was just twenty and their bliss seemed assured. They had two children – a boy named Xander and a girl, Athena. Like their mother, both children are psychic. 'They see what I see,' Irma confirmed.

With no shortage of money, two wonderful children and very much in love, the marriage of Bobby and Irma seemed to be a blessed union. 'Except,' recalled Irma, 'there was one problem.'

'What was that?'

'My husband stopped me doing psychic readings although fortune telling is in my blood. My mother's sisters were psychic and they used to read teacups. But my mother wouldn't let me use my gift – she didn't think it was right for the daughter of Marta Magdalena Beukes to do predictions.

'Now in my marriage, as in my childhood, I had also to suppress my psychic ability. You know what? It made me ill. I was always sick. One operation after the other . . .'

'How is your health now?'

'Since Bobby passed over, I have been doing readings all the time. Not just in Port Elizabeth – I live in St Francis Bay – but at all the esoteric fairs, Cape Town, Johannesburg, Pretoria. I'm very well these days. Just look at me.'

Irma certainly looked in fine fettle – her long brown hair was shining; her long red nails were polished to perfection and she was wearing masses of gleaming gold jewellery. To accompany the rings on her fingers, her necklaces were an eclectic mix that included a large cross, a Star of David and a pentacle. 'All roads lead to heaven,' she smiled when I questioned her on her religious affiliation.

Following Bobby's death, her long-suppressed psychic skills came to the fore. 'These days, not only do I "see" things, I also hear things. I never realised this until I began reading the Tarot for people, I knew things that didn't appear on the cards . . .'

'Such as?'

'Whether the person I was reading for was gay or lesbian. It occurred to me that this knowledge came not from the cards, but from the voices of my spirit guides. I've been hearing voices for about four years now.'

While Irma, or Madame I as she sometimes calls herself – ' "I" stands for the eyes to see it all' – might rejoice in her freedom to indulge her psychic abilities, her voice still breaks when she recalls the circumstances that led to the untimely death of her husband. 'I knew that he was going to die,' she said. 'I had four premonitions of his death.'

After Bobby resigned from the bank, as if in answer to Irma's childish prayer, he bought a bottle store near the Morula Sun Casino in Gauteng. Not just an ordinary bottle store, but an entire small liquor empire, complete with three bars including a ladies' bar, and an off sales section and a discotheque.

At this stage in their marriage Irma didn't really have to work, so she kept herself busy being a housewife and a mother, although she bought stocks for the bottle store once a week.

She also ran her own profitable porcelain factory that produced all manner of mystical creatures – fairies and gnomes and elves and woodland spirits – all created from her clear vision of seeing these little folk as they frolicked in her garden.

'Two months before Bobby died, I had my first premonition of his death,' said Irma. 'I remember that the kids had gone to the café. I was very tired and was lying on the couch. Suddenly I saw his face. It seemed to be drawn in a tree. He was smiling. I went cold and started crying. I said, "I know, God, but please not now." '

'What other warnings did you have of Bobby's imminent death?'

'On the Monday evening – he died on the following Friday night – I was listening to a serial on the radio. Suddenly, instead of the actors' voices, I clearly heard the message coming out of the radio: "He's going to die." I said, "God, you can't do this to me now." '

'What happened next?'

'Bobby used to go to the bottle store but if he wasn't busy there, he would come back home. I think it must have been on the Tuesday that I heard his footsteps in the hall. When he came in I ran to him and, as he held me in his arms, I told him that I wasn't depressed, yet I wanted to cry and I was scared.

'He comforted me as best he could. You know, I think he might have sensed something bad was going to happen because his star sign was Pisces and this made him deeply spiritual.'

'Were your children aware of your forebodings?'

'On the Wednesday while I was packing some things away Athena came to me and said "What's that smell?" I replied that it was "Death". She asked who was going to die. I shook my head and said that I didn't know.

'On the Thursday night, Bobby should have gone back to work to close the discotheque. However, friends suddenly arrived at the house to visit him. So one of the managers locked up. Later that night I went to bed. I was woken by a loud noise like a bang on the stairs. I started crying: "God, I know. But it's not the time." '

'Did your husband sense your uneasiness?'

'Yes. He asked me what was wrong and I told him that somebody was going to die. He asked me who I thought it was. I knew, but I didn't want to believe it. I told him that it was a man with dark hair who was very close to me.

'On the Friday we went to Johannesburg on business. On the way we saw a hearse in front of us. Putting his hand on my knee, Bobby said, "Baby, you know that when my father died my youngest brother was the same age as Xander is today."

'I felt a shiver go through my spine. That night when he went to lock up the bar, they shot him. It was around ten o'clock. The phone at the house rang at about eleven o'clock. When we answered it, a voice said simply: "Hulle het hom geskiet."* That was on the 21st of July 1995 . . .'

'Do you still miss him?'

'Yes. Bobby was my soul mate. An astrologer I went to told me that it was not his time. He should not have died. Thus Xander's first child will be the reincarnation of my late husband.'

'It's more than six years since your husband died. Have you met anyone else?'

'Yes. My new partner is Colin Kemp. Thank God he came across my path. He is attractive, very intelligent and very understanding because he allows me to travel a lot – my work often takes me to different places. You know, Saturn's in my Tenth House. I am a sun rising Aquarian. My moon's in Leo with Pluto.'

'What does that mean?'

'It means that I will lose all my husbands. Bobby passed over for me to go on with my psychic readings. It is the debt that I must pay for having this God-given ability.'

Irma looked at me sadly, tears welling in her eyes. 'It is a high price. A very high price indeed!'

*Afrikaans: 'They shot him.'

I first met Irma at one of the monthly esoteric fairs held at the Parkhurst Recreation Centre in Johannesburg. Over the weekend of the event it was impossible to get a reading with her. With her flamboyant appearance and ready smile, people seemed to gravitate to her table. Thus I was not surprised when I received a testimonial that corroborated this impression.

Last year, round about June, I was on holiday in the Eastern Cape. I had always heard about the wonders of the Grahamstown Festival, so this time I decided to go and take a look for myself.

There were loads of different stalls, but one with a blue and white striped tent, with a curtain at the entrance bedecked with moons and stars, stood out from all the others. I walked over to the table where there were leaflets promoting Madam I, Psychic Tarot Reader. I thought no, this is scary, but then Irma appeared from behind the curtain. I don't know exactly what it was, but there was a kind of energy flowing from her that immediately made me feel relaxed and comfortable. I decided that I would have a reading after all.

She radiates positive energy and when she laughs, you laugh. All the things on her table looked so amazing – her crystals, her gleaming crystal ball, her lit candles and her burning incense with the exotic aroma. I began to feel really excited when she told me to shuffle the cards. She looked at me intently as she asked me whether I wanted to hear everything or whether there were some things that she shouldn't tell me. I was trembling as I told her 'Tell me everything.'

Then she started with the reading. Well, let me tell you, this woman is brilliant! She even picked up on a personal problem that was bothering me at that stage – something that I hadn't even discussed with my best friend.

She mentioned the names of people that I know presently and the names of people that I knew years ago. That should tell you how good she really is! She also told me that she saw a lot of travel ahead

for me. I told her that she must be joking, but do you know what? After the reading I was away for almost the rest of the year.

The best thing is Irma gave me the dates when things would happen and ninety per cent of the time she was accurate. It's ten months since I had my reading and things are still happening to me as she said that they would.

I was so impressed with her reading, that I also asked her to do my astrological chart. She then asked me for my name, my date of birth, the place and the time. When my chart arrived, I was astonished by what Irma had managed to work out from these few details. She told me the position of my sun and moon and she pinpointed various aspects of my character correctly. She told me where my destiny lay. What I found remarkable is that when I read through my astrology chart, Irma had picked up on a lot of things that she'd told me in her readings.

I will certainly contact her next year for a new astrology chart as well as for a psychic reading.

Karen

Irma's interest in astrology began about six years before I interviewed her when she started studying with French-born Julie Sweet, a fellow psychic and astrologer, in Port Elizabeth.

'There was a lot of studying, really a lot, although I didn't find it difficult, probably because of my psychic abilities,' said Irma.

Today, thanks to the miracle of the Internet, Irma is able to do astrological readings for people around the world. Working with the person's name – just the first name will do – their date of birth, the place of birth – 'This is very important as it explains the position of the sun and planets' – and the time of birth Irma is able to do a detailed astrological chart.

'What if the person does not know the time of their birth?'

'Then I will ask them to pinpoint various milestones in life, such as when they got married, when they had a miscarriage, things like that. This information helps me work out, more or less accurately, their time of entering this world.'

Once these facts have been established, with the aid of a specially formulated computer program, Irma will print out an astrological chart, which she is then able to fill in with the information provided.

Her astrological charts can take one of two forms. It can be a birth chart that highlights the type of person you are and the things you need to watch out for, or it can be a predictive chart that highlights the things that will happen to you, month by month, during the course of the year.

Irma explains that your birth chart is a very individual *mandala** that holds instructions and indications on how best to realise your potential by identifying trends throughout your life, which accordingly bring with them happiness or sadness.

Not only does Irma do astrological charts for people who do not necessarily have to be present, she also does psychic readings via the telephone.

'How does this work?' I want to know.

'First the client will phone me for an appointment. After they've paid my fee into my bank account, they'll phone me at the appointed time. I will then shuffle the Tarot cards and I'll start channelling. I begin to see things almost immediately. I will tell the person things like the colour of their hair and I will pick up on small details like the veins in their legs. Just so that they know that I've really got their image before me.

'Oh, by the way, I'm a bit colour blind. I can't tell the difference between navy and black. So I might say: Those slacks you're wearing. Are they black or are they navy? Then we'll both have a good laugh. Telephone readings last anywhere from half an hour to an hour.'

'Whew! Even though your fee is reasonable, that can work out to be pretty expensive.'

'Yes. But many of my clients are professional people – lawyers, doctors – so their main concern is not financial, it's more about finding answers to their questions.'

Today, Irma is in a happy space. Her two children are grown up. Xander is a successful businessman in Pretoria and her daughter Athena works for the police. Irma sees that in a couple of years' time Athena will have an important position within the forensic department, using her psychic powers to help with investigations involving murders and missing people.

Meanwhile Irma herself, occupied with psychic readings and astrological charts, finds that she often works almost around the clock. Not that she is complaining. 'I love the work that I do. And I must continue to work hard. There's so little time. So little time upon this earth.'

*Mandala: Hindu or Buddhist art of various designs, usually circular, symbolising the universe.

Rod Suskin – Astrologer and Sangoma

Interpreting the heavens on earth

Photographed by Jaco Wolmarans

'As I understand it, the entire universe is one conscious spirit expressing itself in manifold ways. Each one of us is a vital part of this universal consciousness. I also believe that this consciousness manifests itself in many levels for human beings. I know for certain that we all have our spirit guides and that we come back to this earth again and again.'

Rod Suskin

The great esoteric teacher Alice A Bailey, who lived on the borders of Tibet and who, at times, presided over a large group of Tibetan lamas, described Astrology in the following way:

Astrology is essentially the purest presentation of occult truth in the world at this time because it is the science which deals with those conditioning and governing energies and forces which play through and upon the whole field of space and all that is found within that field.*

Of the many astrologers practising in South Africa, undoubtedly one of the best known and most respected is Rod Suskin, founder of the astrological magazine Sidereal Times, the official newsletter of the Cape Astrological Association.

Rod was born in Johannesburg on the first of January 1963. The youngest of three boys of a liberal middle-class Jewish family, Rod grew up in the small suburb of Kentview and after attending Fairways Primary School, he went on to Highlands High School, ultimately matriculating at Eden College.

His spirituality manifested itself at a very early age. 'I can clearly remember that as a small boy I had a dream of an old man taking me to a river and playing cards with me. When I was older and I recalled this dream it occurred to me that this old man was a rabbi and that as he sat next to me, he taught me to read the Tarot cards. When I discussed this with my Israeli-born mother Mina, she said that there was indeed a rabbi way back in our family tree.'

With his interest in Tarot, it was no surprise that when nine-year-old Rod walked past a shop displaying a pack of Tarot cards, he immediately demanded that his mother buy them for him.

'However, in my family you didn't get what you asked for,' recalled Rod with a laugh. 'Although, if you had enough money saved up, they couldn't stop you buying anything you wanted. So

we had a nice balance. I remember that I had R14.95 in my moneybox. There was no VAT in those days. This was exactly enough money to buy the pack . . . you can see how long ago that was!

'Only I had a terrible dilemma. My late grandmother always told me that you must never take the last five cents out of your moneybox. You must leave it there so your money can grow. After much deliberation, I finally took my entire savings and bought the cards.

'Now that I had the cards, I needed to know what to do with them. Consequently, I wanted to buy a book called *The Tarot* by Alfred Douglas. Unfortunately, that cost another R6.95. So, heaven knows how long it took me to get that . . . my pocket money was about five cents a week.'

'Do you use the Tarot now?'

'Not for my astrology reading. However, I do use the cards for my work as a *sangoma*. Those who instructed me told me that this is what I must do.'

While he grappled with understanding the Tarot, other strange things were happening to the young Rod Suskin. Sometimes, he had the odd sensation that he was leaving his body.

'Am I dying?' he asked his older brother, Joey. With a smile, Joey handed his anxious brother a book entitled *The Projection of the Astral Body* by Carrington and Muldoon and told him to read it in order to allay his fears.

In other ways, too, the young Rod was flying high. At the age of about eleven, the ingenious boy put a sign above his desk *Hypnosis Shows Daily.* As fortune would have it, the child who sat next to him in the classroom was able to juggle. So, while Rod was perfecting his skills as a hypnotist, his classmate would be furiously juggling his collection of erasers.

Rod had learned his hypnosis the easy way. He sent away for

*Esoteric Astrology: The Seven Rays, by Alice A Bailey.

a plastic disc that he saw advertised in a comic that guaranteed to teach you everything you needed to know on the subject.

After diligently reading the instructions, he used to go around to his friends' homes after school in order to practise his new-found skill.

'I was fabulous at it,' he remembers with a laugh, 'although I don't think their parents were exactly thrilled when they popped their heads around the bedroom door to see what we boys were up to.'

By 1972 Rod had established his own printing company, The Rod Suskin Printing Company, and he was freely distributing his literary outpourings to his classmates. 'I worked out that I wanted to be a writer. This was my ambition and it's never changed.'

As an eleven-year-old boy, Rod had an extraordinary experience that convinced him of the reality of reincarnation. 'I know that we come back, not once, but again and again.'

'What happened to make you so sure of this?' I asked.

'In those days, there was no television in this country. So my friends and I used to go to the cinema in order to watch the movie of the FA Cup. We were all ardent Leeds supporters. I remember that on that particular occasion Leeds were playing Liverpool.

'As I watched, I had this eerie experience that my home team was Liverpool and that my parents lived in Liverpool. I sat watching the match wondering how my parents were going to fetch me after the movie if I was in Johannesburg and they were in Liverpool. Only later did I learn that zillions of children have had the same experience.'

To emphasise his point, Rod then quoted the following extract from the Zohar, the book of Jewish mysticism based on the teachings of the Torah, the book of divine knowledge and law found in the Old Testament:

*The Zohar, Volume 11, p.99ff.

All souls are subjected to the trials of transmigration; and men do not know the designs of the Most High with regard to them; they know not how they are being at all times judged, both before coming into this world and when they leave it. They do not know how many transformations and mysterious trials they must undergo; how many souls and spirits come into this world without returning to the palace of the divine king.

The souls must re-enter the absolute substance whence they have emerged. But to accomplish this end they must develop all the perfections, the germ of which is planted in them; and if they have not fulfilled this condition during one life, they must commence another, a third, and so forth, until they have acquired the condition which fits them for reunion with God.*

With his obvious knowledge of Judaism, I asked Rod where religion fitted into his life. 'As a child, on Yom Kippur, the Day of Atonement, I used to fast, although the religion does not require that children abstain from food and drink. However, when I turned thirteen, I stopped fasting. I suddenly found that Judaism was too confining in its doctrine.'

Rod's lifelong interest in astrology began when he was eleven or twelve. He went on holiday to the Eastern Transvaal with his uncle and aunt and a cousin. They happened to meet an old friend who was working out astrological charts. Fascinated, Rod asked the man one question after another until finally the man said: 'Son, you'd better buy yourself Derek and Julia Parker's book *Complete Astrology*.'

Back in Johannesburg and equipped with the book, Rod began drawing charts and interpreting them. When he was about fifteen, his brother Joey decided to impress his girlfriend with a chart drawn by Rod. 'He really liked this girl and he hoped that the chart would say that they would marry each other and live happily

ever after. I drew up the chart and typed out my findings: *She will marry someone else and be very unhappy.* I forgot all about this chart until we found it in the boot of Joey's car about five years later. It was entirely accurate. From that time, I have always believed in astrology as a predictive tool.'

It was around this time that Rod started growing all manner of medicinal herbs – sage, rosemary, camomile, amongst others – on his balcony. 'I had the belief that I could "fix" people with these things.'

At nineteen Rod went to the University of the Witwatersrand to study psychology. In his second year of study there was a module on African Psychology. The professor organised a group of *sangomas* to be in the Social Sciences building for two weeks in order for his students to get some understanding of traditional African culture, its teachings and its medicines.

When Rod arrived for his appointment with a group of five Swazi *sangomas*, they grew silent after one of the younger *sangomas* had thrown the bones for Rod. They all studied Rod intently. Finally, the head of the group spoke: 'Put on these beads, my son. You know, your ancestors have been teaching you their wisdom since you were a small boy. For you, my son, are a *sangoma* like us.'

When Rod was twenty-two he had a dream that he must move to Cape Town. In the dream he was even told where he should live – in a flat at the top of Buitenkant Street.

As soon as he arrived in Cape Town Rod's spirituality blossomed. He continued studying the ways of the *sangoma*, this time from the perspective of the Xhosa people. He also studied Jewish mysticism, or the Kaballah, and magic.

To keep body and soul together, he worked as an assistant in a video store – which is not all that surprising when one learns that one of his sub-majors in his BA degree was Film. When the store wasn't busy, Rod did astrological charts for customers.

After a six-month sojourn in Amsterdam in order to avoid conscription to the army, Rod returned to the video store. One day, as he sat at the back of the shop doing his own chart – 'a very unusual occurrence as I very rarely do a chart for myself – I noticed that there was a configuration in my chart which augured well for favourable publicity in six months' time. I immediately handed the video store owner my notice, saying that I would be leaving in half a year's time.'

'What are you going to do?' asked his boss.

'I am going to become a full-time astrologer,' declared Rod.

Rod was due to start his astrological practice on the first Monday of a certain month in 1989, much to the chagrin of his parents who failed to comprehend how their unconventional son could earn a living from doing charts. 'When are you going to get a real job?' asked his anxious mother.

On the Wednesday before this, a photographer from the Argus newspaper had asked if he could come to Rod's house and take a picture of the budding astrologer working at his computer – in those days home computers were a rarity.

Rod agreed and the weekend before he was due to start work, there was a double-page spread of the young astrological boffin at work on his home computer.

A year before this, a customer at the video shop had written an article and sold it to The Cape Times about the young man who did astrological charts at the back of the video shop. The newspaper only decided to run with this article when they saw the Argus feature about Rod.

With this deluge of favourable publicity, Rod opened for business on the Monday and spent the entire day taking phone bookings. By the end of that first day there was a two-month waiting list for his chart readings.

Since this period of waiting for an appointment to see him has never shortened, it must be deduced that the chart configuration Rod had mapped out for himself was undoubtedly correct.

'Astrology is all about timing and that proved it to me,' he concluded.

Rod believes that he is able to divide the people who come to see him for an astrological reading into two categories – the first are people who have no major difficulties in their lives at the time but are merely curious to know more about themselves, and the second category are people who have a specific problem, be it health, work-related or a relationship issue, that needs to be dealt with.

'How can you as an astrologer help with a relationship issue?'

'By reading the chart that I have prepared for them according to the information they have given me – their name, the place, date and time of their birth – I am able to pinpoint what's gone wrong with the relationship, what they can do to deal with it and what outcome they can expect.'

'How accurate are you?'

'I believe that an astrology reading is about eighty per cent accurate, although my clients appear to perceive this percentage as far higher. Being man-made, astrology does have certain limitations. For example, certain situations simply do not show up on one's chart. Then the choices and actions people make tend to change. Also, the time of birth is often not accurately recorded and an incorrect time obviously influences a reading adversely.

'I personally feel that astrology's greatest strength is as a diagnostic tool. Here, I find it outstandingly accurate. Although obviously if a major illness shows up on the chart, I must break this news with tact and gentleness.'

The discussion of medical diagnosis brings into focus an aspect of Rod's life which, although hidden for many years from his white clients, is now an integral and very important part of his work – his practising as a fully-fledged *sangoma*.

With his interest in using herbs as a way to cure ill health dating back to the time he was a schoolboy, it was a natural progression for the adult Rod to qualify as a Western herbalist, especially as astrology and medicine have a centuries-old relationship.

'Astrologers had an unwritten agreement with the Church that they wouldn't trespass on the territory of the soul – they would deal only with the body and that is why astrology is the only metaphysical discipline that was never eradicated by the Church,' explained Rod.

His interest in black traditional medicine, while dating back to his university days and studied intermittently with the Xhosa people of the Cape and the rural Transkei, strengthened after he met Chris Reid, a fellow white *sangoma* known to his followers as Ntombe Mhlophe.

Chris, who had studied with the Pondo tribe, the oldest and most traditional of the Xhosa-speaking people, was the catalyst that Rod needed to allow his work as a *sangoma* to become as important as his more highly publicised profession as an astrologer.

'African traditional medicines and herbs are excellent for treating illnesses that Western medical practitioners find difficulty in dealing with.'

'Such as?'

'Cancer, HIV and chronic fatigue syndrome. Also skin problems such as eczema. For example, a young white woman came to see me who had been suffering from eczema for most of her life. She had tried many methods of treating this ailment, all based around conventional Western methods.

'I used her chart to diagnose the physical condition as well as to indicate the emotional and spiritual problems associated with it. I then made up a herbal remedy for her based on my knowledge of African herbs and, working with her chart, I outlined certain areas of her present life and her past that were exacerbating her physical condition, such as unresolved issues with her mother. Over a period of two to three months, after using the herbal preparation and working on her familial problems with a therapist, her eczema cleared up and has never returned.'

'Would you elaborate on your use of traditional black herbal remedies for HIV Aids?'

'A black man came to see me. He was suffering from Aids. Under circumstances like this, I see people almost immediately. He came to see me as a *sangoma*, not as an astrologer. Astrology is not part of the black culture. Things like the date and time of birth are not necessarily important details in their lives. I gave him a specially prepared herbal tea. This mixture is excellent for people suffering from debilitating diseases – it gets them out of bed and into the office. So far, he's holding out remarkably well.'

Today Rod Suskin may be regarded as highly successful in his chosen field. Well known as an astrologer, particularly in the light of his regular fortnightly broadcast on Cape Talk Radio, and with a growing following for his work as a *sangoma*, he regards himself as being in a good space.

'My parents quickly saw that I wasn't going to be like other boys, that I was going to follow my own path. My father, a pharmacist, probably wished that I had done a conventional medical degree. Initially, my mother had some difficulty with my initiation as a *sangoma*; until I taught her about the black traditions and what being a *sangoma* means, she thought that I was becoming a witch. Now that they see how much I have achieved – albeit in an unorthodox manner – I guess you could say that both my parents are *klibing nachas*.'*

*Yiddish: Receiving great joy.

Mirabai Devi Jane Blecher – Spiritual Teacher, Healer & Intuitive

Sister of Light; Daughter of God

Photographed by Francki Burger

'I believe that I have been chosen by God to help guide people on their spiritual path, so that they can discover their own hidden perfect state of being and thus their own direct experience of the Light; the Divine Spark that is in each one of us. I guess God chose me to do this work because I am such a normal, everyday person that people can relate to me.'

Mirabai/Jane

There is a story in the Vedic scriptures that is told as follows:

God was looking for a place to hide Himself/Herself. And God said: 'Maybe I should hide myself on top of the highest mountain.' But God's advisers said, 'No, no, the human beings will find you there.'

And God said, 'I know. I will hide myself at the depth of the deepest ocean.' But the advisers said, 'No, no, the human beings will also find you there. For they will bring big boats and dive to the bottom of the sea.'

Finally, God said, 'I know. I will hide myself in the place that they will never look. And that is in each one of their hearts.'

'It is because of this,' said Mirabai/Jane as she addressed the hundreds of people who had come to the Ishta Yoga School to listen to this South African-born, international spiritual teacher, 'that human beings can never find fulfilment until they attain that union with the Supreme Being.

'So this is where each one of us has to go. We have to go within for we cannot find happiness without. The great sages and Masters say that the purpose of life is to be happy. Happiness is the nature of the soul, it is pure bliss – *ananda*. But what happens is that a lot of veils are placed over the soul.

'When this happens, we blindly seek God without, longing to fill the void that only the Supreme Being can fill. We say, "If only I could get a better relationship, a bigger house, a faster car, more money, then I would be fulfilled. Maybe I will try and reach that state of bliss through sex, through drugs, through food, even through alcohol."

'All these material things are a way to seek God. Unfortunately, however, they have a destructive effect on our physiology, our minds and our consciousness. They will never take us to the goal. The Kingdom of Heaven lies within you. It can only be attained by bringing your awareness within to experience the soul; or a power even greater than the soul, the *paramatman*, the Supreme Soul. True bliss can only come from oneness with God.' So concluded Mirabai/Jane who knew, even as a young child, that as an adult she would be teaching spirituality to human beings.

'My life's purpose is to bring people back to God,' she says simply.

Jane Blecher was born thirty-two years ago to a Jewish father, John, a gynaecologist, and a Catholic mother, Leonae, a former lecturer in English and now a macrobiotic counsellor and cooking instructor.

As she lay in her crib in her home in Emmarentia in Johannesburg, the baby Jane was overwhelmed by a great anger.

'In my lifetime previous to this one I had almost received permanent enlightenment. When you reach enlightenment, you merge with God. You stay with Him/Her for ever, thereby ending the cycle of birth and rebirth.

'I remember coming from a planet of light, where the people were all made of light – they shone with an inner light. They looked into each other's eyes and didn't use words to communicate – they communicated with pure love; nobody got ill or old or deformed, yet they lived for hundreds of years. I called these forms "Light Beings". This was the heavenly realm and I longed to go back there . . . yet, here I was on earth, trapped in a baby's body.'

Even as a very young child Jane had access to knowledge from her previous lives. She remembered Sanskrit; she knew the teachings of the Bhagavad Gita, the priceless teachings found in the great Hindu poem of the Mahabharata. She knew that she had come to this earth to do God's bidding; she knew that she was ancient and she knew that she could fly.

'I used to travel in my astral body. I flew every night in dreams. I used to fly above the house; I visited people in their homes. I worked with people on different realms and dimensions. I met with other spiritual beings and Masters. I didn't even have a sleep state. I thought that that was what everybody did.'

'Were you an only child?'

'I have four older brothers. The brother just older than me is very spiritually active – he is an acknowledged spiritual leader. He has just received the World Economic Forum Award. This award is given to one hundred people under forty who have done something to change the planet. He got this award recently in New York. My other brothers, too, are now awakening spiritually.'

Despite the companionship of her brothers, Mirabai/Jane had a difficult childhood. Very different from other children who didn't understand her or like her, she felt she was an alien presence, first in her Catholic primary school, then later at a government high school. 'I absolutely hated school and if I could have left, I would have,' she said.

From the age of nought to nine years, Mirabai/Jane had frequent spiritual experiences. She knew that God was calling her; she knew that she had to perform a huge mission on this earth.

'Dear God,' she prayed, 'please don't give me the same mission as you gave me the last time(s) on this earth.'

'What was your mission then?' I asked.

'I was a nun,' laughed Mirabai/Jane. 'Not just in one lifetime, but in many lifetimes. As far as I can remember, I have been a Catholic and a Hindu nun.'

This unusual child was experiencing other astonishing visions. Around her bed at night, she would see the Enlightened Masters – Jesus, Mother Mary, Babaji, Yogananda and others. They appeared to her both in form and as Light Beings.

'I remember there were seven to twelve Masters in all. They would talk to me and tell me things. I regarded these Masters as my real family. I never understood my physical family to be my family – I regarded my real family as a visiting station.'

A traumatic event occurred when she was three years old – her parents were divorced and her father moved out. As she grew older, both her parents had some difficulty in accepting their daughter's burgeoning spirituality, which she only had the courage to talk about or express from her eighteenth year. Indeed her father would not tolerate the path that Mirabai/Jane was following and was enraged by her beliefs.

'It was only two years ago, when my father was dying from a lung disease that he had a big turn-around in his feelings. He began to come to me asking what would happen when he died. He wanted to know what he would see and what he would experience in the After World. At the very end of his life he became a spiritual seeker.

'Having lived his life as a materialist, with no emotional links to his family and being what I would call a classically earthbound soul, I, together with a great saint named Ammachi – she sees millions of people all around the world and hugs them as she gives them her blessing – took my father's soul to the light. At last he was liberated.'

Unable to bear the spiritual experiences that ostracised her from her peers, Mirabai/Jane decided to become a 'normal' teenager. From the ages of eleven to nineteen she blocked out her spirituality.

Finally, her uncomfortable school career was over and Mirabai/Jane decided that she wanted to be an actress. In 1987 she enrolled at the University of the Witwatersrand to do a degree in drama.

Once again, she found the academic environment to be a death trap. She could not endure the competition, the back stabbing, the criticism and the jealousy she found among the students. The pressure was such that a couple of her classmates committed suicide in the year that she started her degree.

At the age of twenty-one, and finding the outer reality of the world in harsh conflict with her inner spiritual reality, Mirabai/Jane suffered a severe nervous breakdown. For one year she did not speak.

'I shut down. I was suicidally depressed. I didn't believe in any book or any teaching. I believed in nothing from the outside. I wanted only to experience the truth from within. I went into total darkness to find the light.'

It was at this stage that she began to receive great and wonderful gifts from those guiding her progress from the other realms. She began to write spontaneous poetry, covering page after page with beautiful words. Some of the words she wrote were unknown to her and she had to consult a dictionary to discover their meaning.

In addition to her writing, Mirabai/Jane suddenly displayed artistic talents which ranged from designing and manufacturing jewellery and a variety of handcrafts, to painting pictures.

During this period she also received another miraculous gift. 'I would be lying on my bed. Suddenly I would find myself up on the ceiling looking down on my body and I would see a silver cord between my body and myself. I would see the most exquisite colours between myself and my body. I would hear the celestial music of the spheres. That's when I realised and remembered *I am not my body*. The fear of humanity then left me and I felt stronger. Something inside me spoke and told me that I must go to India to find my guru.'

Mirabai/Jane was discovering that if her mission on this planet was ultimately to raise world consciousness of God, to help people around the world to discover the Divine within themselves, she must first find the avatar, saint or shaman who could truly enlighten her.

This enlightenment, she felt, would enable her to achieve her true purpose on this earth, whatever that might be. With a joyous heart and a few possessions – a bottle of malaria tablets, toothbrush, toothpaste and a little bit of money – Mirabai/Jane set off to follow her path.

Noeline is today a successful healer and teacher of the Alexander Technique – a technique which refines the balance of one's body by improving one's posture and assists one in using one's body better with less tension and stress.

She submitted the following testimonial:

It was several years ago that I first met Mirabai/Jane, who was then known simply as Jane. Mirabai, which means pure devotion to God, was the name she received on her travels in America from a disciple of Swami Satchidananda, himself a disciple of the great Swami Sivananda.

By that time Jane was a Reiki Master. I had never been interested in becoming a healer, but when Jane did such awesome healing on us, I found myself asking her to train me as healer. When she agreed, I got two friends together and the course began.

Jane peeled away my emotional issues as if she was skinning an onion. When I told her that I had a numbness in my hip, she worked on the area for a while and then asked, 'Have you had an abortion?' When I nodded and told her that at that time I simply wasn't ready to have a child, she replied that the soul of that aborted child was still holding on to my hip.

'I will take the soul of this baby to the Light,' she said. After she had performed this task, I had no further pain.

You never get to the point where all your issues are resolved. I had had an affair and I had a child from this affair. When I married for the first time, the union was disastrous. My belief pattern was such that I believed that I deserved what I had created.

During my training as a teacher, Jane did a lot of Inner Child therapy amongst other things in order to help me come to a different place. Today I have another kind of marriage – one filled with love and companionship. Mirabai/Jane didn't teach me how to die, she helped me to live.

During my first pregnancy in my second marriage, I nearly had a miscarriage. In despair, I contacted Mirabai/Jane. She immediately connected with the soul of the unborn child. 'Why do you want to leave?' she asked gently. 'You really are wanted and needed and loved.'

She told me that the Light Mother had already come to take away my son, yet thanks to her unique help, I was able to keep this baby, although the pregnancy was difficult and unhappy. Mirabai/Jane continued communicating with the baby and she informed us that the baby's soul and my husband's soul were very close. This gave both of us immeasurable comfort.

When I went into labour, there was a struggle as Marc, my son, didn't descend. I phoned Mirabai/Jane in America and told her something was wrong. Such are her powers that she is able to scan a body, no matter what the distance. She told me that the umbilical cord was not around the neck, but that the baby was not ready to come down. She said, 'Give it a day,' and promised that although she was not with me physically, she would be with me throughout the entire birth process.

Her spiritual help throughout this difficult birth was like having my own personal hotline to God. I have learned so much from Mirabai/Jane. She no longer sees things from a human perspective – her daily life and her spiritual life are one. She is godmother to both my children and I believe that they are truly blessed.

Noeline

'There must be someone on this planet who has experienced the same spiritual feelings as I have,' thought Mirabai/Jane as she set off for India.

Her two-year journey would include many stops along the way. She visited many spiritual communities looking for her spiritual master. Her route took her to England, Scotland where she stayed at Findhorn, Ireland, Greece, Turkey, Germany, France where she resided with the Taizé Christian community, Israel, Holland and Switzerland.

She met Buddhists, Hindus, Muslims, Sufis, and Christian priests of every denomination.

'In each community I could feel the essence was the same. I could feel the Light of God. When I finally arrived in India, I stayed at the ashrams of Sai Baba and of the Holy Saint Sri Aurobindo. While I was with Sai Baba I prayed to God day and night to give me enlightenment. I wanted to experience unity with God. I wanted to experience what God is. My deepest pain was separation from God. My deepest longing was union with The Divine.

'This wish was granted. In 1992 I was given an eight-week state of enlightenment, or *samadhi*, when I merged completely with God's consciousness. While experiencing *samadhi*, I realised that my true purpose on this earth was to become *a teacher of teachers*.

'I was told to impart this Divine knowledge to fellow spiritual leaders, so that they could, in turn, bring the Light of God to their communities. I was also instructed to bring God's Light to all the people.'

'Have you experienced *samadhi* for a prolonged period since then?'

'There are different stages of *samadhi* and I receive this gift intermittently, although it is growing increasingly strong.

'It was during this period that I also received another gift. A

would cry and cry and pray to God to help the person's suffering. After some time, I prayed to God, begging him to take this gift away.'

'Why should you not want to possess such a powerful gift?'

'Remember, I was very young. Only in my early twenties. I could not cope with such an awesome responsibility. I was so terrified that it would go to my ego – that I would think that I had the power to heal and would not admit that I was merely the instrument for God's work.

'Finally, God took away this power and I spent the next four years begging him to give it back to me,' laughed Mirabai/Jane.

It was while Mirabai/Jane was staying with a Shaman in Switzerland that her gift of healing returned with a vengeance, in a completely different way.

'My inner sight was opened. It was as if I had been kicked by a horse in the solar plexus. The pain was excruciating. I couldn't sleep. I couldn't eat. I could hardly breathe. Suddenly I could see inwardly.

'I could see people's souls; hear their thoughts; see into other dimensions and other worlds. See the past, see the future. I could see their auras, see their chakras. I could see Spiritual Masters and the Angels. You know, angels look like explosions of light, some look like sparklers. Some look like big four-pointed stars, others like balls of light. They are so bright. Some are small. Others are huge – as big as three-storey buildings.'

'Of all the great spiritual leaders that you met on your travels, who impressed you the most?'

'I feel that my greatest inspiration came from Mother Meera, the Divine Indian Mother Avatar in Thalheim in Germany, whom I continue to visit at least twice a year, and Visham, a Mauritian-born Indian stigmata saint.'

It was from Visham that Mirabai/Jane received two precious

gift that terrified me beyond any other gift – the gift of instantaneous physical healing. I would put my hands on people and whatever they had physically would disappear immediately in front of my eyes.

'I saw someone with a tooth abscess, with a boil that bulged out like this,' said Mirabai/Jane blowing out her left cheek.

'I touched him and the abscess vanished. I treated someone who had burns all over his legs, scarred from the hips down after having been severely burnt in a fire. I put my hands on this unfortunate and when I lifted them, his skin was clear and smooth. As I felt that current of healing energy come through my body, I gifts – a holy ring that he materialised from the palm of his hand and a *lingam*, an egg-shaped crystal that grew in his stomach and which he materialised through his mouth.

'A *lingam*,' explained Mirabai/Jane, 'is a holy relic that comes out of a saint. He gave me these gifts to help me with my work. This crystal, which only I am allowed to touch, has sufficient power in it to bring healing to people.'

At the end of 1992 Mirabai/Jane returned to South Africa. Because of the healing gift that she had received and not wanting to be thought of as a 'crazy mystic', she threw herself into learning esoteric healing arts – Reiki, Reflexology, Bach Flower Remedies, Touch for Health, Aromatherapy, Colour Healing, Spiritual Counselling, Crystals, Shamanism, Kinesiology and Rebirthing.

'I thought that if people knew they were coming to me for a Reiki treatment, for example, they wouldn't be frightened. I didn't know how to explain to them that God works through me.'

Armed with the certification for all the courses she had successfully completed, Mirabai/Jane opened the Centre of Light, a centre for healing in Johannesburg – just a few blocks away from the house where she was born.

From this centre, Mirabai/Jane started the beginnings of the work that she's doing now – meditation and workshops, spiritual readings and healing, communication with angels and devas and self-healing – but in a low-key manner. She was also a guest healer/teacher at healing centres and yoga schools throughout South Africa.

'In 1997 I was guided inwardly to give up everything in South Africa and go to North America to help the people there. I was told that they were waiting for me. It seemed impossible for me to go. I had no money, I didn't know anyone in the country except one of my brothers who lives there. However, since my path is absolute surrender to God, I must do whatever I am told to do.

'So I said to God: "If you want me to go to America, you tell me where to go and you send me the money." I closed up my centre in Johannesburg. Out of the blue I was asked to do two huge workshops in Durban. Within two weeks I had sufficient money for the air ticket and travel expenses. I went to America with the clothes on my back, a small overnight bag and enough money to survive for one month.

'When I arrived I was immediately guided to a Master Shaman in the desert in New Mexico. I went there within one week of arriving. During that time I was on a "Good Morning America" television programme with the Shaman.

'While I was with the Shaman I went into a vision state. I could go for days without food or water or sleep. I was seeing visions of Divine Beings, I was being told what my mission was, I was being given instructions, knowledge, light. The spiritual beings were doing work on my body. They were reactivating my cellular structure – I was being reprogrammed for the bigger work on this planet.

'At times, while I was in the vision state, I saw my Soul Self, not my human self, hovering over the earth as a great ball of light. Without being told of the visions I was experiencing, many people in the community also saw a great ball of white light in the sky at this time.

'At the community of the Shaman I met some key people who were my doorway to North America. I was invited to teach across North America. Together with the Shaman and some Native Americans we held a World Vision Conference. In addition to the Native American Elders from all the tribes, many Hollywood movie stars were there, of course – this was America!

'From there I was invited to lecture right across the country. I conducted spiritual workshops and healing sessions throughout the United States – California, Chicago, Boston, Oregon, New

Jersey, New York, New Mexico, Colorado, South and North Carolina. I have recently received an invitation to work in Hawaii.

'These days I am constantly travelling. For I also work in Europe and the United Kingdom and, of course, my beloved South Africa.

'It was at this time that the next stage of the gift opened up and that is what I call Light Work where I don't touch the body any more. The Divine Beings do everything. They just work through me as an instrument.

'Some sessions may take an hour and a half, some much less, while I explain to people what's going on, but transmission of Light takes place instantly. However, say a person has a problem or an illness that needs healing. Then, a great deal of my work is teaching, for each person must learn to take responsibility for their own healing process.

'If their problem is taken away from them they do not learn the lesson and the problem will recur. Each person must work through their own karma, but the Light helps them to speed up this process considerably.'

With the growth of her work throughout the world under the auspices of her non-profit organisation, *Serving the Light*, Mirabai/Jane is constantly doing spiritual workshops, *darshan* and healings throughout the world.

Of all the work she currently does, perhaps the most remarkable is *darshan*. 'Darshan,' explained Mirabai/Jane, 'is the direct transmission of the Divine Light through the eyes into a person's soul. I have found it to be the most powerful form of direct healing. It enables the person to awaken from the illusion of suffering and pain to the reality of God's love, bliss and peace, the true nature of their soul.'

With so many demands upon her time – her healing work continues even while she is in the sleep state – it became necessary for Mirabai/Jane to appoint a personal assistant.

Sonja, an experienced trained healer and spiritual counsellor herself, now accompanies Mirabai/Jane on some of her journeys and is responsible for making travel arrangements, for coordinating events and the teacher/healer's overloaded work schedule, as well as managing Mirabai/Jane's worldwide organisation.

This is no small task as it falls to Sonja to alert the organisation's community organisers so that they can inform people when Mirabai/Jane will be appearing in their city or town and what her programme is.

In addition, when the numbers who attend her sessions are too great, Sonja is able to provide some much-needed assistance with healing.

No matter where she is in the world, no matter how much service work she does, Mirabai/Jane religiously follows her daily practice of Bhakti yoga – a combination of meditation, japa/mantra repetition, prayer and silence – believing that Bhakti is the scientific method of obtaining union with God.

'Someone said that God has given me a lot of responsibility,' said Mirabai/Jane. 'Yes, sometimes the burden is heavy. However, mostly my work is pure bliss. For when *Shakti*, the Divine Light, burns through my body, I am filled with unbelievable energy.

'I am totally in love with this Light and I believe that God is using me as a channel to raise the level of world consciousness to the power of His/Her presence and His/Her love. The Light is God and God is the Light.'

Om shanti, shanti, shanti. Peace be unto all beings.

Contact Details

T Dr. Shado Moses Dludlu
E-mail: themngomawalk@wol.co.za
Mobile: 083 360 4695

The Reverend Donna Darkwolf Vos
Donna's e-mail: darkwolf@netactive.co.za
Kerry's e-mail: kerrylion@mweb.co.za
Telephone: +27(11) 440 9930

Lionel Berman
E-mail: third.wave@pixie.co.za
Telephone: +27(11) 648 2286

Jeanne Stock
Address: The Hypnosis and Psychic Centre
Bedfordview, Johannesburg
E-mail: hypnosis4all@yahoo.co.uk
Telephone: +27(11) 455 6147

Evans V Brown
Address: The Hypnosis and Psychic Centre
Bedfordview, Johannesburg
E-mail: hypnosis4all@yahoo.co.uk
Telephone: +27 (11) 455 6147

Hofit
Telephone: +27 (11) 646 3255
Mobile: 083 558 5175

Mouneen Forrester
E-mail: mouneen@mweb.co.za
Mobile: 073 209 1237

Colleen-Joy Page
Website: www.transformationpages.co.za
E-mail: pages@iafrica.com
Telephone: +27 (11) 708 0000

Renée Fouché
Telephone/fax +27 (21) 462 6174

Rozelle Mazetti
E-mail: lmb@new.co.za
Telephone: +27 (023) 313 3489
Mobile: 083 953 4313

Shui Tseng
Mobile: 083 539 1375

Judy Le Cash
E-mail: judylec@netactive.co.za
Telephone: +27 (21) 462 2011
Mobile: 082 777 6005

Alison Effting & Michelle Serafino
Alison: E-mail: allisone@iafrica.com
Telephone: +27 (21) 761 2808

Michelle: E-mail: colour@telkomsa.net
Telephone: +27 (21) 531 0295

Sandy Smith
Website: www.numerology.co.za
E-mail: numerology@mweb.co.za
Mobile: 082 411 9270
Numerology Hotline: 082 231 0111

Mpumi Khumalo
Mobile: 082 443 5511

Dr Mark Harman
Mobile: 072 120 3335

Dr Melanie Polatinsky
E-mail: melpol@worldonline.co.za
Telephone: +27 (11) 453 5415

Jayshree & Mellissa Mallaya
E-mail: mellisamallaya@hotmail.com
mellisa@mysticsisters.co.za
Mobile: 083 536 1520
Telephone: +27 (31) 566 5362/3

Chris Tokalon
Website: www.soundman.co.za
E-mail: soundman@webmail.co.za
Mobile 072 220 3736
Telephone: +27 (11) 726 2223

Halo Gaia Holistic Journeys:
Nelia mobile: 082 563 9744
E-mail: tours@halogaia.co.za

Nandiva (Wendy) Wood
Address: Ishta Yoga Centre,
Atholl, Sandton
Telephone: +27 (11) 887 2027

Durgana/Magda Inglethorpe
Telephone: +27 (11) 849 3143

Corina Loe
E-mail: corina@sybase.co.za
Telephone: 083 749 1179

Bernie Rowen
E-mail: tedbern@icon.co.za
Telephone/fax: +27 (21) 976 5233

Irma Bellingan
E-mail: irma_bellingan@yahoo.com
Mobile: 082 572 5807
072 149 5866

Rod Suskin
E-mail: rsuskin@iafrica.com
Telephone: +27 (21) 461 0992

Mirabai Devi/Jane Blecher
Website: www.servingthelight.org
E-mail: info@servingthelight.org

All details correct at time of publication

Informative esoteric websites
Cara Faye

There are many paths to enlightenment. The list of sites below is intended to help readers to find sites and information that will aid them on their journeys. Our thanks to *Odyssey* Magazine for allowing us to reprint material originally published in Spirit.Web.

At the time of writing all website details were accurate, but the web by its nature is constantly changing and evolving – some sites disappear, others change in content or address. Every attempt has been made to put forward sites that will continue to be available in some form or another.

Please note: generally, viewing a website page is quite safe; however it is best to ensure that you have a virus checker installed when surfing the net, especially if you want to download anything from a site.

Local Publications
www.odysseymagazine.co.za
The home site for *Odyssey* Magazine, a national holistic magazine that has been going since the early 1970s. Since Chris Erasmus took over editorship in June 2001, *Odyssey* has placed a particular emphasis on bringing Spirit and spiritual matters into mainstream life, with articles and features are geared towards real world applications of wisdom. The website is a strong companion to the print magazine, containing the most recent editorial and a selection of past articles, CD and book reviews as well as a web review section, all beautifully presented. Contact, advertising and subscription details are easily accessible, as well as details of current special offers and a 'What's Hot' section with up-to-date event info.

www.namaste-mag.co.za
The homepage for *Namasté* Magazine, the site displays the contents of the current edition as well as previous issues – useful if you're looking for a specific topic. There is also an Editor's Choice section, featuring one article from each issue, interesting reading which gives a good sense of what to expect from the magazine itself. Subscription forms can be posted from the site, and advertising info is provided.

www.renaissancemagazine.co.za
The online version of Cape Town's *Renaissance* Magazine, at the time of writing the site was only a few months old. Included are selected articles from current and past issues, a directory of predominantly Cape-based Healers, Life Skills workshops, Places to Visit and Things to Do. A variety of readings by local practitioners can be ordered through the site. Articles are original submissions, also predominantly by Cape practitioners.

www.elandor.co.za
A small site belonging to the well-known spiritual centre in Durbanville, Cape. There are books for sale, some informative crystal articles and CD reviews, and a list of forthcoming events at Elandor. Book reviews are linked to a list of books on loan from Elandor's library.

Therapies
www.aromaweb.com
A comprehensive aromatherapy resource site. The Archive section contains almost 100 essential oils listed by common and botanical name; with physical descriptions, strength, constituents, uses and safety info on each. There are also sections on carrier oils and hazardous essential oils. The Recipe Box contains about 30 recipes for health and home usage, including a shoe deodoriser and high stress recipe.

www.colourtherapyhealing.com
A comprehensive colour resource for therapists and laymen alike; this is a well-organised and quick-loading site. There is a history of colour therapy, a very readable scientific explanation of light and sight and an interactive colour-aspect section. Chakras and crystals are treated both individually and together, giving a nicely rounded perspective,

and tips on crystal care are included. Bach Flower Remedies can be found in the Colour and Nature section. The author invites articles for submission; you can purchase light filters, power bracelets, crystal figures, posters and flower cards through the site; and there are also a few useful colour charts which you are welcome to download and use.

Gems and crystals
neatstuff.net/avalon/
A well updated crystal reference site, providing a very comprehensive listing with just about every gem and crystal, from the commonplace to the astonishing. The site owner combines gemological knowledge with metaphysical understanding; descriptions cover appearance, physical properties and healing applications of each crystal. Articles cover gem remedies, laying on of stones and Reiki crystals. Crystals can be ordered online, as can gem pendants and bracelets.

Reiki
http://www.angelfire.com/az/SpiritMatters/contents.html
(can also be found on google.com by typing 'reiki + angelfire')
An easily navigable and fast opening site with articles covering all there is to know about Reiki energy healing, what it is and how it got to us, with a focus on Usui Reiki Ryoho. Each subsection (introduction, histories, advanced, and general articles) provides a selection of articles, all well written, covering everything from the different histories, to distance treatments, to Reiki and surgery. Also to be found are inspirational thoughts, spirit art and two chat rooms. The only drawback is a plethora of pop-up adverts, but these are easily closed.

www.learningmeditation.com
A beautiful and simply organised site containing about 25 short meditations including 5 specifically for children. Meditations can be downloaded for anytime playback, otherwise most text versions are available to print and do offline. Meditations for kids cover relaxation, observation, awareness, sensations and validation; others include Fulfilling Your Own Potential, a Work Break meditation, Self-Image/Weight Management and unguided music meditations. There's an article on Learning to Relax, a Suggested Readings section, and an online shop offering meditation tapes, SeiFu meditation cushions, angel cards and more. A very relaxing site to visit.

Forecasting / Divination
www.tarot.com
An online tarot reading site with a small selection of well-developed free tarot readings, and a comprehensive selection of larger spreads available for a small fee ('Karma Coins', 50% of which go to charities). The card interpretations are well written and provide useful advice and insight into readers' current situations. A thorough articles section covers all aspects of tarot history. The support offered is also superb.

www.astro.com
Run by Liz Greene and Robert Hand, this extremely comprehensive site offers a wide range of free horoscopes (daily, short-term, partner, love-life and more) as well as chart options; anyone with full birth information can sign in and retrieve regular reports. Personalised horoscopes covering yearly, 6-year, relationship, child, and career horoscopes, transits, and your horoscope calendar can be ordered through the site.

www.astrologyzone.com
This site is updated monthly with a comprehensive (3 page) horoscope for each sign, addressing all transits and the signs and houses affected, and how these are likely to manifest in your life. For each sign you will also find a thorough overview of wealth, relationship, fitness, vacation and stress insights. The Astrologer's Toolbox contains an introduction to the Planets, Elements, 3 Qualities and 12 Houses.

'Current Trends' describes the effects of Eclipse and Mercury Retrograde periods. A monthly newsletter keeps you informed of site updates.

www.astrology-numerology.com

This simple, non-commercial double-site provides a wealth of information for astrologers and numerologists of all levels. Each section contains detailed descriptions of every possible chart position. The astrology section offers such gems as sun-moon combination descriptions, each planet in every sign and house, cusp placements, and a comprehensive glossary. The numerology section covers everything from number meanings and the core positions to essences and transits. There is also a reading template which you are invited to use, and 'cut & paste' the given interpretations for each reading. A great teach-yourself site that gives method and structure to these occasionally nebulous arts.

Numerology

www.decoz.com

A very strong numerology site. A comprehensive articles section covers every aspect of numerology from name changes to consultation etiquette, in an informed and caring way. Do-it-yourself tutorials give a good understanding of how to approach each element in your analysis, as well as useful and insightful interpretations in each case. You can retrieve free daily forecasts for the month and send day-of-birth e-cards, or order comprehensive readings online. There's also info on downloadable software, and some fairly complex calculations for the experts. Currently the navigation leaves something to be desired.

www.spiritweb.co.za

A growing site which already boasts clearly written and simply laid out pages on hand reading, astrology, crystals, chakras and numerology, as well as tarot and runes; these latter two also have online oracles with informative answers for the card/rune drawn. The Rituals section contains rituals for abundance, healing, relationships and letting go. There are promises of a totem page and dream, chakra & esoteric dictionaries still to come. It loads quickly and is easy to navigate.

I Ching, Osho Zen Tarot
See Chinese Wisdom

Metaphysics

www.crystalinks.com

A huge site covering an inexhaustible number of topics dedicated to linking physical and metaphysical realities. Each main heading leads to a page of extensive links to articles, writings, other sites or further links related to the subject. If you're looking for info on Ancient India, Aids, conspiracies, sacred geometry or UFOs (and anything in between) you'll find it here. However, it's easy to get lost, so advice is to have a particular topic in mind when you visit this site.

www.transformationpages.co.za

A metaphysics site covering a range of topics including intuition, spirit guides, soulful relationships, finding your healing power, life purpose and past lives; these sections all relate to courses run by the site owner. In addition there is a selection of articles on these topics and more which are well written, concisely imparting a vast amount of metaphysical know-how. There has been no skimping, and the combination of straight talk and density of information is both enlightening and empowering. Freebies include an introduction to astrology, a monthly e-mailed soul lesson, thought for the month and an online oracle. You'll also find event info for lectures and workshops on the site, and a range of interesting guest practitioners. An enriching site, it's worth many visits.

www.circlesoflight.com

Directly linked to **askalana.com**, this metaphysics and astrology-based site has an emphasis on self-development. There is a wide selection of interesting and non-academic articles covering prosperity and abundance, relationships, pages of peace, providing both simple, gentle advice and personal insight. The astrology section includes lessons in Vedic astrology and some celebrity horoscopes including that of the Dalai Lama. An aromatherapy section offers recipes to aid your inner work.

Other
www.lucidity.com
The home site of the Lucidity Institute, dedicated to the study of lucid dreaming. There is extensive literature on the subject, including excerpts from the site owner's books, research articles with a fairly academic bent, and a strong FAQ section. Topics covered range from remembering your dreams, 'Dreaming, Function and Meaning' and different lucid dreaming experiences. The newsletter keeps you informed of updates in lucid dreaming research and Lucidity Institute events, also available on the site. Books, tapes and lucidity induction devices are also sold through the site.

Chinese Wisdom
www.iching.com
Linked to **tarot.com**, this is a highly credible and easy-to-use online version of the Chinese I Ching oracle; generating an initial hexagram and interpretation is free of charge. Comprehensive articles explain how to use the I Ching, the concept of synchronicity which best explains it, as well as the use of interval-sensitive measurements used to construct your hexagram. The correlating text is both simply and beautifully written. For a full reading (including changing lines and the future hexagram) there is a small charge of Karma Coins (see tarot.com).

http://www.geocities.com/Athens/Acropolis/5192/wicindex.htm
(best found on Google.com, search for 'Wisdom of the I Ching Geocities')

This non-commercial site is one of the best translations of the I Ching from book to interactive format. There are informed and well-written explanations of the I Ching and how to consult it, as well as an innovative online hexagram-generator if you don't have access to coins. The interpretations are faithful to traditional scripts which makes them a little archaic, but they remain as valid and applicable as ever to daily life. You may have to close a few Yahoo pop-ups, but it's well worth it. A site to visit whenever you have a pressing question, or just for a dip into the philosophic realm of this ancient Oracle.

www.osho.com
A site based on Osho Zen philosophy; it has a number of Zen meditations to try, as well as a monthly horoscope and some vegetarian recipes. It also contains two online tarot options – Transformation and Osho Zen; the card meanings give both quotes from Osho and an interpretation for daily life not dissimilar to I Ching readings. There is also an online subscription library boasting over 220 books of wisdom and humour; for non-subscribers, a few selected talks are available.

www.astro-fengshui.com
Home site of the Feng Shui Research Center, which supports a number of online courses on Chinese astrology and Feng Shui. There are thorough introductions to the *Four Pillars* and *Zi Wei Dou Shu* astrology systems, with sample charts offering clear insight into how each branch works. The Feng Shui section contains FAQs, success stories, and select articles on Feng Shui from basic to advanced topics, including the Five Elements and 'Feng Shui in the Southern Hemisphere'. There's a short introduction to the I Ching, and information on upcoming courses and events. The author's books on the I Ching and Feng Shui are available through the site, as well as Feng Shui compasses and a detailed Feng Shui template.

Spiritualism / Channelling

www.spriritweb.org

A beautiful site to visit, this large and comprehensive channelling, light work and mysticism site provides simple definitions of even the most obscure areas, written in an accessible fashion. The scope is very broad and each section is covered in some detail, with extensive links to related sites, associations and articles, as well as over 60 mailing lists to investigate. A very strong community feel.

www.spiritual.com.au

A site to be visited and revisited, and mined for information and opinions. It provides a wealth of information on most matters spiritual, from angels, ascension, reincarnation to healing and theosophy. It even includes a spiritual dictionary. All sections are comprehensively addressed, and most articles are easy to read – many are channelled messages which make for interesting and enlightening reading. The Short Stories & Parables section incorporates extracts from Kahlil Gibran and Neale Donald Walsch amongst others, and the Healing section covers Feng Shui, Crystals, Chopra and even 'Healing a Broken Heart'. This is a simple and sometimes beautiful site you could spend hours on, and the quality more than makes up for occasional slowness.

www.askalana.com

Predominantly a channelling site, in which an extensive number of channelled answers from Alana can be read. Answers are organised into clear categories, ranging from life purpose, manifestation and decision-making to earth transformation and departed loved ones. A new question is answered each week, and you can submit your questions through the site. There is also a free comprehensive numerology course, and full numerology readings are offered.

Fairies

www.mythicalrealm.com

A beautiful site dedicated to the beasts and folk of the mythical realm. Here will ye find dragons, gryphons, mermaids, unicorns and gargoyles; wizards, fairies and phoenixes; and Arthurian myths & legends too. The descriptions and histories of each are well written and the text is interspersed with well-placed poetry. It is large, which means you need a reasonably fast PC to get the full benefit, but it's great for anyone with a love for the Faery Folk, and entertaining even to those with a passing interest. Some of the images are available as e-cards too, with a wide range of customisable options (music, text, colour, etc), and magical products from posters to writing sets and fantasy games can be purchased through the site. A rare treat to visit.

International Practitioners

www.myss.com

An information and advice-driven site with a strong community feel; the home page for Caroline Myss's hard-hitting healing philosophy. It's a large site which loads quickly and is well organised. Most informative is the 'Power, Energy and Healing' section, covering her sacred truths, archetype definitions, daily practices for healing, a comprehensive chakra section, and ideas for taking charge of those aspects of life most commonly out of kilter – money, creativity, health, relationships, and spirit. Each section includes thorough exercises and questions for self-examination. She also offers interactive online courses. The Community section shows a human side to the teachings; there are discussion forums, answers to readers' questions, postcards to send, and a photo gallery of Caroline's tours. Join the mailing list to receive regular updates and letters to what feels like 'the Group'.

www.chopra.com

Primarily the website of the Chopra Center for Wellbeing, this site is based mostly around the services, seminars, workshops and teaching programs of the Center. The Daily Wisdom section offers meanings for each day of the week and a daily quote. Deepak's Q&A has answers to readers' questions, and there are prayer/message boards on relationships, spirit, success, education and health with public participation. Hidden well inside the site are the archives (easiest route is through the recipe archives) containing selected excerpts & sound bytes of Chopra's work under Seasonal Dharma, and a Culinary Consciousness section.

Health

www.healthatoz.com

A large site that addresses standard health issues in a positive and proactive manner. There are four main sections – Your Family (covering women's and men's health, parenting, over 60s and more), Condition Forums (covering some 70 health-related conditions), Wellness Center (alternative medicine, fitness, smoking and an invaluable Mental Health Center), and Healthy Lifestyles (tips and advice on eating, travel, home and back to school); newly added is a comprehensive oncology center. Advice is thorough and holistic, and the site is well presented and easy to navigate.

www.vegkitchen.com

A nice, simple site by the author of some 8 books on vegetarian cooking. A number of recipes are published on the site, as well as Tips for Vegetarians which are both informative and well-informed. The author shows an understanding of food that goes beyond merely preparing meals, and the advice is enlightening to cooks of all foods.

Healing/Other

www.anxieties.com

This very useful site provides comprehensive information and advice on different forms of anxiety from simple phobias, obsessive compulsive disorder and fear of flying, to outright panic attacks. It's well written and produces an instant calming effect. The self-help sections give clear step-by-step methods for overcoming fears, from understanding the causes to gaining control over them. You can order the author's products and related books as well.

www.metagifted.org

This is a very on-the-ground site, providing a particularly empathetic look at giftedness; it's large, slow-loading and rambles a bit, but its composition of categorised letters and stories of direct experiences sheds a lot of light on these special and often misunderstood lives. All aspects of gifted awareness are addressed, including a large section dedicated to Indigo Children. The site owner discusses Indigo Wisdom, characteristics, and what to expect. Issues around education are also discussed, as well as the often negative attitudes experienced by these children, but predominantly it is left to the individuals to share their stories. There is also a fair selection of exercises and games to stretch young minds.

www.bnuniversity.com

Linked to Barnes & Noble's online bookstore, this site offers a large number of free courses covering a lot of ground, including a number of alternative topics. Astrology, Buddhism & Everyday Life, Feng Shui for Your Home, Yoga for Novices and Tarot for Beginners all cover conceptual topics; on the self-improvement side there's Stress, Sanity and Survival, Total Memory Workout, and End Your Addiction Now. Registration is simple, courses run for about 10 weeks each, and the format is thoroughly organised for distance learning. You will generally need at least one book available through the site.

www.advisorteam.com

Anybody looking for some direction would do well to visit this site. It's dedicated to helping people see themselves clearly and make empowered career and relationship decisions. At its heart is the Kiersey Temperament Sorter, a quick (5 min) online questionnaire, which produces an accurate personality description, and a thorough assessment of each personality type's strengths. A good place to start investigating, or use it to complement other types of research.

Directories

www.bodyandmind.co.za

At the time of writing, the most comprehensive South African directory. There are extensive links to South African therapists and practitioners of most disciplines around the country – well organised and easy to access. The What's Happening section covers Gauteng, KwaZulu Natal, Western Cape and Other (the rest of SA) and each contains many current and upcoming events. There's also a large and well-written Information Centre – angels, the mythology of trees, and most of the therapies all find a place. Other sections to explore are the Medical Centre, Baby Centre, book reviews, and there's also a selection of vegetarian recipes.

www.naturalhealth.co.za

The home site of the South African Natural Health Network, providing a good introduction to many therapies, and contact details of practitioners, retreats, resources and product distributors around the country – a useful site to search for a therapist or learn more about a discipline.

www.spirtualworld.co.za

More of a portal than a directory, this site is a central holistic advertising and communications point, bringing together an eclectic mix of healers, practitioners and other resources locally and internationally, linking to independent sites and individual pages. By its nature it is far more diverse than a dedicated information site, and everything from artwork to pet care can be found here, as well as a variety of free introductory online readings.

www.holisticonline.com

A huge site covering alternative therapies in depth. There is an extensive list of diseases and disorders (arthritis, hormone replacement therapy and stress management all find a home), along with alternative methods of treatment. The Alternative Medicines section itself is comprehensive; you'll find Biofeedback, NLP, Shiatsu and much more. A separate section covers Holistic Living where you'll find everything from nutrition to spirituality, including healthy veg and non-veg recipes. There's also a Herb Knowledge base covering hundreds of herbs.

Other Useful Resources

www.google.com

The fastest and simplest search engine. The results it returns are structured according to relevance, and you'll generally find something within the first two pages (20 sites). The Advanced Search settings are easy to use for refining your search or finding a specific set of words.

www.kalahari.net

An online bookshop that will simplify your shopping if you know what you're looking for. The site offers a comprehensive selection of books, with both local and international suppliers. The Mind, Body and Spirit section is well represented in most categories, and the search function produces swift results. CDs and wines can also be purchased through the site. So far they have had regular discounts and vouchers for subscribers, and delivery has been speedy and efficient. For book addicts everywhere.

www.kidpub.org

A unique site capturing the magic of children's insight and imagination, this is an archive of completely unedited children's writings from around the world – you'll even find South African contributions. Try the Publishers' Pick, Newest Stories, or pull one from the Hat. Alternatively search through over 40 000 (and growing) original submissions. The site is open to all aspiring authors for a small monthly fee, with a privacy policy tailored for young contributors, which makes for a great read itself. Schools can join as well, and members get a chance to contribute creatively to an unusual chat-like story.